The
American
Connection

The
American
Connection

*Profiteering and Politicking
in the
"Ethical" Drug Industry*

by JOHN PEKKANEN

𝓯 Follett Publishing Company
Chicago

Library of Congress Catalog Card Number: 73-82196

ISBN: 0-695-80419-7

First printing

For Lynn and the children,
Robert, Sarah and Benjamin

Contents

Acknowledgments

APPROXIMATELY eighty people were interviewed in the preparation of this book and to all of them I express my appreciation for their time and help. To two people I owe a special debt: my wife Lynn, whose encouragement and work on this project more than anything else made it possible; and my editor, Patricia Meehan, whose persistent and thoughtful criticism helped to shape it. I would like to single out several people who gave me hours of their time as I gathered information for this book: Larry Reida, Paul Perito, and Carl Perian, all of whose efforts are detailed in the book; Robert Rosthal, Deputy Chief Counsel of the Bureau of Narcotics and Dangerous Drugs (BNDD); Kenneth Baumgartner, a former counsel with BNDD; Benjamin Gordon, staff economist for the Senate Subcommittee to Investigate Juvenile Delinquency; Nancy Chasen, legislative aide to Senator Thomas Eagleton; Dr. John Leventhal, clinical instructor at Harvard Medical School; Dr. Frederic Wolff, Deputy Director of the Endocrine-Metabolic Division of the Bureau of Drugs at the FDA and also Professor of Medicine at George Washington University Medical School; Dr. Russell Leaf, associate professor of psychology at Rutgers University and the MacDowell Colony.

I particularly thank Margery Schauer, researcher for the House Select Committee on Crime, for her invaluable help throughout this project.

The
American
Connection

Prologue

If relatively mentally healthy people want to take drugs then that's their problem. If they get caught up in it without realizing the price they're going to have to pay for it, then I think it's somebody else's problem.
                              A DRUG ADDICTION RESEARCHER

THE working premise of this book is implied in the quote that begins this prologue. Too many people took too many legally and medically sanctioned drugs, and, because they did not realize the hazards to themselves, it became "somebody else's" problem. The drug industry was unwilling to restrain itself and accept any social responsibility, so the somebody else became the government. For many years and continuing today the drug industry has overproduced and oversold drugs whose hazards were buried beneath mountains of advertising and promotion. The easy availability and wide use of these drugs helped create and certainly worsened our national epidemic of drug abuse. When the government intervened—usually belatedly—to dampen the abuse, the drug industry manipulated these attempts to its own advantage. This manipulation of federal regulations was often waged with the help of those in positions of public trust and political power. This then is essentially the story of this book; it is a book about political power, political influences and political personalities.

The drug industry's willful manipulation of these controls—done to maintain profits—has created social consequences that are only now becoming fully understood. T. Donald Rucker, formerly a senior health analyst with the Social Security Administration, estimates that two-thirds of the total drug abuse problem in this country—exclusive of alcohol, which is acknowledged as being the most abused legally produced drug—involves legitimately produced drugs. Other authorities give similar estimates. The most abused drugs, the drugs which will be discussed in this book, are amphetamines, barbiturates, and some tranquilizers. All fall under the general classification of psychotropic or mood drugs. They are prescribed for a variety of reasons—good and bad—and they have one common characteristic: they alter consciousness.

Man's desire for such mind-altering drugs is not unique to this country or to this era. All societies—primitive and modern—have concocted and consumed drugs of some kind. The temptress Circe in Homer's *The Odyssey* is described as "polypharmakos," or one who knows the use of drugs. *The Odyssey* was written centuries before the birth of Christ. But whereas primitive societies derived their drug potions from their natural environment, today large corporations combine and mix tons of very profitable synthetic chemicals in huge vats. From there the mixtures are poured into high-speed stamping machines that shoot out scores of these potent pills every second. The pills are then promoted and distributed in a way that no primitive society—or even any other modern society—could begin to rival. We have become the biggest drug-taking nation in the history of the earth, according to several surveys. Therefore the use and abuse of drugs is not merely a modern extension of an old human custom; the intervention of modern chemistry and automation, coupled with sophisticated marketing techniques and a lust for profit, has helped turn what was once a diversionary pastime into a widespread social plague.

J. P.

1: The Origin of a Crisis

Barbs make you want to go out and kick ass; speed gives you the energy to go out and do it.

A YOUNG DRUG ADDICT

SENATOR Thomas Hennings, Democrat of Missouri, was a large man. Handsome, articulate, he was considered by many to have had one of the best legal minds ever to sit in the Senate. His wardrobe was just short of a dandy's. He fancied Panama suits in the summer, and with his dark hair slicked back over his large rugged face, he often cut a spectacular figure, catching everyone's attention when he burst into the Senate chamber.

But behind the public facade was a deeply troubled man. Hennings had a severe case of alcoholism which had begun in his Navy days and continued to plague him. When on one of his periodic benders, his contact with his Senate office would be minimal. He would call in during moments of clear thinking and then go back to liquor. "It is difficult for other people to understand," one of his aides reflected, "but he felt that nobody loved him. He would get almost manic, then sink way down, and he'd start on the booze."

But in his sober periods Hennings was a highly respected Senator. "Even Lyndon Johnson (then Senate majority leader) was quite wary of him. Hennings was no man to trifle with when he was right," said the same aide. One issue for which he was always an enduring and compassionate advocate was civil rights, despite his border state constituency.

Some time late in 1958, almost accidentally, Hennings was reading a home state newspaper when he came upon a minor news story describing how two young boys had shot amphetamine into their veins. It astonished him. He had not realized that one could shoot up amphetamine by needle, and he was further disturbed to read that after shooting up the amphetamine, the two young boys had summoned enough nerve to commit a crime. Hennings made inquiries around Washington and found the only federal control over amphetamines was a prescription requirement. Amphetamines and barbiturates, another class of drugs subject to abuse, were produced in enormous quantities by many legitimate drug companies. Despite the powerful interests and big profits of the drug industry, Hennings decided to challenge its almost complete lack of public accountability in the mass production of these drugs. He set in motion what was to be a major test of corporate conscience.

In the next session of Congress, which convened in January of 1959, as Chairman of the Senate Subcommittee to Investigate Juvenile Delinquency, Hennings introduced a bill requiring closer scrutiny of amphetamines and barbiturates. In submitting his bill, Hennings offered only a brief reason: "Police report many youngsters often admit they take the drugs in order to get up the nerve to carry out some illegal act." The purpose clause of the Hennings bill stated it was "to protect the public safety by regulating the manufacture, compounding, processing and distribution of habit-forming barbiturate and amphetamine drugs." Hennings' drug abuse bill was different from most others in challenging the legitimate drug companies and their well-financed lobby.

Amphetamines are simply synthesized, man-made drugs which have a natural counterpart in the drug cocaine, a derivative of the coca leaf. They are a class of stimulant drugs which includes *d*-amphetamine, methamphetamine, dextroamphetamine, and other variations of the same basic drug. The basic chemical, amphetamine, was first created in Germany in 1887 but was not introduced in this country until 1927 when Gordon Alles, a California pharmacologist, synthesized amphetamine sulfate and acquired a patent on it. Shortly after that Alles sold the patent to Smith Kline & French Laboratories, a Philadelphia drug house which converted this scientific discovery into a financial bonanza and has remained the leader in amphetamine sales to this day. Its decongestant properties were recognized very early and in 1932 Smith Kline & French introduced the Benzedrine Inhaler on the market. It was recommended for treatment of head colds, hay fever, asthma and other respiratory problems.

New uses for amphetamine were quickly found. In 1935 amphetamine was successfully tested and used for treatment of narcolepsy, a rare disorder in which a person falls asleep involuntarily many, many times a day. In 1937 it was also noted that amphetamines appeared to calm some hyperactive children, an apparent reversal of the drug's expected effect that is still not fully understood. At about this time amphetamines became available in tablet form. Subsequently they were included in survival kits in the Spanish Civil War to ward off fatigue. During World War II they were used by all sides and this is when large numbers of the u.s. population became exposed to the drug. In 1944 in the *Air Surgeon's Bulletin,* an item titled "Benzedrine Alert" endorsed their use by saying amphetamine "is the most satisfactory of any available (drug) in temporarily postponing sleep when the desire for sleep endangers the security of a mission."

There is no evidence that during the 1930s or early 1940s there was widespread abuse of amphetamines in this country. Students took them to cram for examinations and other abuses were recognized but it was not a serious social problem. The American Medical Association (AMA) issued warnings about possible misuse but they were mild. Mostly the AMA, which had enormous influence over the drugs doctors chose through its Council on Drugs Seal of Acceptance program, sanctioned amphetamine use and reassured doctors that "no serious reactions have been observed." In the early 1940s the striking similarity between cocaine—which had been prohibited since 1914—and amphetamines was documented. Both create euphoria, which increases if the drug is shot into the vein by needle, both over-stimulate the body, decrease the appetite, bring on hallucinations and can increase sexual activity. They both cause rises in blood pressure. Convulsions, pupil dilation and circulatory collapse followed by death have been documented with both drugs. Like cocaine, amphetamines create dependency, creating in the user a need for the drug to the point that his whole life revolves around his desire to get it. The question of whether or not it is physically addictive has been debated for years. During the 1940s the weight of opinion strongly suggested it was not physically addictive. This was really a semantic argument since psychological addiction is considered much more difficult to treat because of the powerful underlying emotional factors involved.

After World War II amphetamine abuse rose markedly. The source of much abuse was the Benzedrine Inhaler which could be bought without prescription at the corner drugstore. The inhaler core could be removed and the strips chewed, dissolved in soda pop or coffee. The fad spread and was written up in the popular magazines of the day. One called *Everybody's Digest* ran an article in 1946 called "On a Bender with Benzedrine." There was a gay and lighthearted acceptance of amphetamines. "Who put the Benzedrine in Mrs. Murphy's Ovaltine" was a joke of the times and a newspaper ad featured a charm bracelet with a pill box attached and the copy read: "Benzedrine if you're having fun and going on forever; aspirin if it's all a headache."

In 1947 in a landmark study published in the *Journal of the American Medical Association,* it was reported that one out of four military prisoners at Fort Benjamin Harrison in Indiana was abusing amphetamines. The prisoners told the researchers that they had gotten hooked on amphetamines during the war and that they now wanted them constantly while they were in prison. They were supplied amphetamine from inhalers which were sold to them by the prison guards. One guard in fact was found with 300 empty inhalers in his room. The prisoners were creating serious disciplinary and psychiatric problems, a predictable phenomenon since ten years earlier it was noted that two narcoleptics treated with amphetamine had become extremely paranoid and hostile. It introduced a new disease into the medical textbooks called "amphetamine psychosis," a serious disorder which was documented repeatedly in the medical literature. Suggestions were made to ban inhalers and a bill was introduced in Congress in the late 1940s to make them a prescription item. The bill died but two years after the AMA article, Smith Kline & French withdrew Benzedrine Inhalers from the market and replaced them with Benzedrex, a non-stimulant still sold over the counter today. Other amphetamine inhalers remained on the market to fill the void and since no laws were passed prohibiting or restricting them, the pattern of abuse flourished. The drug companies only encouraged the trend.

There was almost a competition between the warnings about the hazards of amphetamine, which grew more ominous, and the reports that suggested it was a wonder cure for a multitude of ills. These reports, often backed by incomplete or suspect data, were so appealing and plentiful that by one count in 1946, amphetamine was recommended for no less than thirty-nine divergent ills from a smoking cure to head injuries to weight loss to hiccups to heart block, schizophrenia, morphine and codeine addictions. It was a snake oil to cure all ills, sold not by a traveling medical show huckster but by the respected and revered medical-pharmaceutical establishment. As Dr. Lester Grinspoon wrote in an article entitled "Amphetamines Reconsidered," for the July 8, 1972, issue of *Saturday Review,* "Somehow, supporting articles and thinly disguised testimonials invariably appeared in 'reputable' medical organs, such as the *Journal of the American Medical Association,* just prior to the publication of advertisements extending the reasons for prescribing amphetamines. Although only a few of these reports were exposed as fraudulent, most of them were clearly biased, did not use random sampling or double-blind techniques, and frequently drew dubious conclusions." In the competition, amphetamines and the drug companies which were mass producing them were the clear winners.

Under the 1951 Humphrey-Durham Act, federal law required that amphetamines, barbiturates and a number of other drugs be prescription items. It was only a modest first step at regulation. The inhalers, which contained upwards of 150 milligrams of amphetamine, or ten to twenty times the dosage in most tablets, still required no prescription. Moreover, there was no refill limit on amphetamine or barbiturate prescriptions under the Humphrey-Durham Act so if anyone wanted to abuse amphetamines, he could do so legally either by buying the inhalers over the counter or by asking his doctor to prescribe them. The doctors were more than willing to comply.

During the Korean War amphetamines were again included in survival kits and another generation was exposed to amphetamines. Some G.I.'s took them and then stopped later, others took them at the time and then continued to take them. Some Korean veterans came back with new twists. They mixed amphetamine with heroin into one shot and called it a "speedball." Back home, they continued to shoot amphetamine and spread the word. The shooting of liquid amphetamine, commonly called speed, was spreading throughout the country in the 1950s. The drug industry was the major supplier since the great percentage of amphetamines used and abused was of legitimate origin. It was easy to get, legally or illegally. The pills could be popped, crushed and snorted, or dissolved in water and shot up, and the inhaler still abounded. Amphetamines felt good, extremely good; it was one of the very best highs.

Ed is a former speed user. Tall, very thin, he has a delicate, expressive face. He sports a large bushy red beard and as he talks he squints through square, wire-rimmed glasses. He is married and has a small family now, a steady job and a successful career. He recalls the time when he shot up speed. "I was always careful to get good stuff, legitimate stuff," he says. "I remember the pleasure. It was orgasmic ecstasy, the most incredible rush I've ever had. The pleasure was absolutely staggering, better than heroin. With heroin I got mellow, everything went slow motion; but with speed I felt all electric, I felt this sense of becoming total electricity. I felt I could hurl thunderbolts."

Ed's experience is not peculiar to him. Amphetamines do give users a heightened sense of their power, let grand illusions tumble wildly in the imagination—each one more supreme than the last. Visions of flying or floating come as the body jolts to full speed. It is a physical and mental adrenalin, pumping up the body and mind to undreamed-of heights. Olympian fantasies are played out. But it ends. And the withdrawal after a speed run can be a nightmare of hallucinations as vivid as any with LSD, can bring on a desperate wish to commit suicide but not leave enough energy for it; it can create paranoid delusions that the world or anything in it is out to get you. But getting up there, on top of everything, makes it all worth it.

It was almost inevitable that any drug with this potency

and this kind of euphoric kick, coupled with its wide and easy availability and the lack of any restraint by the drug companies selling it, would be discovered by many, first used and then abused. And by the time Senator Hennings had read his newspaper and introduced his bill, this process was already in full gear. A fad was becoming a serious social problem.

But the problem was by no means limited to amphetamine abuse. Seven years earlier, in April of 1951, the Narcotics Subcommittee of the House Ways and Means Committee had held hearings on barbiturate hazards. During those hearings barbiturates had been described by several medical experts as extremely toxic and addictive drugs, a finding later evidence has only substantiated. Barbiturates are primarily prescribed for insomnia, tension and anxiety and although they had been marketed and used since 1903 in this country, no widespread abuse or misuse was reported until the 1940s. They were called "goofballs" and "thrill pills." Abuse was confined to the short-acting barbiturates— such as secobarbital and pentobarbital—because the effect is quicker and stronger.

They were recognized as potent drugs, but with far more legitimate medical uses than amphetamines. But taken in excessive amounts, an overdose can sedate the respiratory system to the point where it just stops functioning. This made it a drug of choice for suicides, and several hundred barbiturate suicides were reported each year.

Taken in high doses for a long period of time, physical addiction develops. A barbiturate addict, unlike a heroin addict, cannot be withdrawn suddenly, for convulsions, delirium tremens and even death can result. A user under the influence of barbiturates becomes drunk, slurs words, staggers, and like drunks, some will lash out violently. "Barbs make you want to go out and kick ass," a user once said of them, "and speed gives you the energy to go out and do it." In most respects, barbiturates are more life-threatening than amphetamines although they do not produce the same euphoric high. During the 1940s and the 1950s, barbiturates were abused and misused but not apparently in the numbers that amphetamines were. On the street both drugs are dangerous to the user and to society.

But as serious as street abuse of these drugs was becoming, it was in the home that the real human damage happened. Housewives taking amphetamines to lose weight or to combat depression found themselves too charged up to sleep. What better remedy than a barbiturate? But then comes the morning barbiturate hangover—tired, still sleepy. What better way to get going again than an amphetamine? It was the barbiturate-amphetamine shuttle—down and up, up and down—hooking unsuspecting housewives, truck drivers, students, artists, athletes, doctors, and a whole segment of society whose lives would not splash in the headlines but would quietly disintegrate in the home. This was and is the "gray market" of drug abuse that generally goes unnoticed but which in sheer numbers far exceeds all the junkies strung out in the street. Many people became addicted blindly. In fact a New York State Medical survey taken in the late 1960s by the New York Narcotics Control Commission, when interest in and knowledge of drugs was greater than in the 1950s, concluded that the general population still had no knowledge of the harmful effects of amphetamines and barbiturates or what knowledge it did have was inaccurate. "Approximately one-third were also unaware that a person could become *psychologically* dependent upon amphetamines and that barbiturates were *physiologically* addicting drugs," the survey found. More than 60 percent of this survey either believed marihuana was addictive or did not know if it was. (It is not.)

The public's ignorance is not surprising nor is it blameworthy. For years the medical profession, the drug industry and the police had called amphetamines and barbiturates "soft" drugs—a semantic palliative that suggested they were not nearly as hazardous as the "hard" drugs such as heroin or marihuana. It was a costly misnomer. Most people never leaped into amphetamine or barbiturate abuse; it sneaked up on them and took hold before they ever really recognized it. It was, after all, what the doctor ordered.

There is another semantic confusion. The words *use, misuse* and *abuse* take on different meanings when legitimate drugs are concerned. Even one shot of heroin is drug abuse; it has no recognized medical use in this country. On the other hand, with either amphetamines or barbiturates, any prescribed dose taken per day for ninety or 150 days is a legitimate and sanctioned medical use, no matter what its consequences to the patient. Then there is misuse, the taking of the drug above prescribed limits. This includes both the people who get multiple legal prescriptions, and those who, instead of taking the one pill as prescribed per day, take two, three or four. "That's how many I need," is the usual explanation for this. But these people still have limits to the number of pills they will take. Amphetamine or barbiturate abuse, however, goes one step further, and the distinctions are clearer. More and more of the drug is taken, in higher doses and for longer periods, and the dependency grows until the need for the drug outweighs almost every other consideration in the person's life. When the slide into abuse happens to enough people, it is no longer the problem just of those individuals, but becomes a problem for society and those who govern it.

However, that 1951 Congressional hearing, which suggested that a more rational look was needed at how we regulate and classify drugs, only gathered dust at the Library of Congress, and the pill-popping public continued to get as much barbiturate and amphetamine as it wanted, either with a prescription or without one.

The exact quantity of barbiturates and amphetamines legitimately produced during this period is difficult to come up with. But estimates by the Food and Drug Administration

(FDA) based on bulk production suggest that four or five *billion* barbiturate pills and the same amount of amphetamines were available. This gives a grand total of about eight to ten *billion* pills which were legally produced and distributed. How many were illegally diverted? That again is difficult. There was little regulation and since the FDA could only see records if a company volunteered them, again we must accept an estimate. But the FDA estimates that 50 percent of these legally produced drugs were diverted to the black market. Whatever the exact percentages might have been it was indisputable that these pills were reaching illegal markets in the tens of millions.

In the mid-1950s the Narcotics Subcommittee of the House Ways and Means Committee again held hearings, chaired by the late Hale Boggs (D.-La.). Individual witnesses from a variety of fields testified. Earlier, in 1952, a report by the Expert Committee on Addiction-Producing Drugs of the World Health Organization had recommended increased national controls over barbiturates and amphetamines, such as refill limits and careful record-keeping. So the Subcommittee had expert backing; however, it placed heavy reliance on the testimony of police officials in the hearing. One of these witnesses, Lois Higgins, the famed "lady cop" of Chicago and then director of the Crime Prevention Bureau of the State of Illinois, testified that the amphetamine habit was "more insidious than the more publicized drugs, and is increasing among our teen-agers." A young user told Boggs and the Subcommittee that amphetamines were "worse than marihuana because after you take them, you are ready to do anything." The fact that marihuana is far less toxic than amphetamines was obscured by the efforts of Harry J. Anslinger, then commissioner of the Federal Bureau of Narcotics (FBN). Anslinger regarded marihuana as an indicator of moral and social decay. He asserted at different times that it was highly dangerous, as powerful as the atomic bomb, and he suggested it could lead to heroin use. Amid this kind of thinking there was little likelihood that much attention would be paid to pills.

Boggs' Subcommittee recognized the seriousness of the pill problem but did nothing about it. The Subcommittee report issued in 1956 stated: "The abuse of barbiturates and amphetamines is of recent origin. Evidence received by the Subcommittee indicates that the illicit traffic in these drugs is endangering the health and welfare of our citizens, and presents a problem that has increased in seriousness in recent years." The report even suggested in one sense at least that the traffic in these drugs posed a more serious danger to the society than narcotics. "Unlike the narcotic traffic, which is concentrated in our larger metropolitan areas, the illicit traffic in barbiturates and amphetamines attacks both large and small communities. The traffickers are individuals operating independent of any underworld organizations. According to authoritative sources, the places of illicit distribution are many and varied, such as: roadside taverns, service stations, houses of ill-repute, bars, hotels, restaurants, retail drugstores, and unscrupulous physicians."

So Congress had identified the problem by 1956, even before Hennings became involved. Although there had been a lag of twenty years from the time when the drug was introduced to the time when it was placed under a prescription restriction, and a lag of ten years before the warnings in the medical literature had come to the attention of Congress, it had come. State controls were a chaotic patchwork of laws with no uniformity. Some still required only prescriptions for the drugs. In the great majority of states possession of amphetamines or barbiturates or the peddling of them was a misdemeanor, often with a maximum fine of $100. No other controls existed. No shipment invoices were required, no inventory controls, no duplicate copies of purchase orders were required nor were they available to federal inspectors except on a *voluntary* basis. In other words, there was no system or procedure to monitor the billions of these pills that were shipped from the manufacturer to distributors, to drugstores, to private doctors and to hospitals.

The Subcommittee report turned itself inside out. It concluded on the one hand that the "increasing abuse of amphetamines and barbiturates and the resulting dangers to the individual and to society demonstrates the need for stronger legislation and more rigorous enforcement to eliminate this serious problem," which was all true. Then it said: "The Subcommittee believes that the primary responsibility for control of the abuses of barbiturates and amphetamines *rests with the states.*" What happened?

After the hearings were completed, Hale Boggs and the ranking Republican on the Subcommittee, John W. Byrnes of Wisconsin, visited Commissioner Anslinger at his office in the Federal Bureau of Narcotics. Boggs told him that it looked like the Congress was going to put him in charge of illegal traffic in amphetamines and barbiturates. Anslinger, a tough, blunt man, bolted. He didn't want jurisdiction in this area and he made that very plain. He told Boggs and Byrnes that he was having enough problems with the growing heroin and marihuana traffic and that if he were given this new responsibility he would not have enough manpower to enforce it. If Anslinger did not want to bend, there was nobody in Washington big enough to bend him. Since his appointment as narcotics commissioner in 1930, Anslinger had built an empire and become *the* national spokesman on drug abuse. He had a cadre of congressional support on Capitol Hill that echoed his sentiments and was as loyal to him as any of J. Edgar Hoover's sycophants were to him. His philosophy of law enforcement was developed during his reign as a deputy commissioner of prohibition when doors were smashed open and police yelled, "Hands up!" That was how he felt you should handle a drug problem. After the meeting between Boggs and Anslinger, amphetamines and barbiturates were no longer included in the then-pending narcotics legislation. That's why the report did a flip-flop by avoiding the obvious conclusions of its findings. In one respect Anslinger was probably right: he didn't have enough manpower. One reason for his manpower shortage, of course, was that he had agents charging around making marihuana arrests. There would always be more newspaper coverage of heroin and marihuana seizures than of a bunch of pills.

Anslinger's wish for a tough narcotics control law was realized in 1956. The law in fact was a crowning tribute to his life and philosophy, and one of the most repressive pieces of legislation ever passed by the u.s. Congress. Called the Narcotics Control Act of 1956, sometimes the Boggs Act, it required that drug addicts register and obtain special certificates when leaving the country and surrender the certificate when returning. It increased the minimum and maximum penalties for all drug offenses to two to ten years for the first offense, five to twenty for the second offense, and ten to forty for the third offense. It provided a ten-year sentence for selling marihuana and a possible death penalty, upon a jury's recommendation, for an adult convicted of selling heroin to a minor. Opponents were derided as "bleeding hearts" by Anslinger, but there weren't many of them. The bill breezed through Congress and was signed into law by President Eisenhower in July of 1956. Court decisions later modified some of the law's provisions.

The full Committee on Ways and Means in its report on that 1956 drug bill made a notable suggestion about amphetamines and barbiturates. It said they should come under the commerce clause of the constitution rather than the tax clause, under which marihuana was controlled. The commerce clause was suggested because the drugs were legitimately manufactured and were legitimately shipped in interstate traffic. So on the opening day of the next Congress in January of 1957, Boggs and Byrnes introduced a bill to regulate amphetamines and barbiturates through the Food and Drug Administration (FDA). Hearings were held but were never completed, nor were they ever published. That's as far as the bill ever went in the House.

In 1958 Senator Hennings read his newspaper story and his interest in amphetamines was sparked. In the House the spark was going out. Hale Boggs, a man of considerable influence, did not reintroduce the bill; the only man who did was Representative James Delaney, Democrat of New York, who chaired neither a committee nor a subcommittee and so had no platform from which to rally support. But Hennings had a great deal of support. Regulating amphetamines and barbiturates was not at the top of Senator Hennings' list of priorities but having introduced his bill in January, he was making plans to hold hearings on it with his Juvenile Delinquency Subcommittee. The Subcommittee had investigative but no legislative power. It could not report a bill to the Senate floor for a vote. It could only submit its bill to the Labor and Public Welfare Committee for its consideration. That committee, which traditionally handles health legislation, could then report it to the floor, or sit on it.

The first apparent effect of Hennings' bill was to jog the FDA into requiring that amphetamine inhalers be prescription items. It was a belated order, coming some fifteen years after very serious abuses were recognized. It was also shortsighted. One company found a loophole and exploited it. The Pfiffer Company of St. Louis put out a methamphetamine inhaler which skirted the ban on amphetamines. Called a Valo Inhaler, it was quickly picked up by amphetamine abusers and addicts. This product was marketed over the counter and unchecked by the FDA despite the findings by Hennings' staff that in Kansas City sales of inhalers were averaging about one thousand above normal, and despite police reports of a marked increase in juvenile crime and arrests. The corporate conscience of Pfiffer being what it was, it was kept on the market until February of 1965 when the FDA finally got around to requiring prescriptions for it. The Valo Inhaler contained 150 milligrams of methamphetamine, a good jolt even by an addict's standards.

In November of 1959 the Juvenile Delinquency Subcommittee went to California, the bellwether of the American drug culture, to investigate a wide range of juvenile problems. Besides Hennings, the Subcommittee consisted of Democrats Sam J. Ervin, Jr., of North Carolina, Estes Kefauver of Tennessee, John A. Carroll of Colorado, Thomas Dodd of Connecticut and Philip Hart of Michigan. Only two were Republicans, Alexander Wiley of Wisconsin and Roman Hruska of Nebraska. The hearings opened at the State Building in Los Angeles. Only Hennings, Hruska and Carroll were present, along with a large supporting staff. The testimony dwelled on marihuana use but as the evidence developed a curious fact emerged. The Subcommittee discovered that the repressive 1956 Narcotics Control Act was killing off some of the supplies of heroin and marihuana, and that in turn the traffic in amphetamines and barbiturates had increased. The Subcommittee's staff investigator, Marvin Fullmer, testified that marihuana was not the only "dangerous habit" enjoyed by young people. "Dropping pills enjoys a surprising popularity among boys and girls of high school age, or even younger," he said. "These pills include barbiturates and amphetamines, which apparently are readily available to youngsters from various sources," Fullmer said, and noted that the pills were more plentiful than marihuana. He told the Subcommittee what had been known for years—that the pills were supplied directly by drugstores, bars, truck stops, gas stations and a variety of other places of business, especially along the Mexican-California border. One reason for their easy availability there was that large shipments into Mexico were routinely made by U.S. firms such as Smith Kline & French, Eli Lilly and other drug companies, both large and small. Also, U.S.-owned companies operated plants in Mexico with loose scrutiny. The pills often found their way to the border where they were sold on the black market, sometimes for as little as ten cents a pill, often for more.

The 1956 narcotics law was having its unanticipated effect. The narcotics supply seemed to be slowed up but springing up in its place was a brisk trade in legally produced pills. The addict population that demanded drugs wasn't making a wholesale switch but it was a significant enough one to warn that everything had not been solved by the 1956 law. When the Hennings Subcommittee was making these findings, some of the medical literature was suggesting that while amphetamines could be a problem, abuse was on the decline. However, even as these sanguine reports were written, the medical profession was creating a new avenue of abuse. Several West Coast doctors, particularly in California, were now injecting Methedrine into heroin addicts as a supposed cure. Methedrine, which is the Burroughs Wellcome brand name for its methamphetamine, is a particularly potent form of amphetamine. Many responsible doctors regarded the practice as at best risky and at worst illegal and highly dangerous. But the "cure" forged another link between amphetamines and the drug culture. Heroin addicts gladly testified to its wonders.

The FDA and state agencies investigated the practice. The violation of the doctor-patient relationship posed a delicate legal question and investigations were confined to cases where the practice appeared flagrant, such as long lines of addicts waiting their turn outside a doctor's office. Besides supplying heroin addicts with Methedrine or Desoxyn, another methamphetamine, some doctors were providing the same happy service for alcoholics. Several successful investigations were initiated during the late 1950s and early 1960s in California, particularly in the San Francisco area. Often, investigators found, doctors would prescribe the speed with a minimal physical examination, sock in seven dollars for the office visit, and write a generous prescription. One Salinas, California, doctor who was convicted was in fact writing the prescriptions without an examination at all. Sometimes he would see 400 patients a day, giving him a grand total of $2,800 for his day's work. As one Methedrine user described it: "You'd get within two blocks of his office and you'd start seeing people you knew from all over."

Sometimes an accommodating doctor would prescribe as many as fifty or one hundred ampules and addicts resold their legal stock of Methedrine on the street at a great profit, thereby supporting their heroin habit. At least mugging and check forging abated. Some pharmacies were also convicted for selling Methedrine or Desoxyn, also a methamphetamine, without prescription, or with phony telephone prescriptions, or with prescriptions so crudely written that a child's gullibility would have been tested. With the outbreak of unfavorable publicity in 1962 and a request from the California Attorney General's office, Burroughs Wellcome withdrew Methedrine ampules from retail pharmacies, although not from hospitals, and Abbott Laboratories of Chicago withdrew Desoxyn liquid ampules from the market.

Hennings' West Coast hearings did not investigate this abuse, since it was just beginning when the hearings were held. The hearings ended in mid-November of 1959 in San Francisco. Hennings' bill on amphetamines and barbiturates was with the Labor and Public Welfare Committee which was chaired by Senator Lister Hill, a Democrat from Alabama. He was, by southern standards, a moderate. The Hennings bill was not oppressive. Its main purpose was to require record-keeping all along the distribution chain. Then, when diversion to a black market was noted, records could be examined and sources could be more readily found. It did not impose production quotas or interfere in any way with the number of pills that could be produced. It required registration of manufacturers to keep track of the legal producers, but this was far less onerous than a licensing requirement. It was, in every regard, a mild bill, seeking only to make enforcement easier but not to interfere with legitimate trade.

Lister Hill let the bill sit on his desk. And although Hennings and other members of the Subcommittee sent letters and memos to Hill asking for action, none came. Hennings, the Congress and the country had to wait. Why Hill didn't act is not at all clear, but the most probable reason is that the problem of pill abuse had not yet caused enough public concern. So the bill languished.

In December of 1959 the Subcommittee staff outlined what it called "an ambitious program for 1960 in relating to some of the more severe problems facing the nation's youth." High on the list of the problems tackled would be the continued probe into the relationship between drugs and youth crime. The hearings began in January of 1960 and focused on the federal narcotics laws. They were to examine fully the amphetamine and barbiturate problem as well, but they were cut short. Hennings had fallen ill, either as a result of his drinking or from cancer; the cause is not clear. In May of that year he was operated on at the Mayo Clinic and his condition after that was serious enough to prevent Hennings from returning to the Senate. His condition worsened in the following months and on September 13, 1960, Hennings died at his Washington apartment at the age of 57. He was eulogized in many quarters and a *Washington Post* editorial called him "one of the past decade's outstanding liberal voices in Congress." With his leadership and direction gone, the Subcommittee confined its investigation to field work, studies, report writing and the distribution of questionnaires. Their work began to uncover more and more of the dangers of and traffic in legally produced drugs, but for the moment at least, the problem dropped completely from public view in the United States. But there were reminders elsewhere.

Following World War II, Japan perhaps more than any other combatant had sunk into virtually total economic, political and spiritual collapse. Surrender was alien to her culture yet she was forced to surrender. Two of her cities were devastated by the atomic bomb and most of her others were in ruins from conventional bombing. Her ancient culture was laid waste and nearly shattered. Like every other combatant in that war, Japan had supplied her armed forces with amphetamines. Japan had also pumped them to large segments of the civilian population. Workers in munitions factories, aircraft factories, laborers working on airfields, thousands of people connected with the war effort were taking amphetamines to work night and day to stave off defeat. When that defeat came the Japanese people sought solutions. Amphetamines seemed to be one such apparent solution. Japanese drug companies had mass-produced amphetamines to keep ahead of the expected demand, and at the war's end they found themselves with huge surpluses of the drugs. Rather than destroy them, they peddled them. They were, after all, known to alleviate depression and now depression was a national state of mind in Japan. So amphetamines soon began flooding the market. They were advertised with the slogan: "For the elimination of drowsiness and repletion of the spirit." They were a hit. There were thousands and then millions of takers. The quantity of amphetamines sold is not certain, but by 1946 the abuse of amphetamines had been detected and by 1948 it was identified as a serious if not grave medical and social problem.

Japan was a country with no tradition of drug abuse. In fact, Japanese health authorities estimated that before 1946 there were about 400 drug addicts in the whole country. The abuse began among artists, writers and entertainers but quickly spread to the young. It created social havoc at a time when the country was already in turmoil. Crime rates soared and by 1955 crimes of violence and juvenile delinquency *directly* attributable to amphetamine abuse totaled 4,866. This happened in a country with a long and honored tradition of respect for elders and respect for law. Roving bands of young Japanese made areas of some cities unsafe. In the mid-1950s, when the crisis was at its peak, Japanese health officials estimated that there were more than one million amphetamine abusers in the country. The Japanese Pharmacist Association estimated the total number of abusers at that time at 1.5 million. The estimates of the number of actual addicts varies from 200,000 to 600,000. It had risen up, a Japanese researcher said years later, "as furiously as a storm." A member of the Japanese Ministry of Health and Welfare commented: "It then spread among the younger generation and soon became a grave social evil, leading to crime and disorder; the number of addicts and the cases of mental disorder due to drug abuse increased alarmingly." Most of the abusers were young men between the ages of twenty and twenty-nine.

Amphetamines were abused in every way. Pills were popped, they were crushed and snorted, liquid amphetamine was shot up. In the midst of the crisis, Japan reacted with decisive action. In 1951, strict controls on amphetamines were instituted which sharply cut down the legal supply. But a black market flourished, since it is a relatively simple procedure to make bathtub amphetamine. Restrictions were then put on the chemical ingredients of amphetamines.

The laws grew tighter and by 1955 they were tough both in regulating production of the drug and in the criminal penalties for abusing it: legal use of amphetamine was restricted to treatment of narcolepsy; only one doctor at any hospital was authorized to dispense it; harsh prison sentences were handed out for possession or peddling. A nationwide educational program began in 1955 and the General Headquarters for the Promotion of Policy Against Amphetamines was established to coordinate the national drive against the drug. The all-out national effort began to show results. In 1954 more than 55,000 persons had been arrested for some violation of the amphetamine law. By 1956 that number had dropped to little more than 5,000 and by 1958 it had sunk to only 271 persons arrested. There were other indications of the success of the national anti-amphetamine drive. In 1954 there were 4,000 persons hospitalized for amphetamine addiction; in 1957 that dropped to only 200 persons. The epidemic was abating but it lasted for nearly a decade. But it was not over. Japan was to have more drug abuse problems. In the opinion of Dr. Maurice Seevers, an eminent pharmacologist and drug researcher and an American drug consultant to the Japanese government, the amphetamine epidemic created a social pattern of drug abuse that has plagued Japan to this day.

The Japanese experience furnished much medical data. One was the full documentation of amphetamine psychosis, a mental disorder that is indistinguishable from paranoid schizophrenia. The Japanese studies did not reveal what it was that triggered the psychosis and for a while it was suspected that the loss of sleep caused by the stimulation of the amphetamine was the cause. Later controlled studies suggested that it was not sleep loss, but something specific in the action of amphetamine on the brain that caused psychosis. What was recognized in the Japanese epidemic and later outbreaks is that a high number of amphetamine users inevitably suffer from paranoia. Often it is more difficult to treat medically than spontaneous disorders, and the psychosis does *not* just occur with borderline psychotics.

In another extensive Japanese study following the epidemic, organic brain damage was discovered in a number of amphetamine addicts. The study showed some portion of the brain was actually burnt out by the constant doses of amphetamine. Of a total of 492 addicts, 69 were found to have chronic amphetamine psychosis that had occasionally lasted as long as fifteen years. Postmortem examinations revealed evidence of organic brain damage in these addicts. Organic brain damage causes confusion, disorientation and memory gaps and is, by definition, incurable.

The Japanese amphetamine epidemic, more than any of the police statistics and medical literature that had preceded it in this country, provided a stark and extreme example of the social havoc amphetamines could wreak if left unchecked, and a grim catalogue of the physical and psychological hazards the drug posed to users. There was conclusive evidence to demonstrate that the drug was very, very psychologically addictive and certainly in some cases physically addictive. Organic brain damage, paranoia, hostility and violence are some of the consequences of amphetamine abuse. Infection, malnutrition and dehydration are among the physical consequences. But the Japanese episode and other reports on amphetamine hazards that appeared in the medical literature were ignored or forgotten at the time. The good news was far more pleasant and the American drug industry was doing a splendid job in spreading that good news and overproducing the pills. But the Japanese experience was there sounding an alarm. It had established that amphetamines were very hazardous to people and society and indicated that other countries should re-examine their policies on drugs. It proved that amphetamine was different from other drugs, different from heroin which was the focus of our national effort. Heroin for most addicts reaches a plateau and the addict comes to need the drug to normalize himself, to "get straight" as they call it. It finally becomes a drug which allows many addicts to function normally and avoid withdrawal pains. But not amphetamines. The Japanese experience showed amphetamines did not normalize people. Amphetamine was, the Japanese revealed, perhaps the drug with the widest range of hazards to mind, body and society yet encountered.

So what did the Japanese epidemic teach us? In 1958, twelve years after the initial outbreak of the epidemic there, a very influential book on amphetamines was written by Dr. Chauncey Leake, a professor of pharmacology at Ohio State University with a long trail of honoraria following his name. In it he declared flatly that "no clear case of addiction to *d*-amphetamine has been reported." But what about the Japanese? Well, the professor confessed at the end of his book that he really hadn't seen the twelve-year-old story until his book was in galley proofs. So he gave it a quick page and cavalierly declared that the Japanese clinicians were apparently "confused" regarding the addictive properties of amphetamine. His book, called *The Amphetamines, Their Actions and Uses* was a warm tribute to amphetamines. Dr. Leake reported that their toxicity was relatively low, and that they might not even be bad for a morning pick-me-up for the depressed patient.

There are a couple of curious things about the book. For one, in the introduction he dedicated the book to Gordon Alles, the chemist who first synthesized amphetamines in the United States and who sold his patent to Smith Kline & French. Alles, Dr. Leake tells us, was a good friend of his. In that same introduction he admitted that the book "will probably disappoint pharmacologists who are expert in the knowledge of these drugs, but it may help physicians to use them wisely." This seems to be an astonishing contradiction. If it "disappoints" those experts who really know something about amphetamines, then why will it help doctors to use them wisely? And one does wonder why Dr. Leake was writing this book anyway, if he isn't and wasn't a pharmacological expert on amphetamines.

Dr. Leake, unfortunately, was not alone. Other medical hoopla made amphetamines sound just as good. It was touted as a cure for heroin addiction, depression, overweight and nearly everything else, and no more dangerous than a cup of coffee.

Yet in the same year Leake's book came out, Dr. Phillip Connell in England, in a landmark study, reported on forty-two cases which indicated that paranoid psychosis, which he said was indistinguishable from paranoid schizophrenia, was a direct result of amphetamine abuse. He also described cases of amphetamine psychosis occurring in people with no previous history of psychosis. Dr. Connell was not "confused." His conclusion has since been substantiated.

There was no easy answer. The strict law enforcement measures enacted in Japan would not have worked here. Presumably they would have had the same result as the stiff law and order measures already taken here to control narcotics—failure. But the hazards of amphetamine use—and more than *ten million of the pills a day* were being pumped out by the drug industry—should have been unequivocally stated to doctors either by the industry or the FDA. Strict record-keeping for all sales and shipments such as Senator Hennings' bill demanded should have been required very early. A real effort should have been made to determine the *real* medical indications for use and, if necessary, a production quota should have been established so that no surplus was available for diversion. Advertising and promotion should have been considered more carefully by the industry, the ad agencies and the FDA. It might have helped. But the drug companies continued with the advertising, promotion and production of this drug, and its potential hazards, such as paranoia, malnutrition, addiction, organic brain damage and hallucinations, remained hidden from the public and ignored by the drug industry.

2: Dodd Takes On the Drug Industry

> *You could never quite say the guy was a total son of a bitch.*
>
> A FORMER DODD AIDE

IN January of 1961 the 87th Congress convened following the November elections. With the death of Senator Hennings that past September, the chairmanship of the Juvenile Delinquency Subcommittee was vacant. Named to succeed him as chairman was Senator Thomas J. Dodd of Connecticut. As chairman he continued to investigate the abuse of legitimate drugs.

Thomas Dodd. The name evokes mixed reactions. He was a loner, a censured United States Senator, a man whose example seems to personify the venality of public office and the darkest aspects of our political system. But Dodd's character, like his public stances, was fragmented into several different parts that never really seem to fit together. He was a contradictory man, caught between good and bad instincts, caught between zealous anti-Communism abroad and social liberalism at home. He was a man whose physical appearance suggested uncompromising integrity. He had swept-back white hair, a granite profile and a steely look from clear blue eyes. There was a determined cadence to his voice, and he carried a pipe that added a final note of distinction. But under the impressive image there was a dark aspect to this man who was abusing a public trust.

Part of the public record of Thomas Dodd is clear: he stole. The facts began unfolding in January of 1966 by columnists Jack Anderson and Drew Pearson in their nationally syndicated column, "Washington Merry-Go-Round." Their most damning evidence showed that Dodd had pocketed vast sums of money collected for his 1964 senatorial campaign. Anderson and Pearson were supplied the documentation for their charges by four of Dodd's former Senate aides, the key one being James Boyd, Dodd's former administrative assistant. As the disclosures mounted in the newspapers, Dodd fought back. He issued a series of denials, sued Pearson and Anderson for five million dollars and floated rumors about Boyd's personal integrity. The rumors were untrue but the evidence against Dodd wasn't. Boyd had been meticulous in documenting the evidence. Anderson and Pearson kept hitting away, column after column, and a national controversy erupted over the conduct of Senator Dodd.

The Senate was reluctant to do anything but, finally, as the evidence seemed incontrovertible, it moved to act. In April, three months after the first column appeared, Senator John Stennis, Democrat of Mississippi, and Chairman of the Senate Ethics Committee—more formally known as the Committee on Standards and Conduct—announced hearings on the conduct of Senator Dodd. These hearings, while they carefully scrutinized Dodd's misuse of campaign money, skirted other issues—such as junkets—which are all part of the Senate game and not to be interfered with. They were hearings designed to rock Dodd's boat, but not the Senate's.

Dodd alternated between declaring his innocence and backhandedly admitting his guilt. Finally, in the fifth and final session of the Ethics Committee, Dodd flatly admitted he had needed the campaign money. That session, held on St. Patrick's Day in 1967, capped the investigations and sealed Dodd's fate. "This has been a cumulative thing over many years," Dodd said that day, "I would pay off one and in order to do so I had to borrow from another. I can't remember beyond that . . . I got in the hole in 1956, and I was never able to get out, and some of these things had to be paid off."

That was part of the explanation. The other part was that Dodd, who was born poor, took more than he needed to pay debts. He had financed the good life and bought the finer things—a country estate, trips to Europe for the family, expensive gifts for his wife and children. But he had not started out that way. His terms in the House of Representatives and his early Senate career had been scandal-free. But he had seen others do it, seen others grow rich off the public trust, and he did it too. He had just been more flagrant about it. He had not sought office to make himself rich, it was a process of learning with him and not an instinct.

The Ethics Committee deliberately and painfully reached the conclusion that a colleague should be censured, and recommended to the full Senate that Dodd be censured. On June 23, 1967, following nine days of debate on the Senate floor, including Dodd's pleading on his own behalf, censure was voted 92 to 2. Standing with Dodd at the end were Abraham Ribicoff, who stood with him out of loyalty to a fellow Senator from Connecticut, and Russell Long, a Democrat of Louisiana, Dodd's self-appointed defender during the floor debate whose antics and emotional outbursts probably hurt Dodd more than they helped. The censure vote was based on the charge that Dodd had diverted $116,038 from campaign funds to his personal use. Following the vote that afternoon, a wounded Dodd retreated to his Senate office where he waited alone with his wife.

This memory of Dodd will remain fixed. But there were other, lesser-known facets of the man which were crucial.

Dodd was born in 1907 to an Irish Catholic family in Norwich, Connecticut. Norwich is in the eastern half of Connecticut, that part of the state that is economically depressed
and far removed from the swank western suburbs that ring
New York City. Dodd was the youngest of five children
and the only son. The family was poor, but not desperately
so by the standards of that day. It was a strong Catholic
family, and for a while Dodd attended a seminary in New
York state. He did not like the life there and left. Then
as in later life, Dodd was restless and a loner; he was not
one to be constricted by rules laid down by someone else.
After graduation from college in Providence, Rhode Island,
he entered Yale Law School. During his final year at Yale
in 1932 Dodd became president of the Yale Democratic Club
and organized a group called "The Flying Wedge" which
debated one another along the campaign circuit of the 1932
election. It was here that Dodd got his first taste of politics
and became accustomed to public speaking.

In the spring of 1933 Dodd was graduated from Yale Law
School and then joined the FBI and started on the road of
public service. Dodd did not last long there. He participated
in the attempted capture of John Dillinger in Rhinelander,
Wisconsin, and soon became disenchanted with the FBI.
Asked by his superior to monitor a neighbor's mail, he
balked. This and other experiences led him to quit the FBI
within a year. He became then the Connecticut director of
the state's National Youth Administration, a part of the New
Deal program. A couple of thousand miles away, another
young and ambitious man, Lyndon Johnson, acquired the
same post in his state of Texas. Their careers were to inter-
twine. They met in Washington on several occasions in the
1930s and their friendship was mutual and lasting.

There appear to be two periods in Dodd's life which
shaped his political ideas. The first occurred in the late 1930s
when Dodd, after leaving the National Youth Administration, was a special assistant to the U.S. Attorney General.

As part of a special unit in the Deep South, he defended the civil liberties of black people, the rights of laborers to organize, prosecuted racists, and chased the Ku Klux Klan. Seeing the plight of people with an entire social system stacked against them kindled a lingering zeal for civil rights and social reform.

Dodd's strong anti-Communist views were also shaped by personal experience. He went to the Nuremberg Trials in a minor role and quickly rose to a position of prominence. Some observers of the trial later said Dodd, always a good prosecutor, held much of it together. But he returned from that experience a changed man. His hair had turned prematurely white and he had developed an abiding anti-Communist world-view. The details of what happened to Dodd at Nuremberg are largely a mystery. "It was the one thing I never heard him really talk about," said a longtime aide, "I think the experience shook him so much he really couldn't talk about it." Dodd apparently came away believing the Russians had been duplicitous and deceitful and that experience seared him. But his anti-Communism was tempered by a real awareness of the damage reckless charges could reap. When he was acting chairman of the Internal Security Subcommittee investigations he found that the New York chapter of the Committee for a Sane Nuclear Policy (SANE) was infiltrated with Communists. Rather than attack the whole organization, which Dodd had no love for, he worked quietly with the national leadership to put their New York chapter in order. Eventually the national leadership revoked the New York chapter's membership. Dodd's concern for civil liberties won the respect of Norman Cousins, then editor of the *Saturday Review* and national chairman of SANE.

Following his return from Nuremberg, Dodd settled in West Hartford, Connecticut. In 1952 he was nominated to run for Congress, won the election in November, and was then re-elected in 1954. After an unsuccessful Senate bid in

1956, Dodd, always something of a maverick in the state party, fought for his renomination in 1958 and this time he won. In January of 1959 Thomas J. Dodd joined the u.s. Senate.

Dodd was mercurial, moody. He drank too much and he was given to nasty outbursts in which he impugned the motives of fellow senators. He once angrily attacked Senate Majority Leader Mike Mansfield, only to sheepishly apologize the next day. He was a raconteur and a better than average mimic. His temper was Irish and so was the gamut of his emotions. He was never a member of the Senate's inner circle and in fact was something of an outcast in the Senate even before his censure. Once on a track and triggered by something that repulsed him, Dodd could be relentless. His absenteeism in the Senate, however, was frequent and many times in his career after laying the groundwork for the investigation of some social ill, he would let it drop. Sometimes, as his former aides-turned-informants suggest, he was doing favors for friends, or for money. At other times he was just lazy.

Dodd was intelligent but not really gifted. He had a more than generous capacity for self-pity, especially evident when his censure was imminent. His lashing out, rumor spreading and claims of a conspiracy out to ruin him were inexcusable, as was his pocketing of funds. But Dodd could be prodded into taking on important and powerful interests. His was one of the early and insistent voices calling for some measure of gun control, even before the assassination of President Kennedy.

And in 1961 with the stewardship of the Juvenile Delinquency Subcommittee, he began an investigation into the abuse of legal drugs that was to pit him against a formidable medical and drug lobby and the indifference of his colleagues. In that fight, Dodd did not quit. He pushed during times when the going was difficult and unrewarding. Clearly there was political capital in it; he needed an issue to run with.

But to Dodd's credit—and to ignore it is historically negligent—he raised an insistent voice when no one else in Congress did about the dangers of legal drug abuse and the culpability of the drug industry in fostering a drug-oriented culture in this country. As a former Dodd aide remarked: "Dodd always kept you guessing. Yes, he took money, he lied, he cheated, he did a lot of lousy things. But he did just enough good things in the Senate to make you unsure. You could never quite figure him out. You could never quite say the guy was a total son of a bitch." In his lengthy drug investigations Dodd would indeed show he was not a total son of a bitch.

He came to the Senate well connected. His old friend Lyndon Johnson was now the powerful majority leader and a man of fierce loyalties. Dodd, as a trusted friend, asked Johnson for a favor. He wanted a seat on the Foreign Relations Committee. This was almost unheard of. No freshman Senator was ever assigned to that prestigious committee. Johnson promised it to him but was unable to deliver, and to assuage Dodd's disappointment he got him named to three highly prized committees—Space, Appropriations and Judiciary. As one Senator remarked about it at the time: "Quite a haul."

Dodd was named to the Juvenile Delinquency Subcommittee under the Judiciary Committee's jurisdiction in his first term. Then when Hennings died and left the Subcommittee chairmanship vacant, Dodd sought it despite his very low ranking on the seniority scale. It seemed unlikely that he could get it, but Dodd had influential friends.

"However he got it, it was definitely a prize, there's no question about that," said a member of the Subcommittee staff during that period. "Dodd had wanted it and I think Johnson helped him get it. Johnson and Eastland were fairly close and Johnson's friendship with Dodd went way back to the New Deal days. Then there was Dodd's support of Johnson for the presidency in 1960. I think the chairmanship may have been the payoff for that support." However he came to it, Dodd got the chairmanship of the Juvenile Delinquency Subcommittee. Others with more seniority on that subcommittee had other chairmanships of other subcommittees but Dodd got the one he wanted.

For several months the Subcommittee staff had been preparing investigations; one of the key ones was on the abuse of amphetamines and barbiturates. The key member of that staff was Carl Perian who was research director when Dodd took it over and was later elevated to staff director. Perian is a hard-nosed guy. He is a recognized criminologist, an expert on juvenile problems and he is a digger. He recognized that the function of a subcommittee investigation was not so much to find information, although that is important, but to arouse public support since that is the only way to get a bill passed into law. These investigations are publicity vehicles and Perian was very good at organizing them. Early he persuaded Dodd to pick up where Hennings left off.

On May 23, 1961, Dodd reintroduced the Hennings bill. He said at the time that "existing federal laws are wholly inadequate to combat the steady increase in the misuses of these drugs." The bill was written with the advice and consent of the FDA which felt it was a necessary step. Its criminal provisions sought to remove the difficult to prove provision that a pill trafficker must be shown to have traveled across state lines before federal agents could make an arrest. It also sought to increase the criminal penalties for each trafficking offense to a $2,000 fine and two years in prison. The provisions which affected the drug industry directly were very mild.

As in the earlier Hennings bill and the similar one introduced in the House by Representative James Delaney, there were provisions which required all manufacturers of amphetamines and barbiturates to list their names and places of business with the Secretary of Health, Education and Welfare. This was because the FDA, which would be charged with enforcing the law, is a part of HEW. All persons or businesses producing, distributing or selling the drugs, with the exception of doctors, were required to keep records. The record-keeping was the guts of the bill. It would permit FDA inspectors to find diversion points. If 10,000 pills were sent from the factory to a distributor, and he recorded receiving 8,000, then the FDA could determine that the diversion occurred en route. This was the point of the bill since these kinds of records were not universally kept. There were no production quotas, no licensing, no criminal penalties for a company whose business was slipshod enough to allow thefts.

At the time the bill was submitted the FDA was estimating that of the nine or ten *billion* amphetamines and barbiturates produced each year, about half were getting diverted from the legal trade into the black market. This was enough to supply twenty-five of these pills to every man, woman, and child in the country from the black market trade alone.

Little if anything was done on the bill for the rest of 1961. Dodd and the Subcommittee were involved in other things but early in 1962, movement was detected. In March of that year Dodd's drug bill was publicly endorsed by President Kennedy and Dodd also received signs of industry support, support that would virtually insure the bill's passage. The administration was working to get controls over these drugs in other ways. The Kefauver drug bill was then under consideration and amid that larger important bill the Administration hoped to tuck in the controls over amphetamines and barbiturates. Deputy Attorney General Nicholas Katzenbach wrote a letter to Oren Harris, chairman of the House Commerce Committee which was considering the larger bill, requesting "more stringent" controls over the drugs. Abraham Ribicoff, then secretary of HEW, wanted it, too. So the amphetamine and barbiturate controls were incorporated into the Kefauver bill and they contained all the basic provisions of the Dodd bill. And then the drug industry supported it, publicly. George Cain, president of Abbott

Laboratories, producer of Desoxyn, a large-selling methamphetamine, said it was a fine bill, but he cautioned that "no
unwarranted burdens" should be imposed. Cain was speaking on behalf of the Pharmaceutical Manufacturers Association, the trade association and Washington lobby for the
drug industry. Eugene N. Beesley, the president of Eli Lilly,
the major *producer* of barbiturates, also said the controls
were needed. With the Administration behind it, with a
Democratic chairman on the House committee in charge of
the bill, and with the drug industry behind it, one would
suspect the time was ripe for passage. But something happened. In an executive session of the House Commerce
Committee, the controls over amphetamines and barbiturates
got lopped off. Why? The Committee explained that inadequate legislative hearings had been held. One wonders what
more might have been needed to get the bill passed. The FDA
which was charged with enforcing it had written it. The
industry it was to regulate said publicly it was for it. And
then it was such a small part of a big bill. Why didn't it get
through? It is likely that in the infighting which went on for
passage of that larger drug bill the amphetamine and barbiturate record-keeping provisions became a part of the "you
give us that and we'll give you this" bartering between the
government and the industry. The industry's lip service at
the hearings apparently meant nothing and the Administration's support was half-hearted. It was enough to make one
wonder, if this bill was such a good idea and if everyone
concerned was for it, why hadn't it gotten anywhere and why
was it purposely dropped when it stood a chance of becoming
law? Perhaps there was something more touchy than was
evident; perhaps the issue wasn't as universally popular as
it had seemed.

In August of 1962, at around the same time Congress
was lopping the amphetamine and barbiturate controls out of
the Kefauver drug bill, Dodd staged hearings in Los Angeles,

Chicago and Washington. Because Dodd chaired the Juvenile Delinquency Subcommittee the emphasis was on juvenile crime and street abuse of the drugs. That was Perian's inclination as well and it was the best way to attract notice.

The most reliable index of street drug abuse is arrest records. It only describes a small slice of what is happening, but it is a guide. Estimates differ on how much arrest statistics reveal, but some experts believe that only 10 percent of the addicts of any one drug come to the attention of police. Toward the end of the 1950s and early 1960s there was evidence of an alarming increase in street abuse of amphetamines. It had not blossomed into a crisis, but it was edging toward one. The Dodd subcommittee, holding its hearings at the Old State Building in Los Angeles with only Dodd and staff members in attendance, heard the catalogue of statistics. Various explanations were offered for the increase. Frequently the effects of the 1956 Narcotics Act, which had dried up much of the heroin and marihuana trade, were cited as they had been to Hennings three years earlier. The pills went by many street names, "pep pills," "uppers," "bennies," "meth," "dexies." Liquid amphetamine was then called "crank," "splash" and "speed," but later both liquid and pills were called "speed." Barbiturates were called "downers," "goofballs," "red devils" and "yellow jackets." They were being gobbled up, Dodd was told, because they were available, cheap, made you feel good, and because such a small legal risk was involved. The Los Angeles police told the Dodd subcommittee of a woman with a long police record as a narcotics violator. In a raid on her hotel room, police recovered 75,000 pills of various kinds. She was arrested for violating the dangerous drug law. Her lawyer appeared in court for her—she did not appear—and he pleaded her guilty. She was fined $50. Police said it was typical. If a few ounces of marihuana had been found instead of the 75,000 pills, she might have gone to prison. The Subcommittee also learned about a Los Angeles doctor convicted by a jury for illegally doling out amphetamines and barbiturates. He had sold them directly to patients after cursory medical examinations with a high profit margin since he was probably paying less than a penny a pill to a mail order house. His nurse testified that he was selling about 8,000 pills a week. Police investigated. One sheriff's deputy who stood a shade under six feet and weighed 136 pounds visited the doctor. He was too fat, the doctor decided, and sold him a supply of amphetamines for weight reduction. The doctor was fined $100 for each of the twenty counts he was convicted on. He was not placed on probation. Then the imposition of all the fines was suspended because the court decided he was not guilty of moral turpitude. The case had been tried in 1958, and when the Subcommittee was holding its hearings in 1962, the good doctor was still practicing medicine in Los Angeles. It was not an isolated example but part of a pattern, part of the double standard governing traffic in corporately-produced drugs. Suppose the doctor had been caught selling $800 worth of marihuana a week?

Dodd heard a litany of arrest statistics that suggested the seriousness of the problem in the Southern California area. Police separate their drug arrest statistics into several categories—marihuana, opiates such as heroin, and dangerous drugs, of which amphetamines and barbiturates were the major items. In Seattle, between 1961 and 1962, police reported a 59 percent increase in arrests for dangerous drugs; in San Francisco for the same two years the increase was 76 percent. Other areas—St. Louis, Baltimore, Chicago, the state of Florida, were all showing this same kind of upsurge.

In the Los Angeles hearings, Captain Walter Colwell, head of the narcotics division of the Los Angeles Police Department, testified that in 1957 there were 181 persons arrested for possession or sale of dangerous drugs. In 1961 this rose to an even 1,300 persons and the rate of increase appeared to be quickening. Captain Colwell also testified that "these legal drugs now represent nearly two-thirds of all juvenile drug arrests." Dodd interrupted him:

> Senator Dodd: "You know, if I may say so—I don't want to interrupt you—that looks like an epidemic."
>
> Captain Colwell: "This is an epidemic."

Colwell reiterated what had become indisputable, namely that the pills were easier to buy than marihuana. While conceding that pills from clandestine labs were a factor in the pill traffic, police officials and other investigators estimated that over 90 percent of the amphetamines and barbiturates found in the black market were of legitimate origin. The ethical drug companies are to the pill black market what the Turkish poppy fields are to the heroin trade. The Los Angeles Police reported that Benzedrine and Dexedrine, both Smith Kline & French products, were the most commonly seized amphetamines. They also reported that amphetamines were often used in tandem with heroin or barbiturates. As one police official told the Subcommittee:

> "Every dope peddler we have picked up has a complete assortment of pills available for sale. Dangerous drugs are a bigger problem for youth than heroin or marihuana."

The California Attorney General dropped 90,000 Benzedrine tablets on the witness table during testimony and said it was less than half of the 190,000 he had bought at a drugstore in Tijuana.

There were newspaper stories at the time which generated publicity that helped Dodd's case. One headline screamed: "Goofballed youths kick old man to death in park." Dodd's subcommittee deliberately dwelled on some drug-related highway accidents to get the message home again. One of these cases involved the driver of a truck who was on amphetamines and hallucinated that he had a co-driver. While the truck was moving he stretched out in the rear of the cab to sleep and let his "co-driver" take over. The truck crashed and the driver lived to tell about it, and to learn that he had been driving alone.

Arrest statistics and sensational news stories of amphetamine abuse told only part of the story. There was reluctance by some police to do much of anything about the pill traffic because the legal penalties were so minor, so they ignored a lot of it. One example was offered by two New York policemen who had made an arrest of a drug peddler who was selling a wide assortment of pills, amphetamines and barbiturates. When they brought him and his pills into the station house for booking, the other policemen laughed. Pills? Why arrest him, why bother? From then on, they said, they hadn't bothered and made no more arrests for possessing or peddling pills.

Other hypocrisies also conspired to diminish the real extent of amphetamine abuse and to submerge the "gray market" of home abuse, the abuse of the respectable middle class. One incident in a northern New Jersey hospital was described by a witness, who was a drug consultant at the hospital: "I was at the hospital when they brought in two people for drug ingestion. They arrived very close to one another on the same night. Both of them had overdosed on amphetamine, in fact they may have even taken the very same brand, I'm not sure. Anyway, one of them was a 19-year-old girl who had been brought in by her friends. They were hairy and freaky looking and they waited around for her. The doctors in the emergency room shot her with tranquilizers and almost immediately the hospital called the police and turned her over to them. She was processed through the criminal justice system. With the housewife they were much more understanding. They attended her, brought her to a hospital room, and kept her in the hospital for thirty-six hours of observation. Then they discharged her to the custody of her family."

What was the real extent of the amphetamine problem in the early 1960s? Were the police reports reliable? In 1963 a careful and very well-documented study confirmed the enormity of street abuse of amphetamines and made the statistics gathered by Dodd and the police agencies appear to be conservative.

Dr. John Griffith, a young psychiatrist who had made studies of amphetamine addiction in the Air Force, and who was to devote much of his time and energy to the study of the drug, was then director of the Oklahoma Mental Health Planning Committee in Oklahoma City when a unique opportunity came to study the illicit traffic in amphetamines. The project began in a very human way. The daughter of a friend of then Oklahoma Governor Henry Bellman became addicted to amphetamines and the governor, seeking answers for this problem for his friend, asked Griffith's group to look into the traffic and illegal abuse of amphetamines. The project began, with full official support. Dr. Griffith, who later reported his findings in the *American Journal of Psychiatry,* found that doctors in Oklahoma City did not consider amphetamine abuse to be a problem of any size although there had been a high number of police arrests for illegal amphetamine traffic. The police department reported a very high increase in amphetamine- and barbiturate-related arrests within the previous three years. The pills could be purchased at that time for about $3 per dozen on the street. Griffith and his associates attempted several approaches but finally decided to make direct contact with amphetamine abusers and peddlers. When they met, in bars, restaurants or other selected spots, Griffith told them he was a psychiatrist studying the problem. He was considered suspect at first, but he eventually established credibility with the addicts and peddlers. He interviewed a total of forty-six abusers and three peddlers. To verify their authenticity, he checked with hospital and police authorities. He discovered that hospital admissions reflected only a small percentage of the total problem of amphetamine abuse. Some of the peddlers he interviewed admitted handling as many as 100,000 pills in a single transaction. The pills were nearly always of legitimate origin, Griffith learned. He concluded on the basis of his study that there were between 1,000 and 5,000 people in metropolitan Oklahoma City—out of a total population of 500,000—who obtained amphetamines illegally on a regular basis. He witnessed an addict inject 250 milligrams of liquid amphetamine at once and noted that the Valo Inhaler, the Pfiffer Company product, which had slipped through the FDA loophole, was a drug of choice for methamphetamine. He attended a "Valo party" where the methamphetamine from the inhaler was extracted and shot up. Violence was almost predictable, and it came. He watched a knife attack by a young man on "his woman" who was a prostitute, whom the man imagined was cheating on him. Griffith noted that "dependence on the use of amphetamine and barbiturate drugs seemed incompatible with social drives leading to gainful employment or education pursuits. As a consequence, crime or prostitution was the main source of the user's income." Griffith later expanded on this study and found that amphetamine traffic was not confined to large cities. "We picked three small towns at random in Oklahoma," he said later. "The smallest had a population of 1,500. We found that some degree of drug traffic was going on in each of these small towns." He also added: "We found, too, that habituation to amphetamines and barbiturates occurs in members of all classes of society. It is not confined merely to people who do not take baths or do not go to church. Once I lectured on drugs to a group of teen-agers at a fashionable Presbyterian church. The response of the audience: 'Tell us something new.'"

Griffith reported that the crime statistics of Oklahoma City parallel the national average "so that one, with a degree of caution, might extrapolate results to be representative." If this is correct, and such an extrapolation is reliable, then in 1963 in this country there may have been about 600,000 to 700,000 serious amphetamine abusers and addicts, and the underworld network that supplied them was dealing in millions of dollars each week. What was also evident was that these drug addicts were hidden and almost unknown to the public and to many officials in charge of protecting public health.

It was obvious from Dr. Griffith's study that illegal traffic in these legal drugs was enormous and uncontrolled and that Dodd was not overstating the case when he demanded a remedy. The diversion of pills from legal channels was enormous to supply such a demand, but more importantly, the overproduction and sloppy distribution of these drugs by the ethical drug companies made diversion easy and a logical consequence. Because the prescription laws were so lax in most states, a prescription for amphetamines or barbiturates, once written, could be refilled and refilled and refilled, even after the doctor who had written it had died. Another avenue of diversion already mentioned was through Mexico. Then there were the mail order divisions: usually a printed letterhead was all the identification needed for someone to order a few thousand pills and get them, no questions asked. Pills were stolen from every place that handled them: military bases, warehouses, the drug companies themselves. They were swiped from drugstore shelves. Trucks were hijacked. They were everywhere and the only limitation was the nerve or imagination of the thief. The Subcommittee found one small West Coast drug manufacturer that had shipped more than three million amphetamine sulfate tablets in a four-month period to a Mexican distributor. That company, Robin-Winters of El Segundo, California, became suspicious and finally stopped shipment. Many more did not. The FDA, with its limited authority, had brought charges against 2,100 firms and individuals in a twelve-year period from 1952 to 1964 but it made no dent in this traffic. Nearly 90 percent of the charges were brought against pharmacists and drugstore employees.

Dodd's drug bill, like Hennings' original version, went no-where with Lister Hill's Labor and Public Welfare Committee. One problem was that Dodd was not on that Committee but had to funnel the bill through it because of its jurisdiction over health legislation.

Another problem was simply that Hill and Dodd were opposites. Lister Hill, then approaching 70 and now retired from the Senate, is a courtly, charming man who spins whimsical anecdotes. He is a history buff, a man of wry wit and keen intelligence. A believer in the old virtues, he is de-scribed by a close friend as a man who is "almost Victorian" in his approach to life and work. "Lister never went on a junket; he felt he had no right to with the public's money."

Hill for many years gave special access to the American Medical Association (AMA). He was himself a frustrated doctor. Another close friend recalls, "His father had been a doctor and Lister had wanted to become one. But the sight of blood sickened him and he turned to a career in law." In fact Hill was named after Joseph Lister, a doctor who orig-inated the principle of antisepsis. Despite the access he always granted the AMA, Hill's relationship with organized medicine was strained and never repaired in 1962 when he ran for re-election in Alabama. He was the single most in-fluential Senator in the area of health legislation, and his Committee was the conduit for legislation which did not sit well with organized medicine, which wanted as little legislation as possible. An Alabama newspaperman recalls: "They began to believe Lister was too radical." The Alabama State Medical Society did not take any official position against Hill in 1962 but it was well known that many doctors had organized on their own to defeat him. This was especially ironic since he had been first elected partly because many doctors had rallied to him as the son of a well-known Alabama physician. Hill eventually won the 1962 election, but by less than 7,000 votes, the closest election fight he ever encountered. He remained wary of the power of organized medicine after that but there was the possibility that the AMA, at the drug industry's behest, might have made a request to Hill to sit on Dodd's bill. Why had the bill not moved all these years?

AMA influence was possible but Robert Barclay, the former professional staff member of Hill's Health Subcommittee, the subcommittee through which the Dodd bill was routed prior to reaching full Hill committee, says that the bill went almost unnoticed. Barclay, now out of government but representing nonprofit health organizations on Capitol Hill, thought back on the Dodd bill: "The bill on amphetamines, yes I recall that," he said, "I'm afraid we just didn't consider that one very important. We were conduits for the administration's health bills. Our responsibility was to see they got acted on, and this one just wasn't that big." Perian, Dodd's staff director, however doubts it was simple inattention. "I communicated with them often enough that they knew what we were doing. There is no question they were being lobbied by the industry." If lobbying and inattention were not enough to kill the bill, there were also the mismatched personalities of Dodd and Hill, who simply did not operate on the same wavelength. Senators need friendships with their key colleagues just as much as lobbyist do to win their points and Dodd and Hill were not destined to be close. Dodd was irascible, not courtly. He was an outsider in the Senate, while Hill was a member of The Club. And no one ever accused Dodd of being "almost Victorian." The best Barclay could say of the relationship between the two men was that it was "cordial but never close."

The bill stayed moribund. In August of 1962, Dodd wrote privately to Senator Hill to plead for the drug bill. He said he could not "urge too strongly" that Hill's committee act before the congressional session ended. Nothing came of the letter. Dodd then made a public plea for his bill. He said, on the Senate floor, that he was speaking in "puzzlement" and not in criticism over the inaction. He said the bill tightened acknowledged inadequacies in the existing law and he stated: "We found that more of these drugs were being peddled illegally than legitimately and that inadequacies in the law were permitting this traffic to flourish.

"Yet," Dodd said, becoming critical, "no committee action was scheduled on the bill. I wrote letter after letter to the chairman of the Committee (Lister Hill) and to the other Committee members. I hand-carried memoranda to the majority leader and the assistant majority leader. I buttonholed everyone whom I thought could help me get action," he said. "Yet the bill has been killed this year by inaction just as effectively as though it had been bitterly opposed. The result is that another year will pass without action being taken to curb an abuse which is deplored by every thinking American who reflects on it."

Conceding defeat in the present Senate session, Dodd pinned his hopes on the Congress that would convene in January. The delay and inaction were crucial, though, and eventually made a prophecy out of a warning Dodd's subcommittee had heard during its California hearings that previous summer. The warning, voiced as a hope, had been expressed by Dr. Joel Fort, a special advisor to the President's Committee on Juvenile Delinquency and an acknowledged expert on drugs. "I think we have a great chance," he told the Subcommittee, "for preventive action before the problem becomes uncontrollable, because we are giving attention to this problem before it gets to the extent that narcotic addiction has."

The chance was slowly slipping away.

3: The Selling of the Public

New drugs called a penicillin for the blues.
A NEWSPAPER HEADLINE

MINOR tranquilizers had exploded onto the American market in the 1950s. Unlike amphetamines and barbiturates, which gained ground over a longer period of time, the minor tranquilizers came in suddenly, with a fury of extraordinary promise, little risk and a hard-sell unmatched in the history of the industry. They were called ataractic drugs by the medical profession, after "ataraxia," a Greek word meaning calm or freed from mental disturbance. Popularly known as tranquilizers, the "happy pills," the "I don't care pills," within a short time after splashing onto the market they became a permanent part of the American vocabulary.

The minor tranquilizers are used in the treatment of anxiety, depression and other neuroses and consequently are commonly placed in the hands of the general public. They are separate and distinct from the major tranquilizers, which are used in the treatment of psychoses, and which are therefore generally used only in hospitals and other institutions under fairly close medical supervision. The first two major tranquilizers, chlorpromazine (Thorazine) and reserpine, were considered pharmacological breakthroughs when their use in the treatment of psychological disorders was discovered in the 1950s. It was the wide success in institutions of the major tranquilizers as an alternative to electro-convulsive shock and other treatment programs that brought about the development of the minor tranquilizers. These drugs then became especially popular because they were believed to be almost completely safe in terms of acute toxicity; you almost couldn't fatally overdose on them. Tranquilizers took hold of the American imagination.

How tranquilizers work in the human mind and body is, like the actions of other mood drugs, difficult if not impossible to determine with complete precision. All that can be truly determined is that while tranquilizers may affect the physical response to anxiety, they cannot treat the reasons for the anxiety itself. Like amphetamines and barbiturates before them, tranquilizers treat symptoms, not causes, of problems.

In the 1950s they became the most hotly pursued chemical formula in history as drug companies worked overtime to discover their own magic formulas for bottled tranquilization. By 1963, the minor tranquilizer business had grown from nothing to about $200 million in annual sales and the market was growing with each day. Everyone was getting in on the act as scores of minor tranquilizers and tranquilizer combinations flooded the market to confuse doctors and dazzle the public.

Three of them led the way, cornered most of the sales market, and had the most by far to lose from any federal regulation, no matter how weak. The companies would lose sales because doctors and the public alike had accepted the tranquilizers as pills of sweet innocence, as mild, non-addictive and good for what ailed you. They were mother love in a pill and if labeled hazardous, the sales boom would surely slacken. The drug that began the phenomenon is meprobamate, which was initially marketed by two different firms under the brand names Miltown and Equanil. Two others, Librium and Valium, came out later but soon took over the sales lead. But meprobamate began the tranquilization of America.

Frank Berger is a tall, thin, pleasant-faced physician. He was born in Czechoslovakia and although he left there as a young man more than thirty years ago, he still retains a middle European accent. He has also retained some of the European graces and still offers a slight bow when introduced. He is rather easy-going, in fact jovial at times, and is a proper and deliberate man. He is also the man who brought Miltown into the world, like a father delivering his own child. He coined the term "minor tranquilizer" and is almost single-handedly responsible for the minor tranquilizer revolution.

Berger graduated from the University of Prague in 1937. As a very bright undergraduate student, he took a keen interest in some pharmacological studies he did there. He went on to complete his medical education at the University and after graduation he worked for the Czechoslovakian National Institute of Health. In 1938, with the Nazi menace spreading throughout Europe, Berger emigrated to England where a sizable Czechoslovakian population was gathering, and began treating many Czechoslovakian nationals.

But his interest in the action of drugs remained strong and while practicing medicine he experimented with penicillin. At the end of the war Berger began intensive tranquilizer research for British Drug Houses, one of the largest and oldest drug firms in the world. While at the British Drug Houses, where he headed the department of pharmacology, bacteriology and clinical trials, he began research on different compounds and developed one called mephenesin, which became the forerunner of meprobamate (Miltown). Although some plants and herbs were known to have calming effects, no artificial synthesis had shown any promise. Mephenesin had a major problem, Berger later recalled, because it was very short-acting. The calming effects of the drug lasted an hour or less, so although Berger published a paper about it in 1946, because of its inability to create a lasting effect, mephenesin was never widely used. In 1947 Berger emigrated once more, this time to the United States, where he settled at the University of Rochester. Ostensibly as assistant professor of pediatrics, in reality he ran a neurological ward at the Strong Memorial Hospital and continued his pharmacological research. "I made it the object of my study to find out why this compound (mephenesin) so rapidly evaporated, because only when you understand why this should be, can you do something about it," he said later. Working with sizable grants from the American Medical Association, the Foundation for Infantile Paralysis and the National Paraplegic Association, Berger continued his probing of central nervous system drugs. In 1947 a paper he had written describing the effects of mephenesin appeared in the *Journal of the American Medical Association*. The article's main point was the observation that mephenesin appeared to be a useful muscle relaxant in mice. Surprisingly, the findings were picked up by the lay press and sparked wide interest. Berger to this day does not understand why. "So suddenly I found myself with neurological patients and neurological psychiatric patients referred to me from all over the country and Canada," he recalls.

Besides the deluge of patients requesting his services— among them people suffering with Parkinson's disease— Berger also received an offer which he accepted to do research for private industry. The offer came from Carter Products Inc., whose claim to pharmaceutical greatness rested on a product then called "Carter's Little Liver Pills." Since then the "liver" has been dropped from the name at the request of the FDA. Carter at that time was a very unlikely candidate for the kind of windfall that was about to come its way. Its wholly owned subsidiary, Wallace Laboratories, had virtually no prescription drug business and was nearly idle when Berger arrived. There was no other medical man on the staff when Berger began and he assumed the dual titles of director of research and medical director. He started at once to try to unlock the secret that would make mephenesin long-acting. Working in tandem with Dr. Bernard J. Ludwig, the chief chemist at Wallace, he labored long hours, diagramming chemical formulas on the blackboard. Ludwig would then make the new compounds himself. In all, some 500 different compounds were synthesized and by late 1950, they hit on one which looked promising. Berger described the animal trials: "We had about twenty rhesus and Java monkeys on hand at the time. They're vicious; you've got to wear thick gloves and a face guard when you handle them, but when we injected them with our compound, they became very nice monkeys—friendly and alert. Where they wouldn't previously eat in the presence of human beings, they now gently took grapes from your bare hand. It was quite impressive." By 1952, after more animal studies, Berger felt the safety of the drug had been established. Combining syllables from the chemical formula of the drug created "meprobamate," the drug's generic name. A new drug application and a patent application were filed; Berger and Ludwig were to hold the patent rights.

Its new drug application approved and the required animal and human testing behind it, meprobamate was approved for marketing. First it needed a trade name. One came. Near Carter-Wallace's New Brunswick, New Jersey, plant was a small village called Milltown. Because place names cannot be trademarked, the second "l" of Milltown was dropped and the newly christened tranquilizer entered the market.

Berger carefully nurtured the first steps of his discovery. He carefully selected doctors to perform the human clinical testing because their medical journal reports would make or break the drug. Clinical testing reports are like *New York Times* reviews of Broadway show openings: a rave means a smash, a pan means a fold. They are, however, controlled much more closely than reviews. The doctors who write them are often referred to as "testimonial writers."

In April of 1955 the *Journal of the American Medical Association,* the single most widely read medical journal, came out with two raves for Miltown exactly one month before the drug was to be marketed. One, written by Dr. Lowell S. Selling of Orlando, Florida, said flatly that Miltown was not habit-forming and that it was a safe and useful drug for treatment of anxiety and for keeping alcoholics sober. Dr. Selling had conducted his clinical trials in 1953 and 1954; they consisted of dispensing the drug to patients and seeing what happened. Berger had kept in weekly contact with Dr. Selling, by phone and letter, just to make sure everything was going fine. When Dr. Selling wrote up his study, Berger suggested judicious cutting which made it palatable for the AMA *Journal,* not wanting to leave anything to chance. Dr. Selling died in January of 1955, three months before his study was published. Berger sent his widow $500.

The second rave review came from Dr. Joseph Borrus, who practiced, coincidentally, in New Brunswick, New Jersey, the home of Carter-Wallace. Dr. Borrus did not disappoint his neighbors. He cited Miltown for its remarkable "absence of toxicity" and its therapeutic wonders. All the pills and other expenses for these trials of course were supplied by Berger and Carter-Wallace.

Miltown first arrived on the market in May 1955, and sales during the first month were only $7,500. The big problem was Carter-Wallace's lack of a reputation in the ethical drug business. Worse than that, they had no medical sales force and none of the promotional machinery to produce the brochures and the attendant hoopla to boost Miltown.

One company, Wyeth Laboratories, a division of American Home Products, had shown interest in Miltown and had offered to buy the rights to it. Wyeth had a medical detail force of several hundred salesmen at that time and could get it into the hearts and minds of the doctors who would prescribe it. Carter-Wallace accepted Wyeth's offer in June 1955, only a month after Miltown came on the drug market. Carter-Wallace, which manufactured neither the meprobamate powder for Miltown nor the finished pill, was however the only buyer of the bulk meprobamate. So it sold marketing rights to Wyeth which then sold meprobamate as Equanil. Carter-Wallace, of course, continued to sell Miltown which cost them seven-tenths of a cent per pill; the cost to Wyeth was one and a half cents a pill; this included materials, finishing and packaging. Carter-Wallace's retail price of 10.5 cents per pill was fifteen times its cost, an extraordinary mark-up in most businesses, but commonplace in the drug industry.

But a funny thing happened. Suddenly Miltown began to move. More and more public attention was showered on it. It was fast becoming a brand name that stood for a class of products and a state of mind. Most of this was happening outside the medical establishment as it somehow touched a national nerve. A product with the right name at the right time had come. It was mentioned in a book title by S. J. Perelman called *The Road to Miltown*. It blared over television: "Hello, I'm Miltown Berle." It was a drink. When mixed with a Bloody Mary it was called a "Miltown Cocktail." The press picked it up and Carter-Wallace hired Ted Bates & Company, a large New York advertising agency, to keep beating the drum for Miltown. "New Drugs Called A Penicillin For the Blues," one newspaper headlined. People were no longer relaxing, they were "miltowning." It was reflected in sales.

By August of 1955, only four months after the initial marketing of Miltown, sales went up more than ten-fold, to $85,000. By December of the same year they had soared to more than a half million dollars a month. Carter-Wallace was making it. In October of 1956 the New York Academy of Sciences held a two-day symposium in New York City where several papers were delivered. The entire proceedings were published and titled: "Meprobamate and Other Agents Used in Mental Disturbances." More than 150,000 copies were mailed free to doctors, courtesy of Carter-Wallace. Carter-Wallace sold these little white pills as fast as they could but there were shortages. People were lined up outside drugstores waiting for supplies and some stores imposed limits on how many could be sold to a customer. A store with a big supply would stick up a sign in the window to advertise it. There were even suggestions that the drug should be rationed on a wartime basis. It was, as a member of the Bates advertising agency said later, a "dream campaign."

By April 1957, only two years after Miltown was introduced, the results of the dream campaign came in. Carter-Wallace's net sales had nearly tripled as a result of Miltown. In 1955 sales stood at $14.5 million. In 1957 they leaped to $41.8 million. Carter was also spending: in 1958 in the AMA *Journal* alone they spent a half million dollars for advertising. In 1955 they had spent a meager $20,000 in that journal. Frank Berger had also done well. Holding the patent rights had made him a very wealthy man. In 1958 he was named president of Wallace Labs.

Carter-Wallace also came out with a series of combination drugs that were as medically dubious as any devised by the amphetamine companies. In fact, they cashed in on amphetamines, too, in 1959, when they came out with Appetrol, a combination of meprobamate and dextro-amphetamine sulfate. Deprol, which combined meprobamate with another tranquilizer, came out in 1958. In that same brief period, Milpath, meprobamate and tridihexethyl chloride, came out for relief of gastrointestinal problems. Milprem was meprobamate and conjugated estrogens for treatment of menopausal problems. Miltrate was meprobamate and another drug to be used to treat anginal problems. It made no difference that these were all chemically irrational drug mixtures; they sold.

Even the AMA later came to regard them as not recommended for anything.

Even in the early days there were some troublesome signs over the Miltown craze, but they were largely overrun in the festive acceptance of these "happy pills." As with amphetamines, the promotion overwhelmed common sense. In 1957 the World Health Organization (WHO) cautioned about the extraordinary popularity and the overuse of tranquilizers. The WHO warned that the drugs might be habit-forming and suggested more controls were needed. While not mentioning Miltown or meprobamate by name, it was clear the WHO had this drug particularly in mind. There was also some negative feedback from doctors who didn't like patients coming into their offices demanding Miltown. It was a backlash over the public popularity of Miltown. But no real injury was done to Carter-Wallace. Instead of Miltown, the disenchanted doctors would usually prescribe Equanil, so Carter still got its percentage.

Dr. Frederick Lemere is a Seattle psychiatrist who treats addiction. In the October 1955 issue of *Northwest Medicine* he published the findings of clinical trials he performed for Carter-Wallace. He reported finding meprobamate effective and non-addictive. But further observation changed his mind and a few months later Dr. Lemere wrote a letter to the *Journal of the American Medical Association,* which published it in the April 21, 1956, issue. Dr. Lemere retracted his earlier findings. He said meprobamate had been tested in 600 patients and he now found many of them had developed "standard symptoms of addiction" from the drug. A spokesman for Carter-Wallace said the Lemere findings were misleading because he had used meprobamate in an alcoholic ward to dry out a "bunch of rummies."

Lemere's reversal stirred a controversy at FDA over the labeling of meprobamate. In 1960 Dr. Barbara Moulton of the FDA told the Kefauver Senate Subcommittee that when she had asked that the labeling of meprobamate reflect Lemere's findings, she was overruled. When more addiction evidence came in in 1957, Dr. Moulton testified she tried again for the cautionary relabeling. This time she went directly to Dr. Albert Holland, Jr., then the FDA medical director, and insisted, she said, on a "strong warning statement about this effect." She was· overruled again by Dr. Holland, who was hired a few years later by American Home Products Corporation, the parent corporation for Wyeth Laboratories, marketers of Equanil.

While Miltown occupied the popular mind, the Wyeth Labs detail men were selling Equanil in the doctors' offices and doctors prescribed Equanil over Miltown by as much as two to one. Wyeth was willing to leave the glamour to Miltown and take most of the sales for itself.

Meanwhile, in Nutley, New Jersey, only forty miles from the Carter-Wallace plant, another tranquilizer boom was in its infancy. Drug companies everywhere were trying for compounds to cash in on the lucrative tranquilizer business.

Dr. Leo Sternbach, now in his mid-sixties, is a Polish-born chemist who first began synthesizing a family of drugs called benzophenones in Poland in the mid-1930s. A thin man with a kindly, avuncular face, he had first investigated these drugs while a postdoctoral research assistant at the University of Krakow. Twenty years later, he found himself a chemist at Roche Laboratories in New Jersey. Roche is the American affiliate of Hoffmann-LaRoche, a Swiss-based pharmaceutical giant. Sternbach began playing around with some of the compounds he had first synthesized in Poland a couple of decades earlier. After synthesizing some forty new ineffective derivatives, he abandoned this line of research. Toward the end of 1955, Sternbach put aside Ro5-0609, a compound which resulted from one of his last experiments, without further testing. Then in May of 1957 during a laboratory clean-up, Sternbach came across Ro5-0609 and submitted it to the pharmacological lab for animal testing. In July, two months after testing the new compound, Dr. Lowell O.

Randall reported excitedly that it possessed "hypnotic, sedative and antistrychnine effects in mice similar to meprobamate." "In cats," Dr. Randall said, "it is about twice as
potent in causing muscle relaxation and ten times as potent
in blocking the flexor reflex." The active ingredient in Ro5-
0609 is chlordiazepoxide hydrochloride. The new drug was
classified as a benzodiazepine—the same general chemical
family Sternbach had synthesized in Poland thirty years
earlier. Further studies were ordered. Roche was on the brink
of something grand.

Like Berger and Carter-Wallace before them, and all other
drug houses, Roche carefully selected a group of doctors to
perform clinical, human trials. This is the most critical phase
of testing and marketing a new drug. Two doctors, the late
Professor Titus H. Harris and Assistant Professor Irvin M.
Cohen, both in the Department of Psychiatry and Neurology
at the University of Texas Medical Branch, were among the
first to be offered this new drug. "You must remember how
these clinical trials are conducted," says a drug researcher
who wishes to remain anonymous. "The drug company
comes to you and says it has selected *you* to do the clinical
trials. Then it names some other eminent people in the field
who are also doing them. You think to yourself, 'Just think,
I'm included with these others' and it is a very strong appeal
to the ego. The trials of course are paid for by the company
and sometimes there are fringes thrown in such as a vacation.
But in my experience the appeal to your ego is the one thing
that will make you look favorably on the company and the
drug." Because of the way these clinical trials are performed
—they are mandatory for a new drug application with the
FDA—there are numerous opportunities for conflict between
honest investigation and fear of offending the drug company.
Dr. M. Harold Book of the University of Pennsylvania
Graduate School of Medicine wrote several years ago: "I
have come to the conclusion that any system in which the
pharmaceutical houses delegate the testing of drugs to physicians of their own choosing will not work."

Drs. Harris and Cohen reported glowingly that chlordiazepoxide hydrochloride was extremely effective as an anti-anxiety agent. (But then researchers had said that meprobamate was, too, five years earlier.) Drs. Harris and Cohen said the new drug had a "qualitatively different" action from other tranquilizers and that Roche's product was superior to meprobamate. Cohen and Harris also said it was more potent for blocking tension. They hinted that it was beneficial as an antidepressant and possessed low toxicity.

Like Miltown, it needed a catchy and descriptive name. Roche chose Librium. Although it was chosen in part because of the drug's effect on the equilibrium, the real value of the name was in its suggestion of liberation, freedom and the good life. Cohen, Harris and others published more reports. They found Librium to be an answer to many ills, safe and useful in the management and treatment of anxiety, depression, phobias, psychophysiologic symptoms and obsessive thoughts. Its most undesirable side effect, ataxia (a loss of muscular coordination), could be "promptly abolished" by reducing the dosage, Cohen and Harris said.

Other researchers claimed it was the best thing yet both to keep alcoholics off the bottle and to ease the withdrawal symptoms of alcoholism. The testimonials just kept mounting.

Roche was establishing a broad base of medical indications for Librium. "The whole idea in these clinical trials is to get as many indications for the drug as you can," a member of a very large drug company admits privately. "Anti-anxiety gives you a huge constituency. There are millions of anxious people out there. If you show it is helpful for alcoholism, that gives you a built-in six or seven million alcoholics who can be treated with the drug. Each indication opens up a wide number of people eligible for the drug and of course bigger sales. But you have the FDA to contend with (since it regulates the industry). They want proof that it will really work for what you claim it will. How good were your studies? How carefully were they conducted? These are incredible sessions. The only thing I can compare it to is plea bargaining in a criminal court. The FDA says you must mention this side effect or that precaution. But that will cut down potential sales and so the bargaining begins. You arrange tradeoffs. You argue if that precaution is stated then give us back the indication you took away. These swaps are kept as quiet as atomic secrets. Some vice-presidents where I work have no idea what goes on in these sessions. And then you wonder why in a couple of years the evidence proves the drug is no damn good for what the company claims or that it causes some side effect that was not on the labeling."

Dr. Barbara Moulton, the FDA medical officer who testified at the Kefauver drug hearings, described these negotiations between the drug companies and the FDA: "Frequently, at such meetings, the investigators who have been lukewarm or cold about the merits of the drug are not invited to participate.

"If the medical officer handling the new drug application is still not satisfied with the evidence of safety, the company will frequently make an appointment with the medical director, who has not seen the data on the new drug application, to present their side of the story to him. I have known such conferences to be followed by an order to the medical officer to make the new drug application effective, with the statement that the company in question has been evaluating new drugs much longer than the medical officer and should, therefore, be in a much better position to judge their safety."

Dr. Moulton summarized the many pressures the drug industry brings to bear on FDA medical officers by saying, "They are an almost insurmountable handicap."

Librium's happy reviews did not come only from Drs. Cohen and Harris. There were many, many more from clinicians, all of them selected by Roche before marketing. Researchers in private practice are flattered, flown to conferences and in a subtle process made to feel part of the company's team. Researchers at universities are awarded grants for research by the drug companies. Now would these companies continue to contribute money to these people if the "objective" researchers said bad things about their products?

Perhaps the best description of this process was given in a statement to Senator Gaylord Nelson (D.-Wis.) who began a long investigation into the drug industry in 1967. The late Dr. A. Dale Console, a former medical director of the E. R. Squibb and Son drug firm confessed:

"Sometime in 1956, when I was still a medical director, the lagging sales of one of our products led management to decide that the product needed a boost. The boost took the form of obtaining an endorsement from a physician who was a prominent authority in the field. We knew that the particular physician was being subsidized by another drug company and so management decided that it would be simple for me as medical director to 'buy' him. I objected since I felt that the doctor was incorruptible and because I felt the product did not deserve endorsement. My business colleagues over-ruled me and I was left with a blank check to win his favor. I was free to offer him a large grant to support any research of his choice 'without strings' or to retain him as a consultant with a generous annual compensation. I was quite certain that the doctor would throw me out of his office if I approached him with any of the techniques suggested by my colleagues. They all had the obvious odor of a bribe. I decided, therefore, to use a strategem that was more likely to be effective and that I thought (at the time) would be easier on my own conscience.

"I took the doctor to lunch, and after the usual two martinis, I told him exactly what had been going on and my disagreement with my colleagues. In this manner we established a physician-to-physician relationship in which we were both deploring the questionable tactics used by the drug industry. Conversation gradually shifted to the product and, to make a long story short, we got our endorsement almost as a personal favor. My travel expenses and the price of the lunch made up the entire cost to the company.

"I recall this out of a hundred similar incidents only because the doctor was, and still is, a highly respected authority. My attitude toward him still is one of profound respect and admiration, since I must confess that the device that gulled him would have fooled me had I been in his place.

"We are still human in spite of being physicians. As humans, we are vulnerable to all forms of flattery, cajolery, and blandishments, subtle or otherwise. The drug industry has learned to manipulate this vulnerability with techniques whose sophistication approaches perfection."

Concluding this part of his statement, Console said: "I know of no effective way to deal with this type of hanky-panky that goes on every day between the medical profession and the drug industry. It seems impossible to convince my medical brethren that drug company executives and detail men are either shrewd businessmen or shrewd salesmen, never philanthropists. *They make investments, not gifts.*"

So with Roche's medical arm successfully establishing a wide range of uses for Librium—including treatment of alcoholism, anxiety, tension, apprehension and a host of other modern ills—the promotional arm was also busily at work. What was needed was a big public sendoff. Nothing tacky like the Hula-Hoop atmosphere that surrounded Miltown, but something quasi-scientific and memorable. A public relations firm hired by Roche contacted *Life* Magazine, then one of the nation's largest circulation popular magazines and the best pop medicine journal in the field. The story was assigned by the *Life* science department to a correspondent in the Los Angeles Bureau, Marshall Lumsden. But Roche was not going to take any chances; a public relations man would "assist" Lumsden. "I have rarely if ever encountered that much outside concern over any story," Lumsden recalled ten years later. "This PR guy was with us every inch of the way, every lunch we had, every drink we drank. He was a very smooth fellow, unctuous in fact, who wouldn't let us alone for the whole time."

In the April 18, 1960, issue of *Life* Roche's efforts were

rewarded. "NEW WAY TO CALM A CAT" the *Life* story headlined. The "cat" was a European lynx. "Tranquil as a tabby after a dose of Librium, the fierce forty-pound lynx shown on the previous page nuzzles a wildflower and shows no more inclination to fight than Ferdinand. In this state it gambols lamb-like in its cage, allowing its ears to be scratched and rolling over on its back to have its belly stroked," the caption read. The *Life* story never said how much Librium calmed the lynx but some researchers say it must have been an enormous dose. Forevermore, Librium was known as the drug that tamed wildcats. The story appeared a month before Librium was marketed.

Librium's first month sales were $20,000 and from then on climbed steadily. Within five years more than fifteen *million* people had taken it and more than six *billion* Librium tablets had been distributed. Meprobamate also maintained high sales and by the end of 1965 more than fourteen *billion* Miltown and Equanil pills were produced. In 1963 Librium's sister drug Valium arrived on a sea of dollar bills and soon overtook them all. In their brief span these tranquilizer drugs had reached unprecedented popularity. Librium and Valium became the greatest commercial successes in the history of drugs. They were promoted as better, far different and less toxic drugs than Miltown or barbiturates. But were they?

The *Medical Letter* is a unique enterprise in the medical and pharmaceutical establishment. It is a nonprofit newsletter which evaluates drugs. The *Medical Letter* is perhaps the single most independent and respected evaluator of drug information published, one reason being that it accepts *no* drug advertising.

In 1960 the *Letter* said flatly that *none* of the many trials that gave Librium its special niche in the drug field were well designed for objective evaluations. In November of 1963 the *Letter* said: "Librium is promoted . . . for use as the sole treatment in anxiety and tension states and also for the relief of acute and chronic alcoholism and some physical symptoms arising from emotional disturbances. Advertisements for Librium state unequivocally that it is superior to 'tranquilizers' and distinctly different in its effects from such central-nervous-system depressants as the barbiturates, chloral hydrate and meprobamate. And many physicians assume that Librium calms without drowsiness or clouding of sensorium and without impairing intellectual or motor skills; it is also considered non-addicting and not capable of being used for suicide. None of these beliefs is backed by convincing evidence." The *Medical Letter* has continued to maintain this position.

So what do you do when the facts go against you? Promote and advertise.

4: Selling the Doctor

The desire to take medicine is perhaps the greatest feature which distinguishes man from animals.
SIR WILLIAM OSLER, AN ENGLISH PHYSICIAN

SHE is standing alone before a darkened background: a young college girl, carrying books. The corners of her mouth are turned down. It is not a grim expression but it exhibits concern and suggests uncertainty. The copy under her picture reads: "A Whole New World . . . of Anxiety." Surrounding her on the background are italicized suggestions of what the anxious world might be. "The new college student may be afflicted by a sense of lost identity in a strange environment." Another suggestion: "Exposure to new friends and other influences may force her to reevaluate herself and her goals." Yet another: "Her newly stimulated intellectual curiosity may make her more sensitive to and apprehensive about unstable national and world conditions." If world affairs and peer pressure don't make her anxious, the ad suggests another cause. Maybe it's "unrealistic parental expectations" or "today's changing morality" and "new freedom" that are doing it. Even though this last problem seems to suggest her need for birth control pills more than anything else, the real answer to her woes is something different. "To help free her of excessive anxiety . . . adjunctive LIBRIUM." Of course. "When mounting pressures combine to threaten the emotional stability of the anxious student, adjunctive use of Librium can help relieve the symptoms caused by her excessive anxiety. Together with your (the doctor's) counseling and reassurance, Librium, if indicated, can help the anxious student to handle the primary problem and to 'get her back on her feet.' "

Valium was receiving the big promotional push from Roche Labs, and the promotion was geared toward recommending it, like Librium, for every conceivable complaint. One of their ads pictured a woman who would have been pretty if she were not so downcast. Attractively dressed, she sat alone at the table in a school gymnasium at the close of a meeting. The copy to the left of her picture said: "Symbols in a life of psychic tension." In large letters, running vertically down the page next to her picture, were those "symbols." "M.A. (fine arts) . . . PTA . . . (president-elect) . . . representations of a life currently centered around home and children, with too little time to pursue a vocation for which she has spent many years in training . . . a situation that may bespeak continuous frustration and stress: a perfect framework for her to translate the functional symptoms of psychic tension into major problems. For this kind of patient—*with no demonstrable pathology* yet with repeated complaints— consider the distinctive properties of Valium."

These drug ads, which ran in the 1960s and later in the most respected medical journals, reached almost every practicing physician in the country. Roche Labs called them the "signs in a life" ads and they were aimed at women because women use about twice as many mood-altering drugs as men. Like the amphetamine promotion for weight control, these ads had a simple message: do not work the problem through on your own, do not face up to it and try to overcome it; take a pill. It won't go away but at least you can forget about it for a while. Roche also pushed Valium, which had been successfully marketed for a wide number of FDA-approved uses, as a treatment for muscle spasms. A series of ads appeared in medical journals with pictures of athletes. A hockey player was pictured slamming into a rink wall. "What's the penalty for Boarding?" inquired the ad. "Painful muscle spasm," which has a solution—Valium. "So, whether you treat sprained backs in hockey players or housewives, your prescription for adjunctive Valium may often be the most helpful in getting them back on the job as soon as possible." One critic of these ads, Dr. Robert Seidenberg, a professor of psychiatry at the State University of New York, said before the Nelson drug hearings: "The drug industry has shown a remarkable boldness in making forays into arenas where angels fear to tread. For instance, the physician is urged to prescribe psychoactive drugs to athletes at the very time that there are national campaigns against such abuse. Medicating racehorses and other sporting animals is a criminal act; tests for such drugging are routine at racetracks. Will we soon have to extend such protection to the football field?"

Roche's advertising campaign was conceived by the William Douglas McAdams Agency in New York, one of the foremost medical advertising agencies in the country. But that agency had a curious relationship to the medical press. The chairman of the board of McAdams is Dr. Arthur Sackler, who also happens to own a controlling interest in the *Medical Tribune,* an ostensibly objective medical news journal. The *Tribune's* masthead motto is "World news medicine and its practice—fast, accurate, complete." The McAdams agency and the *Medical Tribune* even occupy the same office space in New York City and, according to a former employee of the agency, many people when she was there were working for both the ad agency and the *Medical Tribune,* a conflict of interest according to the ethics of the

American Association of Advertising Agencies. Roche Labs, of course, advertised heavily in the *Medical Tribune*. "How can you ever expect anything bad to be said about a Roche drug in the *Medical Tribune* if the company is a client of the chairman of the board?" asked a member of a Senate subcommittee investigating some drug industry practices. "There are many ways such a situation can aid a drug company, such as prominent display of news beneficial to the company and the choice advertising spots in the publication."

Roche Labs, however, was only one among many drug companies which were attempting to push drugs into all areas of normal life. Ritalin, the amphetamine-type drug produced by CIBA, ran a series of ads for "Environmental Depression." One of these depicted a housewife with stacks of dishes to wash, and wearing an exhausted expression; the ad suggested Ritalin to provide the quick jolt to get her through the day "Ritalin Sparks Energy Quicker by a Long Shot," said another ad, with a picture of a cannon superimposed on the text. Never mind that thirty years before the AMA had specifically warned against the use of amphetamines for energy lifts. Children were not spared from mood drug promotion either. Pfizer Laboratories promoted the tranquilizer Vistaril by showing the tear-streaked face of a young girl and suggesting its use for children who are frightened by "school, the dark, separation, dental visits, 'monsters.'"

The whole campaign of the drug industry for mood drugs in the 1960s was to broaden to absurd limits the definition of illness to include every upset, every disappointment, and every vague problem encountered in normal day-to-day living. Each was a ripe candidate for drug-taking. If the facts in their ads were not untruths, then the implications often were. Roche Labs pushed their tranquilizer twins for a wide variety of "illness," although they were careful never to urge the use of Librium and Valium for treatment of the same problem. Librium was promoted for "anxiety," Valium for "psychic tension." But the cumulative effect of the advertising in medical journals was to cover every problem ever encountered in a doctor's office. Tension, anxiety, muscle spasms, even something called the "intervals," described as that worrisome time when one wonders about some dark possibility in the future. Rapid pulse, faintness, breathlessness, missed periods, hot flashes, fear, and depression were all apt candidates for either tranquilizers, stimulants, depressants and anti-depressants, or all of those. There was a chemical solution for everything. The only thing overlooked, said one critic, was a pill for the trauma of birth.

Valium was promoted most of all. One doctor, Richard Rillard of the Boston University School of Medicine, studied journal advertising and concluded that Valium was "the subject of the most extensive advertising campaign which I have ever seen for a psychotropic drug." It is estimated that Roche Labs spent about $150 to $200 million in the 1960s on the promotion of Librium and Valium.

But then the drug makes a huge profit, as do most others. In his book, the *New Handbook of Prescription Drugs,* Dr. Richard Burack compares the cost of Valium to the price of gold. He discovered that the wholesale price of Valium is twenty-five times the price of gold. But that said nothing about the profit to Roche. This was revealed in a patent hearing in Canada, initiated by the attorney general of that country. Here's what was found. It costs $87 per kilo (2.2 pounds) for the raw material for Valium, known by its generic chemical name as diazepam. To put the raw material into final dosage form and to label and package the tablets brings the cost up to $487. This is a generous estimate of production costs; they are probably less. The final retail price is $11,000 for that same original kilo which has now produced 100,000 ten-milligram tablets. The selling price is 140 times the original cost of materials and twenty times the total production cost.

The promotion and advertising campaigns were testaments to the resourcefulness of the mind of man. But the basic questions remained: Why was this kind of advertising, the claims of which were contrary to what many responsible doctors considered to be sound medical advice, permitted to flourish? Why didn't these journals call a halt when it was clear the drug industry was fostering mass drug usage in the ads?

The answers go to the heart of the economic interlock between the medical journals and the drug industry. They explain, in part, why amphetamines had a free ride for so long, why their hazards, once documented, were buried under the deluge of their advertised and promoted wonders, and why so few in the medical profession tried to call a halt to what the drug companies were doing. The journals give the aura of scientific legitimacy to these ads and the drug companies seek this kind of medically sanctioned haven. The journals are boxed in economically; if they fuss too many times over implications, wording, or intent, they may end up losing the ad, and even the entire account; and if they get a reputation as a stickler in the industry, the journal itself may be lost. It is a simple fact that these journals depend on the drug industry for survival. The respected *New England Journal of Medicine,* for instance, in which the "signs in a life" Valium ads appeared, took in more than 2.2 million dollars in advertising revenues in 1968, most of it from drug advertising. This was not a flukish year nor is it a flukish example. That same year the *Journal* took in only $662,328 from subscriptions, which means more than two-thirds of the *Journal*'s income was from advertising, and most of that advertising was drug advertising. This explains why these journals, by running the ads, allow themselves to give the unofficial stamp of approval to ads which contradict much unbiased and responsible medical opinion. The industry wants it this way. As the advertising director of Smith Kline & French said in 1959: "The journal advertising takes on a certain psychological aura of authority by running cheek and jowl with the scientific and expert editorial matter." It has been reliably estimated that drug advertising alone accounts for more than 50 percent of the income of all these medical journals.

Drug companies can and do cancel advertising as a result of real or imagined interference by the journals. It is a situation, as one doctor said, in which the drug industry holds the aces and the journals hold the deuces. Carter-Wallace, for instance, canceled all advertising in the .journal *GP* (General Practitioner) and *The Family Physician* because of an editorial which made a criticism so mild it was barely discernible. Pfizer canceled in the same journals after an article criticized the overuse of antibiotics. For those periodicals in the medical press that do not have subscriptions incomes, 100 percent of their incomes come from advertising. It is a sad but frequent irony to see a carefully researched and written article criticizing a drug or a recommended use of it and then to see, a few pages later, an advertisement heralding the very use that the article debunks.

Do the journals act in the interest of the drug companies by killing or watering down unfavorable articles? A pharmacologist from a major eastern university medical school points to at least one such attempt. He wishes, as do the vast majority of doctors and researchers who speak against the industry, to remain anonymous. Although he explains in some detail the company and the journal involved, he also does not wish to disclose which they are. The journal is a major one. He says: "I had researched the side effects of a particular drug. The side effect was known but I had documented in some depth a part of it that was not complimentary to the drug. In the summary of the article I said the drug should not be taken unless nothing else is available. I submitted it for publication to this particular journal. I was phoned by an assistant editor of the journal who said he wanted to talk to me about my summary statements. He said he wanted to drop the part where I said it should not be taken unless nothing else was available. Instead, he wanted to insert the words 'use with caution.' Well, you can say that with anything. I said no and he said he was coming to my city and asked if I would have lunch with him. I said I would and we had our lunch. He kept ordering drinks and his approach was very subtle and he kept alluding to the change and the fact that the article might not even be published. I held my ground and said I would not change the summary. After he returned home his editor phoned my boss at the university, to gauge his reaction, I suppose. My boss told him he would back me all the way and if the article was killed we would kick up a fuss. They ended up running it the way I wrote it." There is no question in this researcher's mind that the journal was acting solely for the drug company and not for the sake of scientific accuracy. It represents one more avenue in which the drug industry exercises a hidden censorship over what is written about it.

But what about the doctors? They undergo the longest and most intense formal education and training of any profession in the country. Why are they gulled by the advertisements? Why don't they see through the promotional hocus-pocus?

Contrary to their accepted image and contrary to what the public rightfully expects, doctors often know very little about the drugs they are prescribing. Too often all they know is precisely what the drug companies want them to know. Psychopharmacology, the study of the psychological effects of drugs, is offered in only about 20 percent of the medical schools in the country. Pharmacology, the study of drugs, is offered in most medical schools but is usually very limited. A total of one course or even one seminar of pharmacology is not unusual for a medical student. Even supposing it was more extensive, much of his knowledge would quickly become obsolete under the barrage of new drugs and the blitz of promotional campaigns that descend on doctors every year.

So who does the doctor rely on? He relies to some extent

on what his colleagues tell him, on articles in medical journals when he gets time to read them, on the *Physician's Desk
Reference,* which lists current drugs and their indications,
but in which the information is written by the drug companies. But most of all, if we are to believe the doctors
themselves, he relies on the detail men, those ambassadors of
good will from the drug industry who sell their drugs to
doctors door-to-door like Fuller sells brushes. In an AMA-
sponsored study in the 1950s taken in Fond du Lac, Wisconsin, it was disclosed that 68 percent of the doctors there
were dependent on detail men for their drug information.
Industry-wide, there are approximately 22,000 detail men.
Roche Labs, for example, has about 700; Smith Kline &
French somewhat less. The detail man is usually friendly,
reasonably well-informed about his line of brand name
products, but mostly he is a salesman. He is there to push *his*
drug over another and to persuade the doctor to either begin
or continue to prescribe his products. Why can Dexedrine
sell for ten times the amount of generic amphetamines and
still outsell them? Why can Librium or Miltown outsell
phenobarbital, even though many medical authorities consider their sedative and tranquilizing effects to be indistinguishable? The major reason is the detail man who,
through his personal visits, undoes all the objective information available to the doctor. Here is how one detail man
describes his job.

As he talks he is unfolding a large computer readout. He
is tall, rather thin, and has an Ivy League haircut. He supports a wife and a small family. Because he still works there,
neither he nor the large drug company for which he works
can be identified. He has a degree in chemistry and knows
something about drugs, an exception to the general rule
among detail men. He complains that his fellow detail men
have little if any background in the field; "English and
education majors most of them," he says. He points to some

of the sale projections on the computer readout. "Look at those numbers go up. It's selling, just selling," he says. "I'll tell you one thing. When I started with this company five years ago I detailed a low- to middle-income district in the New York City area. At the beginning of every year we get this readout of how many drugs and which drugs we have to sell. Each month we get an updated readout that monitors how we're doing with the sales, whether we're ahead or behind. My first year I had to detail $110,000 worth of drugs. That's what I had to get sold in my area. This year I'm in the same district. It has the same income level, low to moderate, the same approximate size and about the same number of doctors and drugstores. I detail 145 doctors and 75 drugstores. But now I have to sell $230,000 worth of drugs. Next year it will be up to $270,000. We keep wanting to tell the computer there is a limit, that we can't go out and sell more and more every year. But the computer just says keep selling."

What would happen if, say, in October the computer showed you were behind in your sales and estimated you would sell only $190,000 instead of $230,000 by the end of the year?

"What would happen? There'd be no end of the year for you with the company. That's what would happen.

"I'd say," he continues, "the average salary for a detail man where I work is about $15,000 and if you've been there a while about $20,000. But you've also got a company car and a great medical plan. But of course this doesn't include the deals you can make." The deals? "A lot of us started out in this business as idealists. I thought I was going to serve humanity by learning about medicine and getting it to people. Well, that doesn't last long. You're corrupted by the system very quickly, by the drugstores and by the doctors. The druggists are after you all the time to see what you can give them. They want your samples so they can sell them at retail and it's all profit for them. I've done it. I've given a druggist a big supply of free samples and then made a $10,000 sale to him. We both come out ahead. He gets his profit and I get to make my computer happy. Some guys sell their samples to the druggist at a very low price. That's clear profit for the detail man. Then the druggist gets his big profit because his wholesale cost was so low. Almost every drug company marks 'sample' on the cartons and bottles of samples so they can't be resold. But we had some guys where I work try to get around that too. They stayed home with their wives for a few days and took off the word 'sample' with electric erasers so they could sell them to the pharmacists, who could then resell them. They got caught and were fired. But some haven't been caught. There's one guy in this business who's almost a legend. He didn't work for us but he was with a big house. He was making so much money on the side that he bought a big house on Long Island. But then he figured if the company found out about this new place they'd get suspicious because there was no way he could buy a house in that area on his salary. So he just kept his apartment in the city as a mail drop. He was making enough to keep both places. Things like this go on all the time. I'm not saying anything that anybody who's been in the business for two weeks doesn't know." He picks up the company rule book, which specifically prohibits the sale or dispensing of samples to anyone except a doctor. It is also against federal law to dispense prescription drugs to anyone but a doctor or medical institution. How do the doctors figure in this?

"I see most of them every month, or try to. I'll tell you, the average doctor's knowledge of drugs is pathetic, almost nil. I'd say more than half of them rely on me exclusively for their information; the rest listen to their colleagues. I tell it pretty straight because I have a good working relationship with most of them. That's what I'm paid for. But in the sales talk with the doctor is where the truth gets stretched, that's where the company wants you to go because you're protected. The doctor says you said one thing and you can say you didn't. So who's telling the truth? When you talk about patient benefits is where you can do it. Say you walk in with a new anti-depressant. Well, you can tell the doctor that depressed patients recover faster and function more normally within a few days. Or you can go in and say 'give them this and they'll be smiling and whistling within a day.' That stretching is part of our job. I don't do this but it's done. Most of my doctors want to know about side effects more than they want to know about indications. But some companies really encourage their detail men to get in there and tell the doctor as much as you can get away with.

"I bring the doctors a collection of things," he says, looking in his car trunk at a cornucopia of pens, pencils, note pads, brochures and other paraphernalia. "I give them samples, of course. I hand out about a thousand dollars' worth of drugs a month; that's retail value. Some of them want them and some of them don't really care. But there's one I have to bring an armload up to. So I go into his office carrying boxes of the stuff after walking up a flight of stairs, but if I don't he won't write prescriptions. But when I give him samples he writes, boy, he writes."

Would the detail man take any of the drugs he so freely sells and gives away? "Never touch the stuff; never," he says adamantly. "I know what really goes on in this business." His wife mentions an illness he had a year earlier. "He had a temperature of 105 and the doctor told him to take antibiotics. He refused. Finally the doctor had to order it and he [took the medicine], but he didn't want to yet. Sometimes," she says, "it's best not to know as much as he does."

But why does he stay in this business if it's so bad?

Pause. "Can you tell me something that isn't bad?" he answers.

He concludes that the time has come when "we have to stop giving doctors these silly pens and pencils and samples and begin to really have exchanges with them. The detail men will have to improve and to really learn what they're talking about. But this nonsense has got to stop."

The doctor is feted and courted by drug companies with the ardor of a spring love affair. The industry covets his soul and his prescription pad because he is in a unique economic position; he tells the consumer what to buy. Promotion for prescription drugs is so crucial because doctors now prescribe about three fourths of all the medicine we take. This is a complete reversal of fifty years ago when people bought three-fourths of their medicine over the counter. The selling of drugs is apparently more important to the drug industry than is the discovery of new ones. In order to sell the 200,000 practicing physicians on their drugs, the industry spends three to four times as much on the promotion and advertising of prescription drugs as they do on research. The total annual amount spent by the industry is about 4,500 promotion dollars for every doctor in the country.

The promotional trip-hammer begins hitting away at doctors in medical schools and ends at the grave. As medical students, they are supplied with medical kits and stethoscopes by the Eli Lilly company. Roche Laboratories offers a specialty textbook with monographs on sleep, alcoholism, and anxiety, the very things their drugs are marketed for. The medical student may be offered a summer job or have a research project underwritten by a drug company. He is offered trips and tours of the drug plants, sometimes with a gala evening thrown in and most of the tab picked up by the company. Donations for parties, baby supplies, free drugs, and other items are handed out regularly to the medical student by the detail man who from the beginning makes it his business to ingratiate himself with the student. He comes on, not as a hustling salesman, but as a friend. Doctors are not immune to flattery and the many inducements that permeate the medical schools throughout the country appeal to the ego and the wallet. "I can see why they begin on us very early," a young intern said, "because by the time you finally finish medical school you really have narrowed the choice of drugs you're going to use way down for each indication. Doctors usually prescribe by habit after they've decided on a drug, and the company is in there early to see you get into their habit." This early infestation by the drug industry becomes in a real sense a competition between legitimate medical education and the objective practice of medicine on the one hand, and the self-serving indoctrination of these students by the drug companies on the other. The average student leaves medical school with less than ten hours of pharmacological training to help him objectively evaluate drugs and their uses. He will probably also leave with days or weeks of exposure to the detail men, their companies, their drug literature and the other promotional gimmicks available to them. The drug companies are on the road to winning.

After medical school, when the doctor begins practicing, promotion by the drug industry only intensifies. Now he can, as they say in the industry, "write that script." The doctor is deluged with new twists on the old idea. He doesn't have to be gullible or stupid to be persuaded or seduced by them, often they are very well done. He receives direct mail drug advertising and sampling; he is laden with samples from the detail man to ease him into the habit of giving *that* drug. He is invited to slide shows, conventions, workshops, and seminars that are produced and directed by the drug companies. Some of them are excellent and free of a sales pitch. But those that are not as obviously self-serving, one doctor pointed out, are a "mere pittance" compared to the effort and money spent on the hard sell. As Dr. Console, the former medical director of E. R. Squibb & Son remarked, the promotional maxim of the industry seems to be "if you can't convince them, confuse them." One young resident doctor at the Boston City Hospital kept all the unsolicited mail he received in a six-month period. Between the throw-away journals and the drug advertisements, the total weight came to fifty-one and a quarter pounds. He complained to the Sierra Club.

Besides the "hard sell" there is the "soft sell," the "I'll scratch your back if you'll scratch mine." The doctor is invited to drug company-sponsored cocktail parties and invited to "doctors only" golf tournaments. One enterprising promotion man even had the name of his company "Pfizer" stamped on the golf balls, lest the doctor forget who paid his greens fees. Free weekends and plant tours are also arranged for the practicing physician. And lest the reader forget, all of these promotional gimmicks and advertising costs are tax deductible. The cost is passed on to you. Today the annual cost of promotion for the entire industry is about one *billion* dollars for prescription drugs alone. This does not include television and other media advertising for the over-the-counter drugs.

With the industry pushing him from this side, the doctor is also faced with the many realities of his practice on the other. General practitioners in particular are often overwhelmed with patients. Because there is not enough time in the day to give each of them the time and counseling he might need, the office visits often become hurried consultations and quick judgments. In addition, it has been found that of the people who do walk into the general practitioner's office for advice or diagnosis, 60 to 80 percent are there for nonmedical reasons. These patients, often middle-aged women, feel an imagined pain or can describe some vague uneasiness. They are usually lonely, tired, unhappy or depressed. But they are not ill. However, they come, or their family is sending them, demanding something to make them feel better. If the doctor strictly adheres to the medical canon "no treatment without a diagnosis," he can do nothing medically for these people. But aren't these the same kind of people with the same kind of undefined problems the industry says are legitimate subjects for drug therapy? A stimulant to

pep the patient up, a tranquilizer to calm him down, a sedative to help him sleep, an anti-depressant to lift his spirits, all
become an easy choice. Our society has reached the point
where more than half of the total number of drugs prescribed
by the family physician are mood drugs.

Where does the doctor look for guidance in prescribing
such drugs? There are few objective guides. He has the
studies written in the medical journals, but he doesn't have
the time to go through even a fraction of the tens of thousands
that have been written on mood drugs since their inception.
With his work load increasing, he needs quick information.
In 1952, a study revealed, doctors spent three to four hours
a week reading or listening to discussions about drugs. By
1956 that had dropped to little more than two hours, and
it has dropped even more since 1956. So the doctor turns to
his other choice: the detail man who is pushing his company's brand with easily digestible condensed information.
Who better condenses information than the industry, through
their advertising and their detail men? The doctor is likely
to spend more time with and pick a drug from a company
or detail man he likes or respects. He writes down the *brand*
name and the cycle becomes complete. It began in medical
school with the drug industry's indoctrination and friendship
and continued on into the doctor's practice; it ends in the
drugstore with the patient waiting for his or her prescription
to be filled.

Yet another factor is sometimes involved in a doctor's
decision as to what drug to prescribe. A percentage of doctors
are implicated in the most blatant form of an economic conflict of interest by owning drug company stock. How many
own such stocks is difficult to assess, but the Student American
Medical Association, a group that is showing a growing
concern about the practices of medicine and the working
arrangement between it and the drug industry, estimated in
March of 1971 that "available information and prevailing
attitudes, however, suggest that purchase of drug stocks by

physicians is widespread and begins early in the doctor's career." In one study at the University of Virginia, of seventy-three medical students, interns, and residents, six had already purchased drug company stocks; perhaps more significant was the finding that of the sixty-seven nonstockholders, fifty-eight said they considered the stocks good investments.

The drug industry encourages this economic partnership with the medical profession. The March 1972 edition of the *Physician's Financial Letter,* a publication by a large drug house called Sandoz, encouraged doctors to invest in drug firms and gave the reasons why: "The drug field is an outstanding example of the successful marriage of research and promotional talent. By pouring 10 percent of its revenues into research and 30 percent more into marketing and promotion, the pharmaceutical industry has maintained an enviable record for well over two decades. In fact, of the twenty-six most profitable corporations in 1971, seven are in the drug field."

Conflict of interest is as old as civilization. But one does not expect it with doctors, in whom we have bestowed a "sacred trust." Drug prescribing, said the *Journal of the Royal College of Physicians of London* in an editorial in April 1967 should be as carefully considered as a surgeon considering surgery. But it isn't. The editorial concluded: "Prescribing throughout the world is a very idiosyncratic activity, born too often of speed, prejudice and defective information." How much are drugs overprescribed? Several authorities who have studied the question in depth estimate that more than half of all drug prescriptions are unnecessary. Dr. George Baehr, the chairman of the public health council of New York State, believes more than 60 percent of the money spent on drugs is needless. Dr. Console, Squibb's former medical director, estimates it is more than 50 percent.* So not only are billions of dollars spent by the public

*The estimates were made to the Nelson subcommittee.

for no reason, but the drugs they buy are creating a wider and deeper national dependency on drugs.

The doctor's middleman role in this continuing drug cycle is not in most cases a venal or an irrational one. He could probably tell a lot of the patients trooping into his office that nothing is wrong with them and to get out. He could just stop writing prescriptions where there is no medical indication. But a doctor often feels sympathy for such patients; he wants to "help" them. He also wants to maintain the doctor-patient relationship and risks losing a patient if he does not give him something. Also lurking in his mind is often an unwritten canon in the medical profession saying a doctor will be criticized less for *overtreating* a patient than for *undertreating* him. If he tells an apparently depressed patient to go home and gives him no medicine, and that patient later commits suicide, the doctor can come in for more criticism than if he had given a perfectly healthy patient a drug prescription. In fact, in the latter case he probably won't be criticized at all.

The doctor is a human being and therefore susceptible to the same foibles as the rest of us. "There is nothing magic to our work," explains an experienced and respected doctor; "we can be sold on something just like anybody else. And most of us who are honest with ourselves will admit we know very, very little about most of the drugs we prescribe." In the August 8, 1961, issue of *Lancet*, a British medical journal, an unsigned article called "The Pharmaceutical Persuaders" appeared, saying in part: "It might be comforting to imagine that the medical profession on the whole are more clear-thinking and resistant to sales pressures than the rest of the population; but the evidence provided by the drug companies themselves seems to counter such a supposition." The author of the article says nothing has happened in the more than ten years since he wrote it to change his opinion.

It takes a seducer and a seducee to succeed, and what the drug companies accomplished in the 1950s and 1960s and today is two-fold. On the one hand, they have created a climate of easy acceptability surrounding drug use for everyday problems, and on the other, they have carefully and skillfully induced practicing physicians to view the drug industry in the best possible light. "Discomfort is to be avoided at all costs" has been the promotional message coming through again and again. Drug advertising and promotion for both over-the-counter and prescription drugs did not by itself create this state of mind, but it exploited to the maximum our urge to swallow, inject, or inhale something to make us feel better. Nothing of its size or scope acted to point out the opposite side of the picture—not the medical profession nor the FDA. Only faint voices were heard once in a while, telling us to hang in there, to try to work out our problems without a chemical crutch and to not assume a pill would solve the problem. So when the doctor was confronted by a patient with no recognizable medical problem, prescribing a mood drug became the easiest decision. This became his path of least resistance, and because the patient took the drug far too often the doctor became an accomplice. Unfortunately, the doctors who were writing the prescriptions were blind to this trend in themselves. In a recent study of doctors' prescribing habits in metropolitan Boston, 64 percent of the doctors said they thought *other* doctors overprescribed tranquilizers and 67 percent said other doctors overprescribed sedatives and amphetamines.

Someone was doing it. In 1964, with Senator Dodd's drug bill once more hopeful of passage, 149 *million* prescriptions for mood drugs were filled in drugstores at a cost to the consumer of more than a half billion dollars. This did not include hospital sales, military sales, nursing homes, the "obesity clinics" where the pills were sold direct, nor did it include free samples and the multitude of other legal outlets. Nor, of course, did it include the over-the-counter sales of milder mood drugs. It was estimated by national prescription audits and by the National Institute of Mental Health

(NIMH) that one in every four adults was taking a mood drug by the mid-1960s, sometimes more than one, and that fully one half of the adult population of the United States had taken a mood drug of some kind, either a stimulant, sedative, or tranquilizer. These percentages are for prescription drugs alone and have held steady since then. Mood drugs were and are a big percentage of the total drug sales of the industry. Including their combination with non-mood drugs, such as a tranquilizer and a heart medication, they account for about a quarter of the total prescription sales in the United States. And in the mid-1960s their rate of growth of sales was outstripping the rest of the drugs on the market. A pill culture had been created, and the responsibility of trying to undo the damage it would inflict was going to fall, not on the drug industry, but upon society.

Dodd's bill was aimed at drug abuse and misuse, not directly at this economic might of the drug industry. Ten percent of the population is addiction-prone. By inducing a wider and wider number of people to take drugs, the drug industry increased the chances of more and more people becoming addicted, which is what the Dodd bill hoped to reduce. Most of the young people who were turning on to drugs in the 1960s were getting their first taste of them from the home medicine cabinet. Dr. David C. Lewis, then an associate in medicine at Beth Israel Hospital and the Harvard Medical School in Boston, conducted an adolescent free clinic in the Boston area. He made a survey and found that most intravenous amphetamine users took oral amphetamines before they shot speed. Interestingly enough, Dr. Lewis found that "they did not buy these illicitly on the street, but often obtained them in their homes. In that way, use and abuse is connected."

Another subtle but significant connection, which Dr. Lewis hinted at above, has been ignored amid the irrationality and duplicity surrounding the talk about the drug crisis. Several studies have now documented the fact that there is a direct and probably causal connection between parental drug use and their children's drug abuse. Dr. Richard Blum made a study of heavy amphetamine users among young people in California. He found that 31 percent of their parents used stimulants. Nonusers had parents who used amphetamines only 5 percent of the time. Dr. Reginald Smart of the Addiction Research Foundation in Canada, whose study is considered the most complete, found in the late 1960s that if a mother was a daily user of tranquilizers, then the child is three and a half times more likely to use marihuana, ten times more likely to use opiates, five times more likely to use stimulants or LSD and seven times more likely to use tranquilizers than a separate control group of young people whose mothers did not use tranquilizers daily. Dr. Donald Louria, professor and chairman of the department of public health and preventive medicine at the New Jersey College of Medicine, also performed a survey. He said "among the current users of illicit drugs, any one of the illicit drugs, use of tranquilizers among the parents is substantially greater." He found that among young people who were shooting speed, there was five and a half times as much tranquilizer use among their fathers than in a control group who did not shoot speed. "If you look at marihuana, LSD, or heroin, and then look at tranquilizer or stimulant use in the parents, it is two and one half to five times greater than it is among control groups," Dr. Louria concluded.

In his study in Toronto, Dr. Smart said this: "The conclusion is inescapable that the parents who are users of tranquilizers, barbiturates and stimulants are likely to have children who are users of drugs, such as marihuana, LSD, speed as well as prescription drugs and alcohol and tobacco." The above three studies were made at different times in widely different areas and with different populations, but all made similar findings. As Dr. Louria summed up before the Nelson subcommittee in 1971: ". . . all of the studies say the same thing, that if you want your children to use illicit

drugs, then be a user of tranquilizers or stimulants or sedatives yourself, or an excessive user of alcohol or tobacco."

These studies forge another possible direct link between
the practices of the legitimate drug industry and the drug
crisis among the young. Television, radio, and other media
advertising of over-the-counter drugs are also suspected of
abetting a climate of drug-taking, but there are no scientific
studies which can actually link this with drug abuse. However, the taking of the drugs by parents—and Louria said
he was talking primarily about prescription drugs—does
make a link.

But this should not have come as a revelation. Radical
youths are the children of liberal parents, only they took it
a step further. Achievement-oriented children are usually
from achievement-oriented homes. The home environment
plays a profound role in the makeup of human beings. Why
should drug-taking not figure in?

What was the industry reaction to these findings? Did
they seek out Dr. Louria after his testimony? Did they show
a shred of self-doubt? Says Dr. Louria: "I didn't hear a
word from the industry."

5: Legislation by Catastrophe

Our responsibilities extend beyond the manufacture of drugs and delivery to the warehouse—their ultimate disposition is our concern as well.

A STATEMENT BY SMITH KLINE & FRENCH,

BUT NOT A PROMISE

MUCH government regulation of private industry in this country has come about only as a result of some major disclosure of corporate irresponsibility or the occurrence of a catastrophe that so aroused public opinion it forced Congress into acting. It has happened often enough to be called "legislation by catastrophe." The law which currently regulates the drug industry began this way; it is called the Food, Drug, and Cosmetic Law.

In 1906 the first pure food act was finally squeezed out of Congress but not before 190 bills had been introduced on it dating back to 1879. It only passed in 1906 because of a public outcry stirred by publication of Upton Sinclair's book, *The Jungle,* which described the scandalously unsanitary conditions of the meat industry. At the same time it was disclosed that tainted meat had been sold to the Army. It took two disasters thirty-two years later to broaden and strengthen the law. In the 1930s several women were blinded by a cosmetic eye preparation. The incident aroused public ire but apparently not enough to trigger a strong law. Soon after, however, something else did. The S. E. Massengill Company of Bristol, Tennessee—a drug firm still in business—marketed an elixir that had not been adequately pre-tested. By October of 1937 several people who drank the elixir had died and the FDA seized what was left. A total of 108 persons died, including the chemist who developed the potion. He committed suicide. With this emotionally charged issue behind it, the 1938 Food, Drug, and Cosmetic Act passed even though members of industry and their Congressional allies declared flatly that the bill would bankrupt business, end research and require every woman to get permission from Washington before purchasing a cosmetic.

In 1962 the Kefauver-Harris Drug Amendments, which tightened regulations over the drug industry, passed only after scores of European children whose mothers had taken a drug called thalidomide during pregnancy were born deformed.* Congress was prodded into acting only by the revelation that thalidomide was very nearly mass marketed in this country; and it would have been except for the stubbornness of Dr. Frances Kelsey of the FDA. She resisted pressure both from Richardson-Merrell, Inc., which wanted to market thalidomide, and from some of her superiors at FDA who seemed as anxious as the company that thalidomide be marketed.

It now appeared that a similar disaster or revelation would be needed to prod Congress into passing Dodd's bill and taking on the entrenched drug lobby. Dodd persisted and at the opening of the 88th Congress in January of 1963 he resubmitted his bill while Congressman James Delaney submitted the related bill in the House. Dodd also issued a press release calling amphetamine and barbiturate abuse the "number one law enforcement problem in the nation."

*The best account of the passage of this law is Richard Harris's book, *The Real Voice.*

As Dodd's subcommittee staff director, Carl Perian was a constant goad to Dodd. He shrewdly analyzed Dodd's character and knew Dodd would respond strongest emotionally, not rationally, to situations. Reading Dodd a list of statistics that described a problem would yield a yawn. Get him to see one tragic personal result of that problem and he was bound to react. "We'd sometimes take the old man to lunch when he was letting down on us. We knew if we kept pounding him with facts we'd get nowhere," Perian recalls, "so we'd buy him a couple of drinks and point out some lobbyist to him and say, 'You know what he called you?' and we'd be off and running." On one western swing with the Subcommittee, Perian and the press director of the Subcommittee, Gene Gleason, arranged for a trip into Mexico to prove how easy it was to buy drugs there. They took Dodd along. Perian later recalled the trip: "We went across at El Paso. I was dressed in old work clothes and Gene and the old man were dressed in blue business suits. I'd done this before in other investigations and knew what to do. It didn't take long to make a contact and I went in a cab for the stuff. I bought some marihuana and some pills, Benzedrine and Seconal, about $200 worth in all. That's all I tried for. I just wanted to make a buy. It didn't take long at all. (While I was gone Gene and the old man went to a bar and Gene bought some pills.) So we went back to the car to drive back. When we got near the border the old man gets a little nervous. A u.s. senator caught with all these drugs? He didn't want to give his right name but we kept at him. Just say 'Thomas Dodd, u.s. citizen' and don't give a phony name to Customs; that could really get us in trouble. At the border he came through. He gave his right name but he wasn't too happy about it. But when we got back he could go on the Senate floor and tell them from personal experience how easy it was to smuggle drugs into the country."

Perian's motives stemmed from personal experience as well. An accomplished saxophone player, he had seen many

of his musician friends let their lives unravel from drug addiction. "A lot of my old friends are dead now," Perian says
of those days. Perian was graduated in 1947 from Eastern
High School in Washington, D.C., once considered to have
as bad a drug problem as any high school in the country. In
graduate school Perian wrote his master's thesis in criminol-
ogy on drug addiction. A fastidious dresser with a pleasant,
handsome face that makes him look even younger than he
is, Perian also possesses a superb memory. Besides that, he is
highly skilled at the necessary art of maximizing publicity
for his investigations. His work on Capitol Hill and his training have made him a recognized expert on juvenile and
drug problems; he has taught college level courses on the
subject. He looks on the Congress and the lobbyists who flood
it with a healthy skepticism and is one of those who refuses
to accept even a lunch from a lobbyist. He was frustrated
at and often angered by many of Dodd's weaknesses and lax-
ities. Perian was vulnerable as the subcommittee staff director because Dodd had the political leadership. Sam Ervin,
John Carroll and Philip Hart, the Democrats, rarely attended. The Republicans, Alexander Wiley, Roman Hruska
and Kenneth Keating, were no better. The one member who
could have contributed, Estes Kefauver, was involved with
his own drug investigations as chairman of the Antitrust
Subcommittee almost until his death in 1963. If anything
at all was to be done, it had to be done through Dodd. So
Perian worked on him, supplying the groundwork for the
drug investigations, giving them shape and direction and
Dodd a visceral prod now and then to keep him from flag-
ging. It was to Perian's credit that he kept pushing, and it
was to Dodd's credit that he let himself be pushed.

In May of 1963, Dodd received a letter from Senator
Lister Hill. The letter opened with "My dear Tom," but
the message was negative. Hill cited several important hearings coming before his Labor and Public Welfare Committee—on issues such as manpower, education, the HEW

budget—and reminded Dodd that "the schedule of this Committee is extremely crowded at this time." He said HEW "has not submitted any recommendations" on the Dodd bill and concluded by assuring Dodd—after telling him he would do nothing—that he would do "everything that I can to help you. Lister Hill was not budging.

The drug industry had also sent messages to Dodd that convinced him during the early part of his inquiry that he had its support. In Los Angeles the previous summer, the success of these overtures was revealed as Dodd listened to the testimony of Los Angeles Mayor Sam Yorty who had been invited as a courtesy.

> Mayor Yorty: "Senator, I am a little disappointed that
>   our great drug houses themselves have not come to
>   the U.S. Congress asking for legislation."
> Dodd replied: "Some of them have. I have been greatly
>   encouraged, Mayor, by the support of some of the
>   drug houses, the drug industry."

Dodd's optimism was partly based on a letter he had gotten from Walter Muns, the president of Smith Kline & French, who assured him he backed his efforts. Dodd was not a naive man, but was making a naive assumption in supposing that an industry which stood to lose money from government regulation would join hand in hand with the regulators.

The drug industry likes to float the story that government regulation of a drug reduces the sale of the drug by 25 percent. That is undoubtedly true for some regulations of some drugs. But as a general rule it is suspect. Government controls unquestionably do mean sales reductions, although not always as high as 25 percent. The ripple effects of an FDA warning that a drug is hazardous will diminish prescriptions. Doctors will take a more careful look. In the case of amphetamines, annual wholesale sales were big business, at that time in the area of $60 million. The prescription losses could be as much as several million a year, so this was not a prospect the industry would welcome with open arms. But because of the thalidomide tragedy the drug industry in 1963 was in as defensive a position as that industry ever is. So now at least it had to say it approved of regulations that would protect the public health.

Smith Kline & French had a special interest. It had held the first amphetamine patent and was still the biggest marketer of the drug. It was also only one of four major producers of amphetamine base. This base was sold to other companies who in turn marketed the amphetamines under their own brand names. The other bulk producers were Hexagon Laboratories, Inc., Arenol Chemical Corporation, and Roehr Chemicals, Inc., all of New York. Of the four bulk producers, only Smith Kline & French also marketed the finished amphetamine pills. So when Dodd was making noises, Smith Kline & French was listening. The company invited the Subcommittee to visit their large, yellow brick plant in Philadelphia and both Perian and press director Gleason took them up on it. If a snow job was planned, it did not succeed. Gleason remembers the incredible scene of the pill production: "There was this stuff popping out of a stamper like a machine gun. Piles of pills were stacking. You couldn't believe how fast that stuff was coming out of those machines." They were led to the board room and there confronted a group of worthies who represented Smith Kline & French management. "We sat around this big table," Perian recalls, "and we tried to convince them that their pills were getting abused, that millions of them were being diverted and millions more produced by their Mexican plant were pouring into this country. They just stared at us and kept shaking their heads, saying all pills on the black market were from illegitimate producers. They couldn't believe us, they said, or they wouldn't believe us."

Smith Kline & French had grown rich on amphetamines.

It began as a small apothecary shop in 1830. In the 1920s it was expanding its ethical drug line when it bought the amphetamine patent. From then on business boomed. As a former Smith Kline & French executive described the advent of amphetamines: "Amphetamines turned that company around from a small place selling mail order tonic to a pharmaceutical giant. Amphetamines made Smith Kline & French, even though they may not want to admit that now. Many years in the 1930s and 40s amphetamines accounted for 50 or more percent of the company's total sales and it is still big today. It's hard for me to remember a year when they did not sell $15 to $20 million worth of amphetamine products." Smith Kline & French is the house that speed built and the company's genius was in selling, not researching, drugs. Here is a story on the company's rapid ascension: In 1959 a financial guide called *Investor's Reader* told a story that sounded like a fable but was true. It was the story of an Atlantic City druggist named Harry B. Leeds. It seemed Mr. Leeds in 1920 bought ten shares of Smith Kline & French common stock and sat on them. He bought no more. By 1938, the year after amphetamine was approved in tablet form, Mr. Leeds' original ten shares had become forty shares due to a four-to-one stock split and were now worth $4,800. The best was yet to come. As the amphetamines pumped out of the Smith Kline & French factory, Mr. Leeds' investment loomed larger. It split three more times, in 1947, 1950 and 1954. Mr. Leeds died and so could not enjoy his unsuspected wealth. So did his widow Harriet, but in the settling of the Leeds' estate the stocks were found. They were now worth a total of $477,000 on an original investment of less than one thousand dollars.

Smith Kline & French assets boomed as well. In 1938 total assets stood at a mere $2.6 million. By 1958 they had jumped to $82 million. The sales and profit picture was bullish as well. Sales revenues in 1958 were $124 million, profits on that were nearly $21 million or 17 percent, an extraordinarily high figure. But the profits were still soaring. By 1962 they were $20.5 million and by 1964 they hit $38.6 million, making Smith Kline & French one of the most profitable enterprises of any business in the entire country. Smith Kline & French had well over a third of the total amphetamine market even though the field had become crowded by 150 or 160 other firms competing for the same sales now that Smith Kline & French's seventeen-year amphetamine patent had run out. The vast majority of these competitors were small and did only a mail order business by selling directly to doctors. And in league with these doctors the smaller companies sought to cash in on the amphetamine market. One small firm, the Lanpar Company of Dallas, Texas, was proud to say that 10 to 12 percent of the company's stock was owned by doctors who occasionally or regularly purchased their diet drugs. As the doctor peddled the pills, his stock went up. It was estimated by government sources that in the 1960s there were more than 5,000 "obesity clinics" in the country with half of them operated by doctors and the other half by non-doctors. They peddled millions of pills to the gullible and unsuspecting, even young children. Some of them were also guilty of selling amphetamines directly on the black market, probably to avoid those time-consuming office visits. Some of the large companies also sold their pills directly to these doctors even after their unsavory practices were publicized.

As the number of these small companies proliferated, the number of different names for amphetamines proliferated as well. The *Physician's Desk Reference* (PDR) listed fifty-one different amphetamine preparations and these were only the products of the major drug houses. The PDR, as it is usually called, is the doctor's drug bible; the irony of this, of course, is that the drug descriptions are written by the companies themselves, which pay $115 per column inch for the space. One consequence of this is that PDR only lists drugs by brand names and so patients are routinely prescribed the more expensive brand name drugs. In any case, it is reliably estimated that at one point more than 2,000 different amphetamines and amphetamine preparations were available throughout the country. Most of them had only a tiny fraction of the total amphetamine market but they were out there competing for sales. The big firms led the parade. Besides Smith Kline & French there was the R. J. Strasenburgh Company of Rochester, New York, which sold its amphetamine product, Biphetamine, directly to doctors. Abbott Laboratories of Chicago had a brisk trade in Desoxyn. Geigy Pharmaceuticals of Ardsley, New York, was marketing a drug called Preludin. Another drug called Ritalin was marketed by the CIBA Pharmaceutical Company of Summit, New Jersey. These drugs are in the general class of amphetamines and are commonly referred to as "amphetamine-type" drugs. They were recent additions to the U.S. market but already had successfully taken a large share of the amphetamine sales. Semed Pharmaceuticals, a division of the S. E. Massengill Company, was selling Obedrin, a methamphetamine combined with a barbiturate and four vitamins. It is marketed for weight control. Together, these six big companies controlled more than 80 percent of the total amphetamine drug market in the 1960s.

Combination drugs like Obedrin, which had annual sales of $4 to $5 million, are the most profitable amphetamine items. By the mid-1960s, with the major advertising and promotional emphasis on them, they captured more than 50 percent of the total amphetamine market. Again, Smith Kline & French led the way. They marketed Dexamyl, a combination of dextroamphetamine and a barbiturate. Abbott marketed Desbutal, a methamphetamine-barbiturate combination. R. J. Strasenburgh put out Biphetamine T. Why did the combinations become so popular? Because the drug companies advertised their virtues as two-fold. Theoretically, while the amphetamine worked to control weight, the barbiturate would counteract its stimulant effect and allow a restful night's sleep. But a little known study was published in the *British Journal of Pharmacology* in June of 1962—and its findings were later supported by unpublished studies in this country—that suggested a better reason for the popularity of the combination drugs. The study found in several tests on people that the amphetamine-barbiturate mixture made the users feel more "elated" than either drug separately. The drug appeared to produce a kind of euphoria, which is a necessary element for a drug to have addiction potential. The amphetamine-barbiturate combination drugs are "medicine" to get high on. The British study also uncovered one more fact: the barbiturate did not counteract the stimulant effect of amphetamine on the blood pressure and the pulse, for the simple reason that barbiturates and amphetamines act on different parts of the brain. Many drug researchers at the time—and now—say flatly that combination drugs like these are completely irrational mixtures which have no place in medicine and should be banned.

In 1959, Smith Kline & French came out with Eskatrol, a combination of dextroamphetamine and prochlorperazine, an antipsychotic tranquilizer. The sales pitch on Eskatrol said it relieved the emotional distress caused by dieting. It succeeded and the company cornered between a quarter and a third of the entire amphetamine combination market with Eskatrol. Eskatrol pills sold for about ten and a half cents each, or about four times the price of simple Dexedrine. Dexedrine, however, is no bargain as had been pointed out by the *Medical Letter*.

The *Medical Letter,* that unbiased source of drug information which so nettles the industry, in 1961 published a comparison of amphetamine prices from thirty-eight drug companies. The cheapest sold for eighty-five cents per 1,000 pills. The most expensive by far sold for $22.60 a 1,000. It was Smith Kline & French's Dexedrine. The average prices the thirty-seven other companies charged per 1,000 amphetamines were slightly under $2.00, less than a tenth of Dexedrine's price. But the other companies sold their drugs generically and had no brand name like Dexedrine to inflate their prices. The study reported all but three of the sample pills tested conformed to FDA standards and those three had minor variations. But even with the high prices Smith Kline & French was charging for Dexedrine, and the other big companies for their amphetamines, it was very little money per pill. And even though the cost of producing them was only a tiny fraction of their selling price, it underscored the need for big volume sales. That's one reason amphetamines were inundating the country by the billions.

To insure that its brand name products got prescribed, Smith Kline & French, like other companies, employed a legion of "detail men" to persuade doctors to prescribe Smith Kline & French drugs. The kicker here is that in almost every state a druggist is bound to fill a prescription as written. He cannot substitute one brand name for another, even though they are nearly identical drugs, or in some cases identical drugs. Smith Kline & French devised a first for the industry when they began direct mail pill sampling to doctors. They also advertised heavily in the medical journals. "Consider 'Dexamyl,' " one ad said. "Often within the hour 'Dexamyl' works to help dispel such symptoms as apathy, pessimism, loss of interest and initiative and lack of ability to *concentrate*."

The side effects? "Insomnia, excitability and increased motor activity are infrequent and mild," the ad assured us all.

The big push was for weight control. Smith Kline & French was not alone in this. Abbott Labs marketed Desbutal, a methamphetamine and barbiturate combination. One of its ads not only promised weight loss but something far greater. "Two weeks on a new Desbutal gramulet can mean the start of a *new life* for this depressed obesity patient." The "patients" depicted in the ads were usually slovenly housewives in need of a charge.

The use of amphetamine in weight control had been discovered accidentally in the 1930s and has been exploited ever since. In fact, it was reliably estimated that 80 to 90 percent of all amphetamine prescriptions were written for weight loss. It was natural. We are a country in a dilemma. Facing us on one side is an unprecedented food supply. On the other is a compulsive need to be thin, a need drummed into us by the medical profession, the fashion designers and all the young slender people that deluge us in television advertisements. We are also a country that historically and temperamentally has sought quick solutions to often complex problems. What better than a magic pill that would melt off those ugly pounds and require so little from ourselves? That's why it sold. But the entire concept of taking a pill to lose weight is considered by many responsible doctors to be medically irrational. Dr. Morton B. Glenn, chief of the obesity clinic at New York's Knickerbocker Hospital, put it best when he said on April 14, 1971, at a series of amphetamine hearings in New York City:

> If one accepts the fact that permanent weight control depends upon appropriate eating habits together with long-term appetite control, then might not appetite elimination by the drugs actually deter and delay the development of this control? It is somewhat like trying to teach the use of a tool, in this case the appetite, without the tool. Can one teach a child to write without a pencil any more than can one teach an individual to control his appetite without his appetite? I think not.
>
> In my personal experience, I consider appetite depressants as deterrents to permanent weight control.

So could the drug industry possibly be serious about supporting Senator Dodd's drug bill? The drug industry had not plugged any of the leaks in its sievelike distribution system. As many pills, liquid amphetamine and even bulk amphetamines were reaching the black market as were getting to the legal market, the FDA estimated. The truck stops were doing as brisk an amphetamine business as the corner drugstores. Would the drug companies, in the face of this situation, which in many areas was extremely serious and becoming more so, consent to and assist federal controls? Their drugs were deeply implicated. Would they accept some modest loss in sales for the higher purposes of the public health? After all, the Dodd bill was not going to affect their large profit margins on these drugs nor would it cut down on the number of pills they could produce. As Perian said, "All we wanted out of the bill was some accountability. How many do you make, where do you send them to. Since we couldn't keep track of heroin or cocaine, the least we could do was to keep track of what was legitimately produced in this country." Perian, however, expected no industry support. "It's never what the company president says in public that counts," he said, "they say a lot of things to make it appear they are behind you. What really counts is what their hired lobbyists on Capitol Hill do. How they chop up these bills in the committee rooms is what counts." The chopping up was yet to come.

6: The Drug Lobby

It's the old story. They can't win on the merits so they delay it.

WILLIAM GOODRICH,

FORMER GENERAL COUNSEL FOR THE FDA

"BY a faction," James Madison wrote nearly two hundred years ago, "I understand [to be] a number of citizens, whether amounting to a majority or minority of the whole, who are united and actuated by some common impulse of passion, or of interest, adverse to the rights of other citizens, or to the permanent and aggregate interests of the community."

Since Madison's time the word faction has come to be more commonly known as lobby, especially when the group is united in attempting to influence legislative bodies. It has become an American art form. Lobbies are organized factions of professionals paid to seek the "redress of grievances" granted to anyone under the First Amendment of the Constitution. There are about 1,400 paid lobbyists in Washington.

One of the best organized, best financed and most influential of these groups is the drug lobby. It usually does not act with blatant power. It is nothing so blunt and brutal as

112

that. Like most successful lobbies the drug lobby is made up of diverse parts that effect its will through access to key men in Congress. It operates best by persuasion and friendship with those holding power. It is a process of subtle influence, the consequence of which is to consistently shift the balance of power from public to special interest.

A former staff member of a key House committee that handles drug legislation explains: "Just getting past that little girl at the reception desk is the lobbyist's most important job. To do this the member has to know the Congressman. Campaign contributions help. So do entertainment and assistance to the member when he needs it. You also need a reputation for honesty to succeed. If the lobbyist ever misleads a member, he won't have time for him again. The lobbyist also needs the facts to persuade the member to see the light, his light."

These are all legal avenues that favor private over public interest. Drug companies support their important political friends in elections and the favors are returned when legislation is considered. The cornerstone is access. A senator or congressman will not refuse a request to meet with an industry, a private company or a labor union that has made a large contribution to his campaign. Nor will he refuse to meet with a lobbyist who has befriended him. No one is exempt. A dedicated Senate staff member, who has survived many bitter battles with the drug industry, put it this way: "You never see the public take me out to lunch or ask me to play golf. To us up here the public is a faceless, amorphous mass. But the people from the drug industry and the special interest that get to see me are not faceless. They don't offer me money, they wouldn't dare, and besides it doesn't work that way. They work on personal appeal over lunches, drinks and friendly chats. They are men like you, they tell you, they have families, kids in college and so, they tell you, they have to make a buck. Rather than fight each other all the time let's work this out together, they say.

THE AMERICAN CONNECTION

They are usually charming guys, they tell you funny stories and even drop you some information that they know you can use. And how can you attack somebody when you've broken bread with them?

"How is the public supposed to be represented in this? Only when an issue gets big, like thalidomide, does the public get aroused. This kind of lobbying is a very subtle process but it is the most pernicious and insidious kind. The real difficulty you find is that sometimes, even if you are completely opposed to the objectives of the drug industry, and I usually am, you find you like one of these guys they send around and you catch yourself thinking about him and his family and considering the industry's point of view because of it. I've caught myself doing it."

There are many politicians and staff members on Capitol Hill who do not even recognize the adversary relationship and see the special interest lobbyists as friends to be accommodated. Sometimes there is a coincidence of interest: sometimes that industry or union is a major force in the senator's home state or the congressman's district; sometimes accommodation occurs because of political cowardice. But whatever the reason the drug industry knows its friends and depends on them for aid and comfort when threatening noises are made. Usually the special interest only needs to succeed at one point to win. To stop legislation from getting introduced at all is the best way. Short of that, they try to get a key member of a key committee to hold it up, or better still, the chairman of that committee. That can stop it from getting to the floor. Then if it reaches the floor and still does not have what you want in it, try an amendment. If that fails, try for adjustments once more in the House-Senate conference if the bill has passed. A bill protecting the public needs to get over all the hurdles; the special interest only needs to stop it at one. As Gene Gleason, the press director of the Dodd subcommittee put it: "The implementation of the fix is in delay and watering down." This is part of the subterranean tug-of-war that goes on almost daily in Congress. It is the kind of process that as much as anything else determines our laws, our priorities and more often than not, our present and future failures. The process usually passes unnoticed because the working press seldom has the time or inclination to seek out and document the subtle changes that can render a wonderful sounding bill into a worthless law. Besides, to do so is a tedious process often loaded with technical detail that does not render itself into easily digestible stories for lay readers. It is usually years later or in the aftermath of some kind of catastrophe that the loopholes become apparent. This is why changes that castrate a bill go undetected.

The amphetamine and barbiturate manufacturers—with Smith Kline & French pushing the hardest—relied mostly on the Pharmaceutical Manufacturers Association (PMA) to protect the industry's interests. If in 1963 or 1964 the Dodd bill began to look as if it might pass, then it would have been the job of the PMA to make it palatable for the manufacturers. The PMA prefers to be called a professional or scientific society or association, but basically it is a political lobby. It is the information and political arm of the drug industry. Housed in The Madison Office Building at 1155 Fifteenth Street in Washington, the PMA represents about 115 ethical drug companies which account for about 95 percent of the total drug prescription sales in the country. This now totals over $6 billion in sales a year. Like Roche Labs, many individual companies retain a Washington law firm or have their own lobbyist on Capitol Hill. As the PMA works on legislation to mold it to industry specifications, the individual companies work on individual sections that directly affect them. It is a formidable one-two punch.

The PMA was formed in 1958 by the merging of the American Pharmaceutical Manufacturers Association, which represented the smaller drug firms, and the American Drug Manufacturers Association, which represented the large houses. Since that merger in 1958 the staff has grown from under ten to more than seventy, so presumably the drug industry has a lot of "grievances" that need redressing. There are many different divisions in the PMA, and files and background enough to attack almost any allegation made against the drug industry. And that is precisely what the PMA does. It does not defend the industry against charges, it attacks the person making them. According to the PMA, senators or congressmen are not serving the public when they introduce drug legislation or hold hearings, they are making political hay or have a "vendetta" against the industry. The PMA ignores the fact that a politician who takes on such a powerful and organized special interest does so at great political risk.

The eleven largest drug companies pay nearly one half of the PMA's annual budget, which has grown from $150,000 in 1958 to more than $3.5 million today. Dues range from $1,000 a year for the small firms to $175,000 a year for the large ones. The large firms, like Smith Kline & French, Roche, Eli Lilly, Merck & Co. and others control the PMA. The PMA's political tactics were refined considerably during the Kefauver drug hearing which began December 7, 1959, the day the PMA calls its own Pearl Harbor Day. The PMA monitors Congress and the regulatory agencies and has worked over the years to develop warm working relationships with many key members of Congress. Besides its legislative staff, the PMA retains John Kelly as its key registered lobbyist, and the law firm of Wilmer, Cutler & Pickering. Lloyd Cutler, a superlawyer, is the key man there. He has fought off industry foes for years.

As Joseph Goulden described this special breed of men in his book, *The Superlawyers,* this kind of Washington lawyer "is often the interface that holds together the economic partnership of business and government." His job is to help make and shape the law for his corporate clients, to light their way and ease their burden. The PMA's consistent position about its lobbying is that it is seeking only to "perfect" legislation, to make things "workable and reasonable" for the drug industry. The board of the PMA is composed entirely of presidents or chairmen of the major drug companies. The president is the major PMA spokesman. In 1964 the president was Dr. Austin Smith, a Canadian who is a naturalized U.S. citizen. Dr. Smith had previously been with the American Medical Association (AMA) from 1940 to 1958 in an executive capacity and acted as editor and managing publisher of the *Journal of the American Medical Association*. The PMA has long enjoyed a tight working relationship with the AMA.

"The primary goal of the drug lobby is like the gun lobby's," says Carl Perian of Dodd's subcommittee, who has had experience with both. "They want to stop any law at all because they know each time a new one is passed that ultimately they'll be covered in ways they don't want."

The Dodd subcommittee held no new drug hearings in 1963 but the drug bill was not ignored. Perian gave what time he could to the President's Advisory Commission on Narcotic and Drug Abuse, both on account of his expertise and to advance the cause of the Dodd bill faster than hearings could have. The Commission, appointed by President Kennedy, was chaired by the late Judge E. Barrett Prettyman. It came to be known as the Prettyman Commission. Its mandate was broad: to review the problem of drug abuse and make recommendations to combat it. It met regularly in Washington during 1963 and heard the views of all the major federal agencies involved in drug abuse. Meetings were also held in New York City, Los Angeles and other areas where drug abuse was particularly virulent.

But presidential commissions have a way of making excellent recommendations that never see the light of day. That did happen to part of this Commission's report, but another part had some effect. Perian was instrumental in persuading the Commission to single out the Dodd drug bill by name and urge its enactment. It was the only bill so singled out and Dodd was the only senator so mentioned. In an exercise in understatement, the Commission said FDA efforts at curtailing illicit traffic in dangerous drugs had been "unsatisfactory" partly because of the inconsequential jurisdiction the FDA had over what the Commission chose to call "these mind-poisoning drugs." That terminology chilled spines at Smith Kline & French; it was even harsher than what Dodd had used. The Commission repeated a self-evident truth by calling state control of these drugs "chaotic."

Some evidence was building, however, that would cause the Committee to place a quiet time bomb in its Report.

Dr. Carl F. Essig is a quiet, unassuming man. For many years, he was a neurologist at the Federal Addiction Research Center in Lexington, Kentucky, which in the early 1960s was the only fully operating federal addiction treatment center in the country. Essig, now retired, has an extensive background in addiction research and neurology and has written a number of articles on those subjects. In Cleveland, in December of 1963, Essig presented a paper based on a review of the medical literature to the Pharmaceutical Sciences Symposium. He said six new depressant drugs were potentially hazardous and addictive. His paper, published six months later in *Clinical Pharmacology and Therapeutics,* named the six drugs: meprobamate (Miltown and Equanil); Librium; Noludar, another Roche product; Doriden, marketed by CIBA; Valmid, marketed by Eli Lilly; and Placidyl, marketed by Abbott Labs. Essig later said he published the study "as a guide for practicing physicians." His paper noted that the "behavior effects" of these drugs might become "an increasingly important public hazard" and also noted they bore a "striking resemblance" to barbiturates in their "major signs of intoxication and withdrawal symptoms." Barbiturates had long been recognized as perhaps the single most physically addictive drug known. Essig's study suggested that if stricter controls were placed on barbiturates and not on these other depressants, addicts and users would switch to them if the barbiturate supply ever became short. Essig cautioned doctors to be "skeptical about new depressant drugs introduced as not having habit-forming or addiction potential." His findings had already been confirmed and were reconfirmed by later studies but his study was unique in singling out the six drugs comparable to barbiturates. A Roche spokesman privately characterized Essig's findings as "rather primitive." Carter-Wallace and Roche had the most to lose from his study. Essig found "ample evidence" that meprobamate was physically addictive and that Librium, although only very new on the market, had definite withdrawal effects which were, however, less acute than those with meprobamate and barbiturates. But the withdrawal effects did occur.

There was more bad news for Roche and Carter-Wallace later, although not enough to seriously undercut their sales. In May of 1964, the New York Academy of Medicine Committee on Public Health said tranquilizers were involved in "widespread misuses" and then named tranquilizers, barbiturates and amphetamines as the three classes of drugs which were "misused as much if not more than narcotics." Then the u.s. Public Health Service reported children were involved in many accidental tranquilizer poisonings. The "happy pills" might not be so happy after all. "There should be," the New York Academy of Medicine concluded in its May 1964 report, "an educational campaign to change the present public worship of 'happiness' and 'tranquility.' This attitude on the part of many people produces an almost slavish dependence on psychotropic drugs."

So the Prettyman Commission recommended that "all non-narcotic drugs capable of producing serious psychotoxic effects when abused be brought under *strict* control by federal statute." The report not only covered amphetamines and barbiturates, but went one giant step further by saying: "Legislation should not be limited to the barbiturates and amphetamines, but should extend to all non-narcotic drugs capable of producing serious psychotoxic and antisocial effects when abused." Obviously this meant non-barbiturate sedatives and hallucinogens, but more importantly, it meant tranquilizers, the "happy pills." "Experience has proved," the Commission correctly pointed out, "that the drug abuser often turns to other drugs having similar effects when barbiturates or amphetamines become difficult to obtain. Any new legislation should be broad enough to include all hypnotic, stimulant and depressant drugs affecting the central nervous system in such ways as to be classified psychotoxic."

The Dodd bill went back to the drawing board to incorporate this major shift in policy. The bill was redrafted to broaden the bill's coverage of these new "psychotoxic" drugs. If the redrafted bill became law, any new or old drug could now be put under the law's controls if the Secretary of Health, Education and Welfare found that it had a "potential for abuse." Dodd introduced his revised bill in the Senate for the sixth time on March 12, 1964.

The bill still showed no real promise of passage, however, despite the support of the Prettyman Commission and the other authorities outside of Congress. The Administration appeared to be behind it but its support was tepid. The Kennedy assassination was still in everyone's mind and President Johnson was not about to put this drug bill near the top of his legislative agenda. But still it *could* pass.

All this caused unpleasant rumbles back at Roche in New Jersey, at what some irreverent souls call "Our Lady of Librium." Nor was it greeted with wholehearted joy back in Basel, Switzerland, where the home offices of Hoffmann-LaRoche are located. "They want to know one thing back in Switzerland," said one person well acquainted with the Hoffmann-LaRoche operation, "How much money are you going to fly back to the home offices every year?" Now, with the biggest selling product in their entire operation in possible jeopardy in the United States, which was the biggest of all the sixty affiliates in the world, there was considerable concern. If Librium came under government regulation here it would not help increase the money which went back to Basel. The extent of the concern was indicated in a sworn affidavit given a few years later by a Roche Laboratories vice-president who estimated that the kinds of regulations in the Dodd bill would cost Roche more than *$10 million* a year in lost prescription revenues for Librium and Valium. He said doctors would be more reluctant to prescribe a drug deemed hazardous. But it would not have been a $10 million loss in 1964, because sales were not as high then as they were when the estimate was made. The percentage of the loss, however, would have been the same, somewhere around 5 percent. But federal control in 1964 might have been more, not less, costly in one respect. Both drugs were relatively new. Valium had only been marketed for a year then. Roche had spent half of its research budget for three years discovering it. Valium sales might never have soared so high if the drug was placed under federal control so early in its marketing life because of its abuse potential. Some doctors might even have begun to prescribe barbiturates if both were controlled in the same way. After all, barbiturates are far cheaper for patients to buy, and many drug experts believe they have the same effect on patients as Librium and Valium. Roche was not about to let this happen.

Dodd's staff had found itself in a bind in redrafting the bill. There were two ways to put teeth in the bill: the quickest way was to include all the drugs by name in the law. This would be amphetamines, barbiturates, and the six drugs noted by Dr. Essig. Then if Congress passed the bill, the drugs in question would be controlled and there would be no further opportunity for appeal. The second way to regulate specific drugs was through an administrative review procedure, which would go through the FDA, which would be responsible for carrying out the law. The keys to making the administrative procedure—definitely the most likely of the two alternatives—workable were, first, in the definition of the "psychotoxic" drugs which would be subject to the law, and, second, in the type of administrative mechanism written into the law.

The FDA asked for a swift procedure by which drugs could be added to the control list once the bill passed. Obviously, this would enable them to act to protect the public health as speedily as possible once they were aware of a potentially dangerous drug.

Dodd's staff agreed with the FDA that a speedy procedure would be best, but some recent court decisions had suggested that a procedure which was too speedy and which did not have enough safeguards might be declared unconstitutional. "The FDA was absolutely correct that the slower procedure providing full hearings and court review would be too slow," Perian says, "but we had been with this bill a long time and we were very afraid of losing that whole part of it in the courts if all the safeguards were not included." In July of 1964 Perian wrote a memo to Dodd telling him he would "hate to see" part of the bill lost on constitutional grounds. Dodd accepted a change to a review procedure which had been written in the 1930s after industry rebelled against many New Deal decisions. It was the only alternative Dodd's staff had to a too quick and thereby constitutionally questionable administrative review procedure. An experienced lawyer who has worked on both the government and private sides with the procedure calls it "an abomination." It contains about a dozen different steps of review which a company that wants to protest can use to delay the government from making its decision stick. It takes months and years to go from first order to desist to a Supreme Court decision. From the issuance of the first order to control a drug to a company that does not want the drug controlled and which is willing to fight, it can be a minimum delay of four or five years. "The procedure is fair to business and industry, there's no question about that," a former FDA attorney says of this procedure. "It was calculated to be fair to industry."

The other vulnerable part of the bill was the definition of a "psychotoxic drug." The definition in Dodd's bill was inclusive enough to be workable. It said ". . . the use of such drugs, when not under the supervision of a licensed practitioner, may cause a wide variety of acute and chronic changes in psychological functioning, social behavior, or personality, such as difficulties in judgment and coordination, disorderly thinking, disturbances in mood, bizarre and abnormal perceptual experiences, and more severe behavior disturbances such as attempted suicide and antisocial activities." This definition made it clear that this bill was concerned more with controlling a social ill, than directly regulating the legitimate use of medicine. The Dodd definition also included the key words "potential for abuse" which gave the FDA wider latitude: it would not have to wait until the bodies dropped before attempting to control a drug. This was the area where the drug lobby, and Roche Laboratories in particular, zeroed in.

As always, Roche decided to go first class. Their first step in arming for the battle was to hire one of the best Washington "Superlawyers."

By the consensus of both friends and enemies, Thomas J. Finney, Jr., is a very bright, very able, very shrewd, very knowledgeable Washington lawyer, a dependable shaper of laws. As the sounds from Washington grew more ominous, Roche turned to Finney. Finney is a name partner in the firm of Clifford, Warnake, Glass, McIlwain & Finney. The Clifford is Clark Clifford, advisor to Presidents Truman, Kennedy and Johnson and under President Johnson the Secretary of Defense as well. Paul Warnake was general counsel for the Defense Department in 1966–67 and Assistant Secretary of Defense for International Security Affairs from 1967 to 1969. Carson M. Glass was for ten years a member of the Department of Justice. Samuel D. McIlwain was with the Reconstruction Finance Corporation. All were well acquainted with the way the federal machinery works. Even without Finney it is a well-connected firm. Finney from 1957 to 1963 was administrative assistant to Senator A. S. Mike Monroney (D.–Okla. 1951–69). The administrative assistant is a Senator's key aide. He needs to know the inner workings of Congress nearly as well as his boss, and some of them know it better. This Capitol Hill experience gave Finney both insight and contacts, a valuable tool, in fact a necessity, for a successful Washington lawyer. In seeking to tailor laws to corporate specifications, one must know which tailor shop to go to. Finney had also seen the executive side of the federal government when in 1962 he took leave from Monroney's office to become a White House assistant on trade and tariff legislation. Then he joined Clifford's firm in February of 1963. Finney's political background seems to be of mixed ideology. He is both a former member of the CIA and a liberal. He was active in the presidential campaigns of Adlai E. Stevenson and joined the 1968 presidential primary campaign of Senator Eugene McCarthy. Finney managed the latter's Oregon primary, as much as anybody managed anything in that campaign, but there was a parting of the ways with McCarthy over tactics later in the campaign. "Gene says I left and I say I was fired," Finney says of the experience.

Finney has a wiry thinness. His hair is slightly curled and flecked with some gray, and his sideburns are trimmed at the bottom of the ear lobe. He speaks with traces of his native Oklahoma accent, the words soft and drawn out. He has a small-featured, delicate face and rather small delicate hands. His face is very expressive, eyebrows popping up when he is surprised, brow tightly knitting when he is concerned. He chain smokes and consumes large quantities of coffee every day. Finney is a cautious man. A government lawyer who has been up against him on occasion says:

"Finney is the kind of fellow who is very, very careful about everything he says and does. He's a man who bears watching, close watching."

So it was to Finney that Roche Laboratories turned for protection when Dodd's bill came up. Roche's aims were obvious. Their first priority was to keep Librium out of the bill entirely. There was no fear for Valium then since it had just been marketed and was not even cited in Dr. Essig's report. That accomplished, their second priority was to see that the definition of psychotoxic drugs was worded so Librium could not be included. Roche did not want any hint of a "stigma" attached to its tranquilizer, and most importantly, Roche did not want to lose that $10 million a year. Each day it could keep it out of the bill and on sale would mean several thousand dollars in added sales revenues. Whatever Finney cost, he'd be worth it if he could accomplish that.

One of the things to Finney's advantage was that Dodd would ultimately have less control over the bill than Lister Hill, the full Committee chairman. Moreover, while Dodd was not only not a member of Hill's Committee but had also demonstrated how minimal his personal influence with Hill was, Finney's access to Hill's Committee was excellent.

So Finney began to work to revise the definitions of "psychotoxic" drugs so that neither Librium, Valium nor any of the other tranquilizers would ever come under the law. "Finney kept coming back with revisions of his definitions," Perian recalls. "He especially wanted to get the words 'potential for abuse' out of the law." As Finney went back and forth with his revisions, the industry scored its first victory.

The FDA had stated that it thought the six drugs cited by Essig and mentioned again in the Prettyman Report should be included in the bill, but oddly enough the agency put little effort into seeing that this occurred. Asked about this, a former FDA general counsel recalled: "We wanted to name the six drugs in there in the first place, but there was a lot of industry opposition. All of the companies (Roche, Carter-Wallace and the others) with drugs on the list were around. It was clear that their opposition was going to be heated on this. We were more interested in the kind of authority the bill would give us to use in the future so a compromise was worked out and those six went out." The FDA made a precipitous withdrawal from the struggle, and any chance of listing the six drugs by name vanished. Dodd had needed strong FDA support to get them included.

As the negotiations continued, the drug industry was one up, and the bill just waited.

7: The AMA-PMA Marriage

"Mr. Chairman, I do not know anyone who is against it."
SENATOR DODD, TESTIFYING IN BEHALF OF HIS BILL

ON July 19, 1963, an automobile carrying an Air Force sergeant, his wife, their eight-year-old daughter, and their six-year-old son approached a checkpoint established by a highway commission traffic survey near Tipton, Iowa. The automobile pulled to a stop behind a truck. A few moments later a tractor trailer smashed into the rear of the car and rammed it under the truck in front of it, whereupon the car burst into flames. Everyone in it was mangled and charred beyond recognition. The driver of the tractor trailer was not injured. Three bottles of amphetamine pills were found in his suitcase in the cab of his truck. Although he initially denied knowledge of their source and denied they were his, he later admitted having bought the pills and used them during his trip. Blood tests proved he had taken substantial amounts of the pills.

Because a rash of truck accidents seemed to be traceable to amphetamine use, both the Interstate Commerce Commission (ICC), which regulates trucking, and the trucking industry were becoming alarmed by this new hazard. Also, amphetamines were being found more and more frequently during spot checks at ICC roadblocks. Police and trucking investigators were convinced, but could rarely prove, that amphetamines were responsible for many unexplained single-vehicle truck accidents. Amphetamines can cause hallucinations. Another danger is that amphetamines do not supply a person with a new source of energy; they merely push the body to use up what remaining energy supply it has. When the effects of the amphetamines wear off, the collapse is sudden and a driver can fall asleep in seconds, before he even realizes he is exhausted.

In the May 1964 issue of *Fleet Owner,* a trucking magazine, a very detailed, if not overstated, article described the extent of amphetamine abuse by truck drivers. Called "The Deadly Highway Menace," the article estimated that about 90 percent of all illicit amphetamine traffic was routed at one time or another through truck drivers. The article also estimated that illicit amphetamine traffic in the trucking industry alone was a $200 to $400 *million*-a-year business and was a major threat to both the trucking industry and highway safety. Truck drivers were involved in both taking and selling amphetamines. One trucker was arrested for selling 6,000 amphetamines over a four-month period to three teen-agers in Mount Morris, Illinois. The major contact was the truck stop and there were then more than 5,000 in the United States. The article, which was heatedly written, demanded illegal amphetamine selling be made a felony like hard narcotics peddling.

The trucking industry—itself a strong lobby—was now aroused along with the ICC. The Justice Department and HEW now took an active interest in the Dodd Bill. Already it had the support of the Prettyman Commission, and in the summer of 1964 there was some hope that the bill would be dislodged from Lister Hill's grip. Dodd himself made a personal appeal to Hill. Visiting him at his senate office, Dodd told Hill he was up for re-election that fall and, although his prospects were excellent, he wanted something to bring back to show the home folks. He asked Hill for a hearing and Hill relented. "We were the squeaky wheel that needed the oil. They finally had to do something with us," Perian recalls. Hill scheduled a session of his Health Subcommittee on August 3, 1964, to make a legislative record for the bill. Dodd's efforts up to that time had been investigative. This would be the final legislative step before the full Labor and Public Welfare Committee considered it and sent it in to the Senate floor for a vote.

Senator Hill did not bother to appear that day and the hearing was chaired by Senator Ralph Yarborough of Texas, the ranking Democrat on the Subcommittee. Members of the Health Subcommittee staff knew so little about the bill that before the hearings they called Dodd's people to ask about many details of the bill.

Five witnesses were scheduled for the hearing. First among them was the late George Larrick, the FDA commissioner. Larrick, with forty years of government service behind him, had risen to the top of the FDA by not rocking the boat. He refrained from criticizing the drug industry's role in the massive diversion and production of amphetamines. Larrick said the FDA supported the Dodd bill because it could do little about controlling these psychotoxic drugs under the existing law. He approved of the measure in the Dodd bill that would remove the need for proof of interstate traffic in the pills before federal authorities could make arrests. "Since drugs sold on the bootleg market are often packaged in fruit jars, paper sacks, envelopes, matchboxes, or cigarette packages, it is often difficult if not impossible to establish the interstate character of the merchandise," Larrick said. He repeated the now very obvious fact that barbiturates and amphetamines constituted a major drug abuse problem because they were so easily bought and because the penalties for trafficking were so weak, which was not the case with narcotics. Larrick dwelled on the truck crashes and other sordid aspects of amphetamine abuse, and confined his criticism of the drug industry to saying that adequate drug records were not kept. Larrick said the bill was carefully designed to avoid interference with legitimate prescribing. He talked about tranquilizer abuse and said "some of the doctors who were participants (in the Prettyman Commission) pointed to cases where people had become addicted or had acquired the habit of taking these tranquilizers excessively outside of good medical care." They satisfy a "non-medical urge," Larrick said and reasoned that, if controls over amphetamines and barbiturates became stronger, the abusers would "unquestionably turn to other psychotoxic drugs, including tranquilizers."

Larrick went on to speak of the FDA's attempts to find out the size of the amphetamine and barbiturate abuse problem and then made an astonishing admission: ". . . We conducted a survey of all known manufacturers, brokers and distributors of basic amphetamine and similar stimulant chemicals and of barbiturates. We wanted to obtain accurate and current information about the amounts produced, the amounts exported and imported, and the identity of all firms engaged in such enterprise.

"Unfortunately," Larrick concluded, "our survey of production figures was incomplete because records kept by several basic manufacturers were inadequate and also because *two* of the nation's *largest* pharmaceutical firms declined, as was their right, to provide the information requested. Nevertheless, we did learn that at least enough basic material was produced in 1962 to make over nine *billion* doses of barbiturates and amphetamines. Probably half of these end up in the bootleg market." [Author's italics]

The revelation of sloppy record-keeping by the manufacturers, and worse, the revelation that two of the country's pharmaceutical giants—not those small "schlock" houses as the major companies disdainfully refer to the smaller firms—refused to disclose how much they were making was astonishing. Larrick—who should have been outraged—could not bring himself to criticize the companies or to question their social obligation in the face of a serious problem involving their drugs. Larrick could not even bring himself to name the two companies. As later disclosed, they are Eli Lilly, the country's largest marketer of barbiturates, and Parke-Davis. Eli Lilly's big item is Seconal; Parke-Davis markets a barbiturate tradenamed Carbital and an amphetamine combination drug called Amphedase. These refusals came in 1962, the same year an Eli Lilly executive told Congress and the nation that the industry supported more regulations for barbiturates and amphetamines. Here was the gap between the public façade and the private action; it showed the extent to which the drug industry would voluntarily serve the public health.

As Larrick was testifying, Senator Dodd walked into the hearing room. His plane had been delayed and, as he entered, Yarborough invited him up to the witness table. Larrick concluded his tepid testimony and Yarborough, who had co-sponsored Dodd's bill, gave Dodd an effusive introduction—welcome words in an election year—and praised him for his persistence. Yarborough, an unfailingly polite man, said Dodd had faced "indifference at times" with his bill. Dodd began with a capsule history of the bill and the dimensions of the drug problem he hoped it would remedy. And then he gave a litany of his attempts at getting it passed:

"Since May 23, 1961, when I first introduced this bill, it has been subjected to the scrutiny of the President's Commission on Narcotic and Drug Abuse; the Department of Health, Education and Welfare; Treasury; Justice; State; the law enforcement agencies in New York City and the State of California, where this problem is greatest; the Association of Juvenile Court Judges; the International Juvenile

Police Officers Association; the Pharmaceutical Manufacturers Association (PMA); the distinguished representatives of a number of religious faiths. All of these groups, without exception, have approved of or endorsed this bill over the past three and a half years. Thousands of parents have written to me urging passage of the bill. Even the president of the largest producer of stimulant drugs in the United States personally wrote to me and endorsed this legislation."

Dodd continued. He told of more supporters, and he cited the Prettyman Commission findings and the support of "every witness" who testified before his subcommittee.

"Mr. Chairman," Dodd said, "I do not know anyone who is against it."

When Dodd concluded, Yarborough, in a courtroom surprise worthy of Perry Mason, told a stunned Dodd that there was in fact someone against his bill and that opposition had just now surfaced. "We have a letter against it, but it just came in today," Yarborough told Dodd; "the first letter, I am advised. It is from the American Medical Association, dated July 31, 1964, and it is opposed to the bill."

Why was the country's foremost medical organization coming out opposed to a bill designed to protect the public health? This flagrant disregard of medical and social evidence which had shown without question the widespread abuse of amphetamines and barbiturates would have been difficult for a medical association to explain. But the AMA is never to be confused with a medical society. It is a political and economic organization that is beholden to the drug industry, and the drug industry had called on its ally to do its bidding—bidding the PMA could not do in public if it wanted to appear respectable. There is a significant history to the actions of the AMA that day in the Senate.

The interlock between the AMA and the drug industry was not always tight. In fact, there was a time when their relations were very strained. The history of the relationship begins in

1905 when the Council on Pharmacy and Chemistry was formed by the AMA, then a respected medical and scientific organization. The Council was established to evaluate drug compounds. The name was later changed to the Council on Drugs. It was made up of independent doctors who apparently took their trust and their mandate seriously. They expended their energies on evaluating and often criticizing drugs, and in 1929 established a seal of acceptance program for drugs. This seal soon became a coveted prize among drug companies; it could mean the difference between the success or failure of a drug's sales because the Council also had control over advertising copy in AMA journals. But the members of the Council on Drugs gave their approval grudgingly. They examined data, ran their own tests in their own laboratory which they had established, and only when a drug met their standards was it given the seal. Members of the council also inspected drug company plants and did not let a company advertise the brand name of its drug in AMA publications unless that company had actually discovered the drug in the first place. It was all very sticky for the drug companies. The AMA drug council did not hold the actual power of life and death over a drug, but it was close to that, and their power came to be bitterly resented by many segments of the drug industry. By the late 1940s, advertising revenues in the AMA journals, especially the *Journal of the American Medical Association,* began slipping while many competing journals were booming. The revenue loss was coming at a particularly bad time. In the 1930s the AMA had changed from a scientific organization to a political one as it fought many New Deal reforms, and it had intensified its lobbying over the years to keep medicine in private hands. All this took money, and it was not coming in fast enough. The AMA space sales in its publications had dropped off 3 percent between 1948 and 1952 while some competitors had increased by 40 percent. The AMA *Journal* was still leading in ad revenues but its position was deteriorating and AMA people were plainly worried. In 1952 it commissioned Ben Gaffin & Associates, a Chicago-based consulting firm (the AMA is also headquartered in Chicago), to see what might be done about the problem. Gaffin's firm made a proposal of what the survey should be: "To uncover fundamental thinking of advertisers and physicians regarding basic advertising problems in general, and the peculiar problems of medical advertising in particular. This information will enable the American Medical Association, through its publication advertising, to better serve its readers and advertisers and by so doing, it increases its advertising revenues." The AMA agreed: discover how the AMA can make more money. So Gaffin's firm set out to find the pot of gold and on March 6, 1953, Gaffin returned to the AMA with the results of its findings. The drug industry had not concealed its feelings, so it was a rave review for neither the AMA nor the Council on Drugs. The Gaffin report said the drug companies no longer felt they had to "bow down" to the AMA since it no longer held the monopolistic power it once had over drugs. Drug companies could now advertise elsewhere, and that was precisely what they were doing. Why? Gaffin found an almost universal complaint from the drug industry: the Council on Drugs was meddlesome, dilatory, and picky and the drug industry was angry about it. One drug company executive characterized the Council on Drugs as having a "holier-than-thou" attitude. Others didn't like the careful lines the council drew around its ad copy. "An advertiser necessarily doesn't want to say merely that his product is good; he wants to say that it's better. This is the very essence of competition," one drug company executive said, neglecting to mention that this is also often the very essence of misleading advertising. Another drug company executive lashed out: "They want to quibble over copy. They have a regular schoolteacher attitude. The council's attitude is that the industry is a crook. The industry resents this attitude—that the council is always trying to catch it doing something that is crooked. The biggest bone of contention is that they figure you are guilty until you prove yourself innocent." Another called the council's standards "ridiculously arbitrary demands."

Members of the drug industry also did not feel the drug council's Seal of Acceptance had any value anyway, but even if it did they were no longer going to get on their knees to get it. It was this breach between the AMA and the drug industry that was costing the AMA lost ad revenues. In the summation, the Gaffin report recommended that the AMA change its attitude toward the advertisers who, it said, "resent being treated as irresponsible or incompetent." The message to the AMA was to play ball with the drug industry.

The second part of the Gaffin survey revealed an opposite view among doctors. They believed generally that the Seal of Acceptance was more important than the name of the manufacturer, and 79 percent of the doctors said they felt safer prescribing a drug that had the council seal. So the AMA was faced with a split. The industry did not like the seal and the doctors, whom the AMA is bound to serve, considered the seal to be very important.

The choice was not hard and it was made quickly. In 1955 the Board of Trustees of the AMA ruled in favor of the drug industry, ending the council's Seal of Acceptance and emasculating most of the council's power and influence. No longer were advertising emblems given by the council and no longer was the council to be a judge of the advertising copy. In effect, the Council on Drugs would cease to have any influence over the advertising of drugs in the AMA publications. That function was relegated to an advertising committee. No more nitpicking by the AMA. At the AMA annual convention in Atlantic City, New Jersey, in June 1955, the AMA House of Delegates, the national body made up of the state medical societies, rubber-stamped the decision ostensibly on assurances from the editor of the AMA *Journal* that the "same principles and standards" would continue to be applied to advertising copy. If the 1953 Gaffin study was the proposal, then the 1955 decision by the AMA to abandon the Seal of Acceptance and dismantle the vital functions of the Council on Drugs was the marriage between the American Medical Association and the drug industry. Of course, the AMA said at the time that the decision was an "internal" one, just one of those things. The Council on Drugs budget took a whopping cut; in 1954 it was $155,000 and by 1958 it was sliced to $75,000. The AMA chemical lab, established in 1906 to formulate standards for drugs, was abandoned in 1959 for reasons of "overwork and lack of finances," the AMA announced. The AMA did not mention that while the money for the lab could not be found, about a half million dollars that same year was expended for the AMA's public relations department. Image had won over substance. That was not all. All the old drug council functions, such as plant inspections and control over generic names in the ad copy, were ended. A microbiologic lab established in 1949 was also abandoned in 1955. But it was apparently worth it in the eyes of the AMA's medical politicians.

The AMA publicly said the Gaffin report and the industry complaints about the Council on Drugs had "no influence whatsoever on the decision to eliminate the Seal of Acceptance." But as the shackles came off, the ad revenues pouring into the AMA began to soar. In 1949 they had been about $2.4 million for all advertising in AMA publications. By 1960 advertising revenue had more than tripled to reach $8 million. As Ben Gaffin himself boasted later, the AMA netted a return of 3,600 percent in increased drug advertising for each dollar spent on his study. There were other signs that showed how deeply the drug industry had bought into the AMA. In the late 1940s and early 1950s the balance between drug advertising and other advertising—such as ads for medical or hospital equipment—had run about fifty-fifty in the AMA publications. With the AMA standards gone the drug advertising became completely dominant and the AMA *Journal* was running about three to four times as many drug ads as it was ads for everything else. Most of the drug ads came from the big drug houses and the AMA publications reached the point where more than 80 percent of their revenues came from drug advertising. All these revenues are tax-exempt: the AMA is a non-profit organization.

The marriage of the AMA and the drug industry was fully consummated in 1956 when Gaffin did another survey for the AMA designed expressly for the drug industry. The survey was part of what the drug industry had termed the "exchange of ideas" needed between organized medicine and industry. The new Gaffin survey was to find out the best marketing techniques for drugs, and the industry would use the auspices of the AMA to do it. "If this study reveals a tenth of what we have reasonable hopes of learning, it will enable the American Medical Association to *perform a service* for the industry of such magnitude that the industry will be very mindful of AMA publications when setting up advertising media allocation," Gaffin proposed. The survey was made and it showed among other things that the best way to sell drugs was through the industry detail man. This survey was turned over to the drug industry with no strings attached.

Dr. Joel Fort, a respected drug abuse authority, later said that after 1955 the AMA "drastically reduced its standards of accuracy and truthfulness for advertising." The AMA denies this, but if any proof were needed it came in 1960, five years after its marriage to the drug industry. Two ads ran in the AMA *Journal,* one for Equanil and one for Miltown. For Equanil, a Wyeth product, the ad warned: "Careful supervision of dose and amount prescribed is advised, especially for patients with a known propensity for taking excessive quantities of drugs. Excessive and prolonged use in susceptible persons (alcoholics, former addicts, and other severe psychoneurotics) has been reported to result in dependence on the drug."

Compare this ad to one run for Miltown by Carter-Wallace. "Simple dosage schedule produces rapid, reliable

tranquilization without unpredictable excitation. No cumulative effects, thus no need for difficult dosage readjustments.
Does not produce depression, Parkinson-like symptoms, jaun-
dices or agranulocytosis. Does not impair mental efficiency or
normal behavior." No warning of any kind could be found
in the ad. Both Equanil and Miltown, of course, are the
same drug—meprobamate—but one would not know this
from the two ads.

With its advertising standards a thing of the past, the
AMA was willing to accept almost anything to build up its
treasury. The union with the drug industry grew tighter and
tighter.

Dr. John Adriani, an independent medical professor and
anesthesiologist from New Orleans and former chairman of
the AMA Council on Drugs, puts it bluntly: "The drug industry has the AMA in its hip pocket." The drug industry's
demands are funneled through the PMA which deals with
the AMA on a day-to-day basis. Their relationship is so tight
on the policy-making level that since the PMA was founded
in 1958, both its presidents have held prominent positions
with the AMA before heading the PMA. It's the revolving
door policy.

Since the early 1960s the drug industry had annually spent
about $10 million a year on advertising in the AMA publica-
tions, including the lay magazine *Today's Health,* which
means the drug industry supports about one-half of the AMA's
annual budget. The other half of the AMA's budget is made
up largely of dues from members. In about fifty years the
AMA had shifted from being a respected scientific body to
becoming a political organization to becoming a service arm
for the drug industry, forming what could aptly be called
the Medical-Pharmaceutical Complex. In 1964 the AMA was
plainly worried about the Medicare bill and trade-offs were
arranged with the drug lobby in the spirit of mutual self-
protection. The drug lobby was to help the AMA fight off
Medicare, and the AMA was going to help the drug industry

fight off its attackers. This is how the AMA came to be the drug industry's hatchet man and to oppose Dodd's drug bill the morning of the hearing in August of 1964.

The AMA position was spelled out in a letter to Lister Hill from F. J. L. Blasingame, the AMA executive vice-president. Blasingame, a former anatomy professor at the University of Texas, said the need for special controls over amphetamines and barbiturates depended on the extent of the problem. What was the extent of the problem in the eyes of the AMA? "In the United States at this time," the AMA letter said, "compulsive abuse of amphetamines and barbiturates constitutes such a *small problem* that additional legislation to control such abuse does not seem to be necessary."

That statement contradicted virtually every carefully documented piece of evidence gathered on the problem. The AMA letter asserted that the Dodd bill would "create far greater problems similar to those in enforcing existing narcotic laws." The Dodd bill in no way paralleled those narcotic laws. It was only regulating legal drugs and not trying to stamp them out, but this was blithely ignored by the AMA letter. While it denied the amphetamine problem was of any consequence, the letter said it considered education, and local and state laws rather than federal regulation, to be the appropriate solution. The AMA's suggestion of education as a remedy was particularly curious since the medical profession itself, which should know better, has one of the highest rates of drug misuse and abuse of any single group.

Yarborough asked Dodd if he wished to answer the letter. Dodd was caught unprepared since the letter had come in only that morning, a tactic that did not go unnoticed. Dodd said he could find no words "strong enough" to disapprove of the AMA's position. "The house is on fire," he said, "and we do not need a lesson in how to prevent the starting of fires. What we need now is to put the fire out and go on with our fire prevention work."

The AMA letter was designed to give anyone in Congress, preferably a key committee chairman, the authority to say that amphetamine abuse is not a major problem and therefore new legislation is not necessary. After all, the AMA, the country's foremost medical authority, said so. That is all part of the delay, the stringing out of the drug bill. It gives the industry more time to chop it up and more time of uninterrupted profits. That, as Gene Gleason of Dodd's staff had said, is the "implementation of the fix."

The AMA had taken the low road and it was now up to the PMA to take, if not the high road, the high-sounding road. PMA president Dr. Austin Smith, like the AMA, wrote only a letter and did not appear before the Health Subcommittee that day. "The PMA has long been interested in and has consistently supported federal legislation intended to impose additional controls on the distribution and sale of certain depressant and stimulant drugs," Dr. Smith's PMA letter said, but now that it might actually pass, the PMA of course had some suggestions to "perfect" the bill. First, get rid of that word "psychotoxic" in the title of the bill. It stuck in the throat of the drug industry. The PMA said that this was an "unfair designation because it stigmatizes these medically useful drugs." It also objected to the term "dangerous drugs," which also appeared in the bill, for the same reason. The letter said amphetamines "do not produce physical dependence," and argued against calling the drugs "habit-forming." It said such a designation was "irrelevant" and "blurs the objectives of the bill." And what were the objectives of the bill? The record-keeping requirement for drug companies and distributors was the major reason for the bill. The PMA went chopping away at this provision. It argued that since most drug companies and wholesalers already kept records of the names and addresses of their suppliers and customers, there should be *no separate* record-keeping for these dangerous drugs. The PMA suggested the wording of the bill should state this unequivocally, and even supplied an appropriate sentence: "There shall be no set forms or separate files for the records required under the act so long as the necessary information is available." The intent of the bill was not just to have those records lying around somewhere mixed up with all the records for aspirin, cold tablets and hay fever remedies these drug companies marketed. The intent was to make them quickly accessible for the FDA inspectors so they could make quick checks to trace down diversions along the distribution chain. It would take weeks to search through a company's entire records to learn where a few shipments of amphetamines went. The FDA simply did not have enough manpower to do it.

The PMA offered a few more suggestions to "perfect" the bill. It joined with the tranquilizer companies in objecting to the words "potential for abuse" in the bill as being a determining factor for controlling a drug. It preferred that a drug be controlled only if it posed an "immediate" threat. Ralph Nader once called this the "proof of corpses" requirement of corporate law; i.e., let us find out how truly bad it is before trying to do something about it.

The National Association of Retail Druggists (NARD), which often works in tandem with the PMA, appeared before the Health Subcommittee that same day and tried to bore its own loophole through the bill by demanding druggists be exempted from the record-keeping requirement. Said Ralph Rooke, chairman of the national legislation committee of NARD: it would be "unjustly discriminatory" to cover pharmacists and exempt doctors. He also said only a small percentage of illegal drug diversion came through drugstores, something the evidence contradicted. He was correct in accusing many doctors of doing a handsome business in the peddling of these drugs and in arguing they should be covered by the bill. The major reason they weren't was because the Dodd investigations wanted accountability from the companies foremost and did not focus on doctors. As it was written, however, the bill could trace down doctors getting abnormally large shipments of these drugs if the record-keeping requirement were left untouched by the drug industry.

The hearing lasted a little more than an hour and the transcript and the letters and the bill went to the full Committee on Labor and Public Welfare for its consideration. Dodd and Perian considered this alone a milestone. The drug industry in league with the AMA clearly wanted to delay the bill. If that failed, then the idea was to drive in those crippling loopholes in order to continue business as usual.

8:"Potential for Abuse"

What a little thing to ask. And yet ...

SENATOR DODD ON CBS

CONGRESS conducts much of the public's business in private. Perhaps the most secretive aspect of the process is the executive meeting of the congressional committee when they decide on a bill's fate and wording. Here, amid privacy and security, senators or congressmen often change bills and public policy. Their motives may be bad or good, in the public interest or for private interest. If one gets a majority of his committee colleagues to go along, he succeeds and the bill is changed, usually permanently. Records or minutes are sometimes kept and sometimes not. Even if they are, they are kept under lock and key and some committee chairmen have been known to refuse a request from other senators wanting to look at them. The only way the public can learn the details of what actually happened is if someone in the meeting, either staff member or committee member, decides to talk about it. On the morning of August 11, 1964, a week after the Health

Subcommittee hearing on Dodd's drug bill, Lister Hill's full Labor and Public Welfare Committee was meeting to consider Dodd's bill and report it to the Senate floor. Perian discovered that Finney, lobbyist-lawyer for Roche Laboratories, finally had succeeded in placing into the drug bill a change in the definition section that would kill any chance of ever including the tranquilizers or many other drugs. The words "potential for abuse" had been deleted. "The Hill committee really hadn't done much with us after they had full control of the bill," Perian remembers, "and we were not kept fully abreast of any changes in the bill until one FDA lawyer who had been telling us what was going on told us that the definition change had been slipped into the bill." Perian began immediately that morning to keep the change from becoming permanent. He and other members of the Subcommittee staff and Dodd's personal staff joined together in a frantic attempt to change the definition back to the original. A memo was written and Perian brought it to Dodd for his signature. It was written to Lister Hill and in it Dodd said:

"I have just been informed of an eleventh hour attempt to sabotage S. 2628," Dodd's memo said, "which is slated for final consideration this morning by your committee. This attempt is being managed by a Washington lawyer, Mr. Thomas Finney, who claims to represent Roche Laboratories of New Jersey. Mr. Finney seeks to change a key definition in the bill, that of psychotoxic drugs. The result of this proposed change would cripple the attempts of the Food and Drug Administration to classify new drugs as psychotoxic drugs. It would be the cause of *years of litigation.*"

Dodd charged in the memo, but did not explain how, Roche Labs and Finney were using Dr. Nathan B. Eddy as the expert to buttress their case. He accused Dr. Eddy of shilling for the drug industry and of accepting a three-week vacation in Hawaii, plus his original travel and per diem expenses, as payment for testifying in California for

Endo Laboratories on behalf of a drug called Percodan. Dodd's staff had been informed of this by California's attorney general, who publicly accused Eddy of it. "This is the nature of the last-minute opposition to this bill," the memo said. "It could not stand up to rebuttal in the light of day. That is why they have waited until the last minute. I am sure the members of the committee will not be deceived by this tactic." Not only were they not deceived, members of the committee had helped to get some of Roche's wording into the bill. Dodd and Perian were on the phone to HEW lawyers while dictating the memo, and Dodd reported that these lawyers confirmed the "sleeper" in the bill that would "destroy the effectiveness of the bill entirely." He said HEW was going to send a letter to the committee, which it did. Time was tight.

Perian was writing a memo himself to Robert Barclay, the staff assistant on Hill's Health Subcommittee. Perian mentioned a conversation he had had the day before with Finney, in which he quoted Finney as saying "many experts" favor the change in the bill. Perian said Finney mentioned only Dr. Eddy by name. In their haste and anger Dodd's staff did not check with Dr. Eddy. If they had they would have discovered that his name was being misused. Dr. Eddy later said in an interview in October 1972 that he had no part in supporting Roche's or Finney's position on the bill. Dr. Eddy, then in his early 80s but still very alert and keeping abreast with the latest developments in addiction research, is called the "grandfather of drug addiction research." Although a consultant to Roche Labs at the time, he said he felt Librium and Valium should be classified with the barbiturates and had told Roche this. As for the three-week trip to Hawaii, Dr. Eddy said it was not paid for by the drug company but by a professional conference held in Hawaii and to which he was invited. If his name was bandied about during the private meetings it was done so without his knowledge or authorization. "I had even told Hoffmann-

LaRoche that the writer of the report on Librium and Valium had gone out of his way to avoid all the difficulties with the drug," Dr. Eddy added.

When Perian finished writing the memo and talking with the HEW lawyers he was certain it was Finney who had lobbied to put in the crippling definition change. "There was no question. They said it was Finney. The PMA had their people around but it was Finney who got the change in. I don't know who on the committee put it in for him but he got it in." The feeling of being sandbagged filled the Dodd sub-committee, and Perian took the memo and hand-delivered it to Hill's committee. One incident still burns in his memory. "Finney got hold of the memo of course because he had more entree to the committee room than we did. He came out in the hall at one point and said 'Carl, I don't think you understand what we're trying to do in there.' I was really hot at that point and I kept jabbing my finger into his chest and I said 'I know precisely what you're doing in there. Don't you realize this stuff is killing children?' I'll never forget that. He arched his eyebrows way up and said, 'What's that got to do with it?' I told him if he could ask that question we had nothing further to talk about."

What happened next among the members of Hill's committee is unclear. HEW lawyers brought out their argument to keep the words "potential for abuse" in the law and not to restrict it in the way Roche and Finney wanted to restrict it. There was also the specter of Dodd making a public issue of it. The Committee reversed itself on the definition change; Dodd and Perian won their round. The old definition went back into the bill. "But Finney still sandbagged us," Perian said. "His delaying tactics stalled the bill for so long that it was making it more and more difficult to pass both Houses in the 1964 session."

Sitting in his plushly appointed office on Connecticut Avenue, Tom Finney strokes the side of his face with his hand. His expression is rippled with concern. "I told them at the outset if they were going to keep 'potential for abuse' in that bill we were going to fight them," Finney remembers. "You could put just about anything under that law with the kind of definition they wrote." But wasn't Roche Labs really trying to devise a definition that would keep its drugs out of the bill altogether, permanently? "It wasn't the regulations Roche objected to," Finney explains, mustering sincerity, "it was the libel of comparing Librium and Valium with barbiturates which would come when they all were included in the same law." Finney and Roche simply wanted a special law to themselves.

On August 15, 1964, the Dodd drug bill finally reached the Senate floor for a vote. The speed with which it got there, after a three-and-a-half-year wait (actually a five-year wait when Senator Hennings' first bill in 1959 is included), was next to incredible: an hour's hearing on August 3, a full committee meeting a week later, and suddenly there it was, ready for a vote. It seemed so quick and simple. Why hadn't it happened three years earlier?

There was little floor discussion of the bill. Dodd, of course, spoke up for it. He listed the police statistics of the abuse of amphetamines and barbiturates, the wide support his bill had received, and the necessity for it. It was a speech he had given so many times he could have recited it in his sleep. No one voiced any opposition. No amendment was offered to include the six other drugs named by Dr. Essig. To try would have been fruitless and Dodd knew it. Hill's committee had the power over the bill and its position would have held sway on the floor. By a voice vote, the Dodd drug bill passed the Senate on August 15, 1964. Majority Leader Mike Mansfield commended Dodd for his determination and final victory, which, Mansfield said, "he has achieved after fighting for it for so long." The bill was called the Psychotoxic Drug Control Act of 1964."

This was one hurdle; now for the second. It needed to

pass the House where the drug lobby has traditionally had more influence. It would go to the House Interstate and Foreign Commerce Committee (House Commerce Committee) which was chaired by Oren Harris, who for twenty-four years represented the fourth district of Arkansas. A Democrat, and an effective chairman who could get passed the bills he wanted, Harris is also a proud man and, like all committee chairmen, jealous of his domain. His political instincts were to protect business interests. "He might rail against this industry or that," said a veteran House reporter, "but basically Harris' point of view rested with the business community when it came to push and shove. The rest was for public consumption." As chairman, Harris was also a tireless worker and floor manager. He stayed every night in his office until eight or nine o'clock and usually was there on the weekends. He was a quick study, an admiring former aide recalled, able to digest information quickly and make rapid sense out of it. On your side he was invaluable, against you he could be implacable.

"We knew it was going to be tough on the House side," Perian recalls, "because the drug lobby had even told us to our faces that their system is set up for the House's side." Because the House of Representatives is so large and diffuse—435 members as opposed to 100 in the Senate—it receives less scrutiny by the press and less attention by the public. It is not populated with the famous names of the Senate, like Kennedy or Fulbright, Muskie or Goldwater. Because it gets less attention, more special interest pressure goes unnoticed, which is precisely why the drug lobby prefers it. What would Oren Harris do about the drug bill? He did nothing. "We sent letters, made calls; Dodd was very good about sending letters, waiting ten days for an answer, and then writing another letter," Perian remembers. "He was persistent. But nothing happened. Finally we got a form letter from Harris saying he had heard of no urgency from the Administration to pass the bill and he had no time for it in the remainder of the session. This was in spite of the Prettyman Commission, and the support of Presidents Kennedy and Johnson. It was obscene."

The chances for the bill becoming law were now the same as they had been three years earlier. Dodd's people had no control over it and Harris was refusing to budge. Harris, proud, at times even vain, would want credit for the bill, as would Dodd, and pride of authorship is a never-to-be-ignored ingredient in the political process. Harris' committee was also receiving visitors. On August 18, only three days after Senate passage, the *Drug Trade News,* an industry trade sheet, announced, "Some drug interests are known to be trying to kill the bill." It did not name the interests. In the September 1 issue, the same publication reported: "Retail and manufacturing sections of the pharmaceutical industry are pressing hard this week to delay House action on the controversial psychotoxic drug bill . . ." The PMA was among the subterranean opposition now that things could be settled quietly. At about the same time the *Washington Report on the Medical Sciences,* a medical newsletter, said the Dodd bill was resting in the House Commerce Committee with no sign of its being "removed from the shelf." The story continued: "The drug interests failed in efforts to have the control bill modified before (the) Senate voted but (the) Commerce Committee calm suggests they are doing better on the other side of the capitol."

The success of the best laid plans of the drug industry, the AMA, and Oren Harris was not to be. Just as the thalidomide tragedy forced the passage of the sweeping Kefauver drug bill in 1962, now something was happening far away from Capitol Hill that would force Oren Harris to act. Jay McMullen, a CBS television producer, had prepared a feature for showing on Walter Cronkite's evening news on September 2, only two weeks after Senate passage of Dodd's drug bill. It was inspired by Perian, who recognized the need for aroused public opinion to get the bill over all the obstacles. He suggested that a feature on the easy availability of amphetamines and barbiturates would be a worthwhile exposé, and McMullen and CBS picked up the idea. McMullen had rented an office in New York City the previous May and had ordered stationery with the letterheads and envelopes reading "McMullen Services, Export-Import." He then opened a checking account at the First National City Bank of New York and bought a copy of the *Drug Topics Red Book,* which listed drug manufacturers selling barbiturates and amphetamines. McMullen mailed letters to twenty-four drug companies in eleven states requesting catalogues, and received seventeen. He then placed orders for pills, and by the first week of August he had received 297,000 quarter-grain barbiturates and 628,000 five-milligram amphetamine pills. He repeated the procedure with twenty-seven more companies and thirteen replied; he placed orders with seven of these companies and still more pills poured in. One company, and only one, Kirkman Labs of Seattle, Washington, finally alerted the New York State Pharmacy Board, and by the time its inspectors arrived 47 percent of McMullen's orders had been filled. He had a grand total of more than one million pills at a cost to him of only $600.28. It was estimated that street sales could bring him between $250,000 and $500,000. In all, fifty-one companies had been contacted and orders had been placed with nineteen.

The revelation had a dramatic impact. McMullen's resourcefulness had exposed the ridiculous ease by which these drugs could be obtained from legitimate drug companies. The exposé was aired, and the following night CBS asked Dodd to appear and discuss McMullen's findings. In a display of cold anger, rare even for Dodd, he lashed out at the opposition to his bill. By now he realized that Roche Laboratories and Finney had been sandbagging the bill in Congress, and the PMA and AMA were trying to string out the decision process on it. Said Dodd: "I introduced that bill in May of 1961. It's passed the Senate; it's now in the House where it is meeting undercover opposition; opposition that never appeared when we held our hearings in the Senate. And this makes it very difficult for us to get the bill through this year." The interviewer asked Dodd if he had discovered the strength of the lobby that opposed the bill: "I sure have," he said. "I've learned of it in a couple of other fields, too. And it is powerful and it is strong. They don't come forward—we invited everyone who wanted to be heard on this bill to come forward; for over a year and a half we heard witnesses. None of these people ever showed up: that isn't how they work. They work underneath in a sinister manner, and they block these measures despite the fact that a vast majority, I believe, of our people in this country want this bill, for example, and others like it passed. It's a frustrating experience to fight this kind of opposition. It's just what I said it was, it's a national scandal. Now, I'm suggesting, [along with] those associated with me, like Senator Hart and other senators: just give us the simple information, how many are produced, who do you sell them to? What a little thing to ask. And yet we run into a stone wall of opposition."

Dodd's swipe at the "sinister manner" of the "undercover opposition" was not destined to warm Oren Harris to the task of passing Dodd's bill in the House. He took it personally. As James Menger, Jr., professional staff member for Harris' Commerce Committee, said, the statement made Dodd as popular with the Committee as "the proverbial skunk at a lawn party." Now that matters were out in the open, however, there was a discernible shift in Oren Harris' thinking; that drug bill didn't seem like such a bad idea after all. He called Menger, a loyal servant of the Committee, into his office and told him to draft a bill dealing with amphetamines and barbiturates. At the end of September Harris wrote Dodd to say that in view of the "importance of the legislation it will be considered early next year."

Meanwhile, the PMA was putting its publicity machine

to work to smooth over the effects of the CBS exposé. Two days after the initial CBS show the PMA issued a news release saying "any failure of drug producers to check whether all their customers are legitimate receivers of prescription drugs is deplorable." Dr. Austin Smith, the PMA president, was quoted in the release as saying "our members have consistently recognized the social problem inherent in the abuse of amphetamines and barbiturates." He said the PMA had urged controls since 1962. "Just in the past two weeks," Smith added, "PMA has written the chairman of the House committee urging public hearings on the Senate-passed bill providing for additional controls over distribution of certain stimulant and depressant drugs." Yes indeed.

Dodd returned to his Connecticut senatorial campaign with laurel wreaths to spare. President Johnson had invited him to the White House in what was staged as an offer for the vice-presidency, which Dodd said he turned down before it could be made. His drug bill had passed the Senate and his efforts were vindicated by a television exposé. Goldwater's presidential candidacy would not hurt either. Dodd won in a landslide.

9: The Bill Passes –
Too Weak and
Too Late

We appreciate your testimony, Mr. Delaney.
                                  OREN HARRIS, DURING THE
                                  DRUG BILL HEARINGS

THE 89th Congress that convened in January 1965 was the most liberal Congress ever elected in this country. The Democratic and liberal ranks were swelled by the Goldwater disaster of the previous November and President Johnson, still riding a wave of unprecedented presidential popularity, moved swiftly to capitalize on this legislative windfall. It was obvious at the outset, with the McMullen CBS disclosure as the impetus, that a bill to control amphetamines and barbiturates was going to pass. On January 8, the President submitted his health message to Congress. As part of his "Great Society" package he included the need for control over dangerous drugs. "Widespread traffic resulting from inadequate controls over the manufacture, distribution, and sale of these drugs is creating a growing problem which must be met," the message said. The only question now was what kind of law would be passed, as many hurried to occupy the ground that Dodd and a few others had occupied alone for so long.

James Menger of Harris' Commerce Committee staff had spent several weeks preparing the House version of the bill. Menger, who until his retirement in 1972 maintained close and cordial contacts with the drug industry, wrote a bill that managed to incorporate most of what the drug industry wanted.

Oren Harris introduced it on January 4, 1965, the opening day of the new Congress. It was numbered H.R.2, the second bill introduced that session. Dodd, with eight cosponsors, reintroduced his Senate bill but no hearings were scheduled by Hill's Senate committee. All the attention this time would focus on Harris' version.

The House bill included PMA demands which had been voiced in the letter to Lister Hill the previous August. The hated words "psychotoxic drugs" were replaced by the more genteel words, "stimulant and depressant drugs." This removed the stigma the PMA found so offensive. The words "habit-forming" were deleted from the purpose clause of the bill. The words "potential for abuse" were retained but the definition was narrowed considerably.

Many crucial substantive changes were inserted. The PMA demand that the bill specifically state that no separate drug records be required of industry was written into the House bill. It was taken almost verbatim from the earlier PMA letter to Lister Hill. FDA attorneys struggled with the Commerce Committee to keep that statement out of the bill, but the PMA pushed to keep it in. Too burdensome for the companies, they said. "I had Ted Ellenbogen (HEW legislative counsel) wanting me to take it out and the industry people wanted it in there. Finally, a lawyer from Lloyd Cutler's firm (the law firm retained by the PMA) had the last shot at me and I put it back in," Menger says, without apology. That was it. It stayed. The PMA succeeded without an open fight and its public image would remain unblemished. Ellenbogen, now retired, feared such a loose record-keeping requirement would pose too big an obstacle in tracking down diversion. He would be proven right.

Besides embracing most of the PMA's demands, the Harris bill provided yet another favor for the industry. A specific provision now made the counterfeiting of drugs a criminal offense. This would avoid any possibility of civil suits that might arise regarding the infringement of trade. Such a suit might well disclose the enormous markups on drugs, a secret the industry wanted to keep quiet.

The cumbersome administrative procedure of course remained in the Harris version. The FDA would not make a big issue of it. Wilbur Cohen, then assistant secretary of HEW, wrote to Oren Harris to say that with all appeals a full hearing "is not best suited to a proceeding in which scientific and judgmental questions are likely to be primary." One reason no major objections were raised by HEW and FDA was that the major fight to be waged in Congress would be over Medicare. No needless IOUs would be wasted on this bill. Harris wanted a palatable bill, one that would quiet the noise even if it did nothing about the problem. Unfortunately, the bills that slide easily through Congress are often not the best ones, and any drug bill the PMA fully endorses, as it now did, is bound to be weak.

There was no chance of including the six drugs, meprobamate, Librium, Valmid, Placidyl, Doriden and Noludar, in the bill by name. The FDA was not supporting it and Harris certainly wouldn't. There was somebody who wanted it, however, and was fighting quietly for it. McNeil Laboratories, which ranks close to Eli Lilly as the leading barbiturate marketer in the country, wanted those six drugs in the bill. McNeil and Lilly each make about 30 percent of the more than $30 million from annual barbiturate sales. If the above drugs stayed out and Butisol, McNeil's leading barbiturate, went in, McNeil would lose competitively. Enter Thomas "Tommy the Cork" Corcoran. Corcoran, a fabled Washington lawyer-lobbyist, was hired by McNeil to see what he could do about listing the six drugs in the bill. With his flowing white mane, his perennial tan, and his deeply seamed face all a trademark in Washington, Corcoran could get access. He was a member of the FDR inner circle until he and Roosevelt had a parting of the ways. Since those New Deal days Corcoran has managed to stay on good terms with every administration that came to town and his gift for helping corporate clients in the Washington jungle is legendary. He is able to leap high obstacles with a single bound, or a single telephone call. Corcoran is a man of energy and charm and he would need lots of both to win this case. He tried. He took the list of the six drugs to the FDA, to Capitol Hill, and "to damn near everybody who would listen," a competing lobbyist remarked. Corcoran's magic failed him. Nothing came of his work. The other six drugs had already been amply represented and Corcoran could not get them included. But he would try again.

Oren Harris, the man who could see no urgency in controlling these drugs the previous fall, now moved swiftly to hold hearings and report the bill out. Hearings were held in late January and early February 1965, and Harris made it plain he didn't care for the Dodd bill. He complained that he had been "advised that you could even control aspirin with the loose definition in the Senate bill." One can only guess who his "advisers" were. Harris' feelings about the Dodd bill coincided with the drug industry's thinking. In a story published on January 27, the opening day of the hearings, the *Wall Street Journal* quoted an unidentified industry spokesman as saying the Dodd bill was "far too severe." The industry liked the Harris bill better, but it still wasn't a love affair. The record-keeping, said the spokesman, would be "onerous" but at least many of the "industry objections" had been met in that bill. "The way the legislation is worded and the way those officious bureaucrats at FDA work," the industry spokesman told the *Journal,* "they'll be inquiring into every sale of any drug that's subject to misuse, and that takes in nearly everything we sell." The *Journal* also spoke with pharmacists. They did not like the bill and said so both publicly and privately. One pharmacist in the *Journal* article referred to the FDA inspectors as a "lot of federal snoops" who came in and harassed druggists.

An improvement was written into the bill on the House side. A prescription refill limit was inserted which would prohibit the continued refilling of amphetamines or barbiturates, a practice that had been going on for a long time and was one of those "legal" avenues of diversion. Now a prescription could only be refilled five times in a six-month period. After six months a new prescription from the doctor, either oral or written, would be required. A modest step but still an easily skirted one. Many experts at the time felt each and every prescription for these drugs should be a new one with no refills allowed at all.

The leadoff witness in the House hearings was FDA Commissioner Larrick. He mentioned that he was "personally proud to be an honorary member of the American Pharmaceutical Association and the National Association of Retail Druggists." Both of these organizations often work in league with the PMA. The PMA in fact had honored Larrick in 1958 for his "devoted service to the public welfare" and his understanding of industry problems. Larrick had often expressed the role of FDA as sharing in a sort of partnership with industry. A benign-looking man who usually sported a bow tie, Larrick began to recite his reasons for supporting the Harris' bill. Larrick was not a venal man, he was simply a weak man and out of his depth. He was not a doctor nor was he even a college graduate; he was a career bureaucrat. The revolution in synthetic drugs, a former co-worker said, was beyond Larrick. When he should have been demanding regulation, he seemed content only to politely request it. He did not make public issues of anything. Now before Oren Harris' full Commerce Committee, Larrick said calmly that there was not enough law on the books to do much about the legal drug traffic problem. He talked around the PMA insert requiring no separate drug records. As had become his custom through forty years of bureaucratic survival, his criticism was almost indistinguishable from his praise. He said the provision would "sometime place an undue burden on both the FDA and the establishment being inspected." The companies apparently did not think so. Larrick offered, but did not insist on, a compromise. He said the bill should require all drug records to be "readily and conveniently available." He said the FDA investigations into legal drugs received little attention because of the enormous work load on inspectors. Larrick said less than one-twelfth of an inspector's time was spent on these investigations in 1964; in terms of man-hours, this meant the FDA had only a little more than one man per state to deal with the problem of legal drug diversion, barely enough time to keep abreast of the problem, much less to stop it. In one state one inspector would have to deal with hundreds or possibly thousands of drugstores, hospitals, distributors, manufacturers, if there were any, in order to find the sources of diversion. Larrick gave an example of what kind of work load was involved when there were no separate records for amphetamines and barbiturates. In New York, he said, FDA inspectors required 250 man-hours to look through the drug records of a small company which had grossed only $250,000 a year. It was a tip-off that without separate records for dangerous drugs, that law would probably be useless.

Harris showed some flashes of real ignorance about the bill he had in front of him and the drugs it was to control. He wondered at one point whether Miltown was an over-the-counter drug. It had been a prescription drug for ten years. Harris, whose committee was and is the major conduit for health and drug legislation in the House, asked Commissioner Larrick at another point what an amphetamine was. Larrick told him it was a powerful stimulant.

"A harmful stimulant?" Harris asked.

"Powerful," Larrick assured him.

This at times was the level of debate between the executive and legislative branches of the federal government.

Congressman James Delaney of New York, who introduced the same bill in the House several times that Dodd introduced in the Senate, testified. He recognized the industry change in the record-keeping for what it was, an innocuous-sounding sentence that would in fact cripple the bill. "Failure to keep adequate records has been found by the Senate Subcommittee to Investigate Juvenile Delinquency and the Senate Labor and Public Welfare Committee to be one of the principal inadequacies in the present law," Delaney declared. "If this exemption is not abolished, we are providing a sanction with an ineffective remedy for enforcing it," Delaney concluded. Harris glanced around the committee. "Are there any questions?" he inquired. "If not, we appreciate your testimony, Mr. Delaney." Thanks but no thanks, Mr. Delaney. The clause specifying no separate records stayed in the bill.

Harris also dismissed complaints about another industry-inspired portion of the bill. It required the Secretary of HEW, who would make a decision about controlling a drug and pass it down to FDA, to form an advisory committee of impartial experts to collect findings and make recommendations to the secretary about controlling a drug. Such a committee, to be chosen by the National Academy of Sciences, would be still one more hurdle to leap before a drug could be controlled. The industry was erecting these hurdles in the bill, hoping that the government would trip on one of them and any company could delay or avoid regulation.

Harris dismissed any suggestion that the six depressant drugs be included by name. Dr. Tim Lee Carter, a Republican Congressman from Kentucky, a medical doctor, and a member of the committee, opined that meprobamate "might be habit-forming" but suggested the bill only include amphetamines and barbiturates. "Thank you very much, Dr. Carter," Harris hastened. So that issue was delicately dropped.

Next something surprising happened. The AMA, which six

months earlier had said it did not recognize any medical or public health problem with amphetamines or barbiturates, nor had it seen the need for any new law, now thought there might be a problem. But the drug industry had already shaped the new bill to its liking in many crucial sections. Dr. Henry Brill from the AMA's Committee on Alcoholism and Addiction testified. A psychiatrist and neurologist, Dr. Brill said "it has become increasingly apparent that the concern regarding the abuse of barbiturates and amphetamines may be well-founded." Six months earlier the AMA had said it was "such a small problem." Whatever developments had come to light since then were not explained by Dr. Brill. He did say he thought the bill ought to control only amphetamines and barbiturates, not the other sedatives. When he completed his turnabout testimony, not one member of the Commerce Committee asked him why the AMA had come to see things so differently in so short a time. James Menger of the House committee staff, who solicited Brill's views when writing the bill, took pride in the fact that the AMA did not find anything objectionable.

Following the AMA testimony that day was, naturally, that of PMA President Dr. Austin Smith. Now that the bill had been "perfected," Smith could say it was "workable and, we believe, needed legislation." The only objection the PMA could find was the wording "potential for abuse," the same words Roche Labs wanted dropped. Smith said a drug should be controlled only if there has been "substantial actual abuse constituting a public health and safety problem." In other words, wait until abuse gets completely out of hand. Harris' Commerce Committee did not incorporate this final PMA request; apparently it was the only industry request not placed into the bill.

The committee had previously heard from Dr. Lawrence Peters, executive vice-president of scientific affairs for McNeil Laboratories. With "Tommy the Cork" Corcoran's failure to quietly slip the other six nonbarbiturate depressant drugs into the bill, Peters went public in demanding that they be "automatically" included. He said the evidence was clear "that some of these nonbarbiturate drugs are subject to the same abuses as some of the barbiturates." He was right. He argued that to regulate barbiturates and exclude the others would be "competitive discrimination and a continuing hazard to the health of the public . . ."

The late Dr. V. P. Mattia, the executive vice-president of Roche Labs, testified. He said that what Peters said wasn't so. "I find it difficult to believe that where there is conclusive evidence to warrant inclusion of a drug under this act, that responsible manufacturers will oppose such measures," Mattia said reassuringly.

The hearings ended in early March and, in an exercise in myopic reporting, the *New York Times* told the American public on February 28 that usually industries fight government regulation. "An exception has turned up this year, however, in the drug industry's almost united stand in support of federal legislation to control the manufacture and distribution of barbiturates (sedatives) and amphetamines (stimulants)."

On March 8, President Johnson, in his crime message to Congress, gave the bill one more push. "Sensational killings, robberies, auto accidents, have resulted from the radical changes induced by the indiscriminate use of these drugs." On March 10 it reached the floor of the House for a final vote.

There was a chorus of effusive support for the bill, now that it was a foregone conclusion it would pass and become one of the building blocks of the "Great Society." Oren Harris put in a few words. He said it would not eliminate all illegal traffic in amphetamines and barbiturates, a fact his committee helped make possible. "There will still be some unscrupulous individuals and firms that will deliberately try to evade the law. But the bill will make it possible to detect points of major diversion in a way that is not possible today.

It will be a tremendous aid to controlling the problem." More statistics were cited on the *billions* of pills diverted and then it came to a vote. The bill, now called the Drug Abuse Control Amendment of 1965, passed by a vote of 402 to 0. The bill then went to the Senate side for passage there. The Dodd bill had been forgotten by now. The Harris bill would be the one the Senate considered. It went to Lister Hill's Labor and Public Welfare Committee. Dodd was annoyed by several things, the biggest of which was having been completely frozen out of the bill. He made noises that he would offer amendments and would demand hearings. Finally Dodd was visited by Robert N. Hills, who was a special assistant to Wilbur Cohen, then assistant Secretary of HEW. Dodd wanted some of his changes—changes which would toughen the bill—put back in. According to a memo written March 19, 1965, by Perian, Hills told him that "the department (HEW) saw no real validity in the objections to the Harris bill . . . . He related," the memo continues, "how Congressman Delaney was euchred out of any credit for the dangerous drug bill in the House and that, in view of the fact that Dodd had done the major work on dangerous drugs, he would hate to see the same thing happen to him." Hills told Dodd he received a commitment from Lister Hill to "allow" Dodd to floor-manage the drug bill in the Senate and the bill would be officially identified as the "Harris-Dodd Act." "Let's face it," Hills told Dodd, "you aren't the Chairman of the Labor and Public Welfare Committee and you really don't have any say-so in the matter." Dodd was to be frozen out completely if he persisted, Hills said. Dodd erupted. He told Hills he did "not appreciate being offered a carrot and a stick" and that his major concern was in having a good bill, not just any bill. He said he would make it "hot" for the Administration and concluded by telling Hills to leave his office. "In the end," Perian says, "we were really steamrolled into accepting what they wanted."

"Tommy the Cork" Corcoran was not finished. He visited

Dodd on behalf of McNeil Labs, the barbiturate company. Dodd and Corcoran were friends. They had visited one another's homes and knew each other well. Friendships are a large part of Corcoran's effectiveness. He asked Dodd to write a letter to Lister Hill requesting to list the six other sedatives and tranquilizers in the bill. Dodd agreed for his friend. Corcoran wrote the letter on Dodd's stationery and Dodd signed it. Then it was turned over to Perian to deliver to Hill's committee. Perian put it in his file drawer: "I knew it was the right thing to do but Dodd did it for the wrong reasons and I didn't want it to go out." A few weeks later Dodd's secretary called Perian and asked about the letter. Perian admitted it had not been sent. After the call it was delivered. Corcoran had used their friendship to get Dodd to send the letter. An unseemly method for a good end. The letter urged Hill to use his congressional prerogative and put the six drugs, meprobamate, Librium, Doriden, Noludar, Placidyl and Valmid, into the language of the law. Dodd said in the letter that experience had shown "that the overworked and understaffed Department of Health, Education and Welfare cannot always act expeditiously enough to protect the public health and welfare from a clear and present danger. It is therefore suggested that these drugs be specifically included within the statutory language." Hill ignored the letter, and that was all Dodd was to do for Corcoran. When the bill reached the Senate floor, without Senate hearings, Dodd did not even bring up the six drugs as an amendment; only amphetamines and barbiturates were covered. The bill passed the Senate side by voice vote on June 23, 1965. Dodd said on the floor that "these drugs are cheaper, deadlier, and more plentiful than such commonly known narcotics as morphine and cocaine." The Senate did not substantially change the House bill. The record-keeping loophole remained. The Senate report on the bill said only "ordinary business records kept by legitimate businessmen will be considered as adequate records for the purposes of this legislation." The industry had won nearly every concession it wanted. The House accepted the minor changes of the Senate and there was no House-Senate conference. The bill went to President Johnson and required only his signature to become law.

At a signing ceremony, with Senator Dodd and executives from the drug industry in attendance, President Johnson signed the bill into law on July 15, 1965. He singled out Dodd for his "courageous public leadership" and then spoke directly about the new law.

"I cannot express too strongly my determination that this good and decent and law-abiding society shall not be corrupted, undermined or mocked by any criminal elements, whether organized or not. I believe that most Americans share this hope and share this determination.

"I think it noteworthy," the President continued, "that this legislation received very widespread support from various citizen groups, from the drug industry, from organized medicine, and others." On February 1, 1966, the law went into effect.

10: The Drug Industry Wins Everything

You do as much as you can, and then you leave it up to the FDA. I wondered at times what they were doing with the data.

Dr. James Nora

IN 1967, a little more than a year after the Drug Abuse Control Amendments of 1965 (DACA) became law, the President's Commission on Law Enforcement and the Administration of Justice, chaired by then Attorney General Nicholas Katzenbach, issued a report on drug abuse called: "Task Force Report: Narcotics and Drug Abuse." It said flatly that the record-keeping loophole lobbied into the 1965 law by the drug industry made the law unworkable. The report gave these reasons: "The record-keeping and inspection provisions of the 1965 amendments are at the heart of the Federal dangerous drugs regulatory scheme. They are designed to serve several purposes: To furnish information regarding the extent of the dangerous drug problem and the points in the chain of distribution where diversions of drugs occur; to facilitate the detection of violations; and to deter violations. Yet at present the 1965 amendments specifically state: 'No separate records, nor set form or forms for any

of the foregoing records (of manufacture, receipt, and disposition), shall be required as long as records containing the
required information are available.' "

Why that sentence crippled the law was made plain by
the Commission. "There are about 6,000 establishments, including 1,000 manufacturers and 2,400 wholesalers, which
are required to register and keep records under the amendments. In addition, there are about 73,000 other establishments that are required to maintain records but not required
to register. This group includes some 54,000 pharmacies or
other retail drug outlets, some 9,000 hospitals and clinics,
some 8,000 dispensing practitioners, and some 2,000 research
facilities. The Commission simply does not believe that a
proper and productive audit of such a mass of records is
possible without, *at the very least,* a provision requiring the
records to be segregated or kept in some other manner permitting rapid identification and inspection." The Commission then recommended that the 1965 law be amended "to
require that records must be segregated or kept in some
other manner that enables them to be promptly identified
and inspected." The total came to 79,000 separate establishments that handled amphetamines and barbiturates,
along with a multitude of other things such as cotton, Band-
aids, aspirin, and toothpaste. An FDA inspector was now
required to wade through all of those records to find a
shipment of amphetamines and then go through some more
at another point to try to find where the shortage happened
and to pinpoint the source of diversion. Therefore, from the
viewpoint of enforcement and protection of public health,
the law was unworkable.

The President's Commission recommended that the FDA
increase the manpower in its Bureau of Drug Abuse Control
(BDAC), the new bureau formed to enforce the 1965 amendments. FDA continued to operate with what it estimated to
be about one man per state to watch the illegal flow of
amphetamines and barbiturates which now totaled about

twelve or thirteen billion pills a year. And the FDA field inspectors—Congress imposed a limit of 200—were left to make do, along with the public. Only the drug industry fully understood the insurmountable task of sorting out these records, and the virtual impossibility of effective control of the drugs represented by these records.

As for the industry's feeling about the law—it was quite satisfied. Probably expressing the general mood, a Smith Kline & French executive remarked at a drug abuse conference in September of 1965 that his company "does not consider it a hardship." It was good news for the drug industry, but not for most others.

An opportunity was arising fast, however, to reopen hearings on DACA. A frenzy was gripping the country in the wake of an alleged LSD blinding. This bizarre hallucinogen seemed to seize young people and estrange them from their parents and society. The press riveted attention on it. Timothy Leary was fired from Harvard after he advocated its use and claimed it was less harmful than tobacco or alcohol. The Senate held two separate LSD hearings in 1966, one by Senator Robert Kennedy and one by Dodd. With the shouts of "soft on crime" and "crime in the streets" becoming *the* Republican war chants, the White House moved to blunt the rhetoric. In early February of 1968, President Johnson requested amendments to DACA by asking that "Congress immediately enact legislation to make the illegal manufacture, sale or distribution of LSD and *other* dangerous drugs a felony and the illegal possession of these drugs a misdemeanor." Not to be outdone, Congress submitted its own bill. Harley Staggers, a white-haired West Virginia Democrat who succeeded Oren Harris (who had become a federal judge in Arkansas) as chairman of the House Commerce Committee, introduced the Administration bill and one of his own. However, neither the Administration's bill nor the bill introduced in the House mentioned amending or changing the record-keeping requirements in the DACA law.

The two drug bills before the House in 1968 were law-and-order bills: Stop the epidemic of LSD and get the addicts and peddlers in jail.

Congressman Paul Rogers, a Florida Democrat and fast becoming the most influential member of the House on health matters, would hold hearings before the House Subcommittee on Public Health and Welfare, a part of the full Commerce Committee. John Jarman (D.-Okla.) was and is the chairman of that subcommittee, but Rogers has always been the moving spirit. A tall, energetic man with a protective instinct for the drug industry, Rogers' hearings concentrated exclusively on a discussion of LSD and the need for stiffer criminal penalties.

An important witness at the hearings was Dr. Cecil B. Jacobson, a geneticist and instructor in the department of obstetrics and gynecology at George Washington University. He reported on ten cases involving pregnant women who had taken LSD; two babies had been born with broken chromosome chains, and a third mother lost a deformed fetus in the seventh week. "At the present time LSD shows a definite embryopathic effect," Dr. Jacobson testified. Future studies of LSD's effect on chromosomes would be about equally divided as to whether or not the drug damaged them.

But there were certain recently published studies of the effects of amphetamines on fetuses that were not reported at these hearings. The evidence may not have sounded as convincing as that of the LSD study, nor was it as sensational, but it was every bit as important because it affected more pregnant women.

Dr. James Nora, then a teacher at the University of Wisconsin and a practicing pediatrician, saw three mothers in a short space of time who had given birth to babies with transposition of the great vessels, a heart defect in which the aorta and pulmonary artery are reversed at the heart. If not operated on, the defect is fatal. Dr. Nora left Wisconsin soon after seeing the three mothers, but knows two of the babies died; he is uncertain of the fate of the third.

"The alarm bell had rung," Dr. Nora said of his visits from the three mothers. He questioned them and found one common pattern: they had all taken dextroamphetamine (Dexedrine is Smith Kline & French's trade name for the drug) during their pregnancies. The dextroamphetamine was prescribed for weight loss. Dr. Nora left Wisconsin and went to the Baylor University School of Medicine in Texas and there performed amphetamine experiments by injecting more than one hundred pregnant mice with large doses of dextroamphetamine. He found the mice offspring injected with the amphetamine had a significantly higher incidence of malformations than did a control group which had not been injected. A heart defect appeared; cleft palate, lip and eye abnormalities showed up in 11 percent of the mice, and the drug-treated group was generally stunted in size. A total of 38 percent of the mice with amphetamine injections were born with detectable abnormalities. Only 5 percent of the mice not given amphetamines were born with abnormalities. In 1965, Dr. Nora published the study in the British medical journal, *Lancet,* which is also read by medical professionals in this country. The advantage of *Lancet* was the speed with which it could publish the article. Although Dr. Nora is a cautious and understated man, he believes a "mild" precaution should have been issued by the FDA for prescribing amphetamines for pregnant women after that 1965 report. None was. The dose given the mice for the 1965 study was about 200 times the usual human dose, but this, coupled with the evidence of the three babies born with heart defects, did not convince Dr. Nora that the unborn were immune to the effects of amphetamines even if he could find no causal relationship. One drug company eventually contacted Dr. Nora and said it was "concerned" about his findings. As far as Dr. Nora is aware, however, no attempt was made by the company to contact the FDA or to insert even a mild warning into advertising or labeling.

Dr. Nora persisted with his amphetamine study. In the December 18, 1967, issue of the *Journal of the American Medical Association,* the single most widely read of all the medical journals, Dr. Nora and his colleagues again said no *positive* link could be found between various birth defects and their causes, but went on to say of his amphetamine research that he was also unable to feel confident that this drug could not be responsible for human malformation, if it acted on individuals "predisposed to the malformation and sensitive to the teratogenic effects of the drug." The article concluded by saying that a large percentage of pregnant women are still exposed to drugs which are avoidable. "We wish to emphasize the magnitude of drug exposure and urge involvement of physicians in the conscious reduction of this exposure." The article inspired a letter from a California obstetrician who objected to the "implication" of Nora's article. He said the suggestion that drugs should be prescribed to pregnant women "only in life threatening situations does not, in my opinion, represent a medical advance."

Because this was the same kind of thinking that had permitted thalidomide to reach the European market, Dr. Nora was moved to reply, and in so doing, he reached the core of the issue. While it is logical to insist on conclusive evidence, he responded to the *Journal,* "it is frivolous to ignore even a small potential hazard which can be so easily removed." It was also frivolous, if not criminal, to ignore the possibility of including even the mildest warnings on the labeling of amphetamines. Still thinking did not change. The labeling required by the FDA in the *Physician's Desk Reference* in 1968 regarding amphetamines during pregnancy read: "There has been *no evidence* of any deleterious effect in pregnancy." Included was the caveat, which appeared with many drugs since the thalidomide tragedy, that amphetamine should be "used cautiously" during pregnancy, especially the first three months. Take them, but take them cautiously, was the message. Dr. Nora is uncertain how many expectant mothers took amphetamines, but he estimated at least 10 percent of the women in the country were taking them at the time of his study. At one clinic where he observed, 21 percent of the pregnant patients were prescribed amphetamines.

In 1970, Dr. Nora, apparently the only researcher publishing at the time in medical journals on the possible link between amphetamines and birth defects, made a final and more conclusive report in *Lancet*. He had studied a number of women who had taken amphetamines and some who had not during pregnancy, and found that more women who had taken amphetamines gave birth to children with congenital heart defects than those who had not taken them. It led Dr. Nora to believe amphetamine during pregnancy is a "trigger" for congenital heart defects in families predisposed to the disorder. It also caused him to retract his earlier published statement that "no causal" connection could be found between heart defects and amphetamines. This study was published in June of 1970.

As a result of a general review of amphetamines, a warning was belatedly put on them in August of 1970 by FDA. The accompanying report noted that reproductive studies on mammals "have suggested an embryotoxic and teratogenic potential" and that "safe use in pregnancy has not been established." The new labeling was not due to Dr. Nora's latest report, however. Although Dr. Nora had forwarded all his findings to the FDA, it was clear from the wording that the FDA in 1970 was only now reacting to his 1965 study.

Dr. Nora had been extremely cautious with his data; he had not ventured beyond what it allowed him to say and he kept himself well within safe limits. He did not issue a bold and final proclamation that amphetamines cause birth defects. Also, the birth defects linked to amphetamine use were not oddities like the broken chromosomes with LSD or the

172 THE AMERICAN CONNECTION

flippered limbs from thalidomide. "You do as much as you can," Dr. Nora said of his findings, "and then you leave it up to the FDA. I wondered at times what they were doing with the data."* Dr. Nora's findings ask the hardest of questions. Why was it that an outside researcher operating independently with research grants was the one to bring to light the potential dangers of amphetamines in pregnancy? And why did the awareness not come until twenty-five years after amphetamines were first marketed? Why didn't the industry, with its well-financed and -staffed research facilities, investigate this area thoroughly instead of directing their research only to those products which could be commercially marketed for profit? One also wonders why it took the FDA five years to put even a mild warning on amphetamines. And one wonders finally how many children may have been born with needless heart defects, because their mothers and their mothers' doctors were not cautioned about the possible hazards of amphetamines. This episode of genetic roulette in the history of amphetamines is not an exception; rather, it is a part of its pattern.

The 1968 House drug hearings held by Congressman Rogers ignored Dr. Nora's findings even though three of his amphetamine studies had been published by the time the hearings were held. A staff member said only that they had not heard about them. Neither was corporate accountability a major concern in Congress or at the FDA. The annual report of the Department of Health, Education and Welfare in fiscal 1967 (issued in mid-1967) said part of the FDA's drug effort was devoted to diversion of legal drugs, but it noted "*a considerably greater share* is given to undercover investigations of drug peddlers and counterfeiters." [Author's italics] HEW claimed the DACA law was effective, but pill

---

*A full evaluation of Nora's studies, for the purposes of this book, was requested in writing from FDA. FDA officials said one was done and suggested verbally that Nora's 1965 study "was not the best." No detailed written evaluation, as requested, was ever submitted to the author, despite repeated requests.

seizures remained at about the same level as that achieved before the law.

The Rogers hearings surfaced other facts as well. Amphetamines were still included in Vietnam survival kits for Special Forces and the Air Force. About 7,000 amphetamines a month were sent to United States medical authorities in Vietnam.

Rogers was particularly zealous in pushing for stiff criminal penalties and eventually this latest drug bill passed the House on July 12 by a vote of 320 to 0. On October 24, 1968, it passed the Senate by a voice vote. President Johnson signed it into law the same day.

The bill stiffened the penalty for *peddling* these dangerous drugs, LSD, amphetamines, barbiturates. A person under twenty-one peddling to someone over eighteen could now be punished by a $10,000 fine and five years in prison.

In setting repressive federal penalties for *possession* of amphetamines, barbiturates and LSD, Congress had again reacted too late with the wrong remedy. A $1,000 fine and a year in prison, or both, was the penalty for possession in first and second offenses. Subsequent offenses were punishable by a $10,000 fine and three years in prison.

In its zeal to penalize the small-time peddlers and possessors of these drugs, Congress ignored new penalties or restrictions of any kind on drug companies or corporations that mass-produced these drugs and sent them to illegal sources.

The maximum penalty for a corporation which shipped pills to an illegal seller was a $1,000 fine. This would equal the profits realized in only a few minutes at any major drug house. But a kid with a pocketful of pills could now be imprisoned by federal authorities for a year and fined $1,000.

But even these minimal corporate penalties were not exacted in court. A few years earlier the FDA had charged the Calbiochem Company of Los Angeles with "shipping stimulants to unauthorized persons." The company pleaded guilty to four counts in court. The penalty? A total fine of $800.

11: Buying Time

FDA ATTORNEY: *"Doctor, can you tell us, year by year, the amount of money that has been paid to you under any licensing agreement?"*
DR. BERGER: *"I consider the question improper and refuse to answer."*

CONGRESS did not become the stepchild of the federal government by any one big decision or by any one turn of events. It happened through a series of small concessions of power that, at the time they were made, were eminently rational and explainable. As the culmination of these little decisions, made over a long period of time, Congress came eventually to realize that much of its power was gone and many of its options closed. In the passing of the 965 Drug Abuse Control Amendments (DACA), Congress made one of these small, unnoticed abrogations of its power to the executive branch when it refused to regulate any specific drugs in that bill other than amphetamines and barbiturates. The Congress, which had enough authority and evidence to make the decision, passed the buck to HEW and the FDA to do administratively what it would not do legislatively. The report by the Senate Labor and Public Welfare Committee on the bill, noting that tranquilizers had a poten-

tial for abuse, said the secretary of HEW "should not be required to wait until a number of lives have been destroyed or
substantial problems have already arisen before designating
a drug as subject to controls of the bill." The House Committee report also urged controls over other drugs by means
of speedy FDA hearings. This double-talk did not obscure the
fact that the bulky mechanism available to the FDA to regulate
the other drugs provided for anything but speedy controls.

On December 28, 1965, the FDA Advisory Committee,
chaired by Dr. Frederick Shideman, announced its "unani-
mous opinion" that several drugs which had escaped regulation in Congress be brought under the DACA law by
administrative action. There were the six originally named
by Dr. Essig more than two years earlier: Librium, meprobamate (Miltown and Equanil), Placidyl, Doriden, Noludar, and Valmid. Also added were Librium's twin drug,
Valium, and two other sedatives, chloral hydrate and paral-
dehyde. Two stimulants were also named, Preludin, the
amphetamine-type stimulant, and Desoxyn, a potent methamphetamine that escaped legal controls because of DACA's
restrictive wording. The advisory committee said "there is
sufficient evidence at this time to support a finding of 'potential for abuse' " for the drugs. FDA Commissioner Larrick
retired at the end of 1965 and Acting Commissioner Winton
Rankin acted quickly. The FDA issued orders in the Federal
Register on January 18, 1966, to control these drugs.

"As far as I'm concerned," one of the FDA attorneys says of
the attempts to regulate the drugs, "we were just repeat-
ing everything Congress should have done in the first place."
The FDA wanted to regulate these other drugs, partly because
it anticipated a tightening in the availability of barbiturates
with the arrival of the DACA law, and therefore users would
turn to other tranquilizers for depressants; and partly because
of its goal of placing similar controls over drugs harboring
similar potentials for abuse. To this day, that goal is unreal-
ized. Although Librium, Valium, and meprobamate may not

be as deadly or as addictive as are barbiturates and amphetamines, they are in the same general class in regard to their
effects and potential for abuse. This was what the FDA wanted
to have understood.

All the delaying mechanisms built into the administrative
procedure for the drug law would now work to the benefit of
the drug companies. Just to reach the point of beginning the
hearing took months. Unlike a criminal case, in which delay
can work to the disadvantage of the defendant, delay for the
companies meant uninterrupted profit.

Two companies with the most to lose, Carter-Wallace
and Roche Labs, decided to fight the new law. Their
"minor" tranquilizers were very big money-makers. In June
of 1966, the FDA granted Carter-Wallace a hearing after
judging the company had offered "reasonable grounds" for
one. In the race of the turtles, Carter-Wallace's case had
moved faster. Wallace Labs would be defended by the New
York law firm of Breed, Abbott & Morgan. The FDA cases
would be handled by two young attorneys, Walter Byerley,
a Texan with six years' experience at FDA, and Axel
Kleiboemer, a lawyer trying his first case. As one FDA official
said about government hearings in general: "People believe
the myth that the government comes in with an arsenal
against these poor companies but the opposite is usually the
case. The companies hire very high-priced legal talent and
they come up against usually inexperienced government
lawyers. Often our guys have little if any trial experience
and they're up against lawyers who've been trying cases for
years. The only things the government usually has in its
favor are broad investigative power and the fact that they're
right and the corporations are wrong. The corporations
usually realize that. They're only putting up a fight to string
it out."

Axel Kleiboemer, the youngest member of the FDA legal
team, points out now that the FDA was woefully unprepared

for the meprobamate hearings. "It was inexcusable," he said. "I was literally stopped in the hall one day and told I was going to work on this case. I knew nothing about drugs and I had to get a quick course in drugs from our FDA people. We had to go out and hustle every witness we got for our case. We had to beg and persuade many of them. Some of these drug experts flatly refused us. The basic question they'd ask is 'what's in it for us?' You must remember these drug companies give a lot of money to these people to do their research projects. We were offering fifty bucks a day and travel expenses." Although the federal government also awards research grants, it has no economic interest in a drug. If a researcher comes back with a negative report, the government, unlike a drug company, loses no money, Kleiboemer suspected many researchers to be reluctant to stick their necks out because they feared loss of research money from the drug industry. In 1968, the last year industry-wide figures were made available by the PMA, the drug industry awarded grants totaling $12.3 *million* for academic and medical school research.* This represents a lot of projects and a lot of researchers involved with drug companies. Many researchers have their projects almost fully supported by drug industry money. If any of them testifies against a drug company or one of its prized products, he could very possibly see his grant dwindle or disappear altogether. This fear of retribution is pervasive and profoundly disturbing to many scientists, even though they will not openly talk about it. One drug researcher, now in the drug abuse research field, says: "A drug company can have any of us twelve different ways. I won't even discuss them. Let's just say they have a big economic investment and they know how to protect it and they will protect it." Another academic re-

---

*The PMA no longer specifically identifies the amount of money the industry spends for academic research. A PMA spokesman explained, "it's just one of those things we no longer itemize." The reason? "No particular reason."

searcher at a prestigious eastern medical school, who wants to remain anonymous, says: "One thing a company can do is spread the news that your work is dishonest and try to ruin your reputation. This happened to me after I had written up an article describing a bad side effect of a particular drug. It got back to me because one of the people to whom the rumor spread knew me and knew my work and told me what was happening. It shows the lengths the company would go to protect that drug." The drug industry exerts control over many medical and academic researchers the same way it exerts control over the American Medical Association. By controlling the purse strings, it controls many of the policies and people who depend on drug industry money.

On June 27, 1966, six months after the initial FDA order to control the drugs, the meprobamate hearings began. The hearing examiner was William Brennan, a cautious and meticulous man who, because of the nature of the proceedings, unfortunately had no real power. Hearings such as these are often called "playing court." The examiner has no subpoena power, no contempt power, and no final arbitrative power. Witnesses have been known to yell or just get up and walk out if they did not like the line of questioning. The examiner is powerless to stop them; he can only make a recommendation to the FDA Commissioner after the hearing, and the Commissioner can accept or reject it. These flaws, plus the delays built into the procedure, have demanded reform for decades, but none has come. But then, to corporate interests, the flaws are the real point of it all.

Meeting on the fifth floor of one of the HEW north buildings, and attended by a small contingent of the lay press and trade press, the hearings began during the hot Washington summer. Despite problems in lining up government witnesses, the FDA had in its corner some impressive addiction experts. A key witness was Dr. Frederick Lemere, the

Seattle psychiatrist who had tested meprobamate for Wallace Labs before it was marketed and had published a report on his findings in October of 1955 in *Northwest Medicine;* that report said meprobamate was nonaddictive. However, a few months later Lemere wrote a letter to the *Journal of the American Medical Association* retracting that earlier statement and declaring that meprobamate was addictive. It was this new statement that had set off the earlier relabeling controversy at FDA. Walter Byerley, who did most of the questioning for the FDA, asked Dr. Lemere if he knew of people taking meprobamate "in amounts to be detrimental to their health?"

"Yes," Lemere answered. "To my personal knowledge, being very, very conservative, I have known at least sixty patients who have taken it to the point where they were drunk on it, they would have auto accidents, would fall asleep and get cigarette burns, they were staggering around, were not able to work sometimes because of it. I have had a couple [patients who] . . . were arrested for drunk driving, [where the police and their attorneys] asked me to come and testify that they were on tranquilizers, meprobamate, instead of alcohol, and I refused because if they had taken the prescription as I prescribed they would not have been drunk."

Lemere's description of meprobamate intoxication could have fit that of barbiturate intoxication or plain drunkenness. Lemere, who had treated many alcoholics with meprobamate to keep them off liquor, also said: "In my general experiences with alcoholics or other addiction-prone individuals, I would, as I say, say conservatively, oh, that there would be maybe 4 percent, perhaps many more, alcoholics [who], if they had free access to meprobamate, would take too much. There are six million alcoholics in the country. So what is 4 percent of six million? I think 240,000 perhaps potential meprobamate addicts, if they had free access to it."

Lemere said access to meprobamate was easy. Doctors were

lax and so were drugstores. Byerley asked if he felt stricter controls were needed. "Very definitely," Lemere answered.

Lemere had brought with him a former meprobamate addict who testified. The man, who at the time was holding a responsible and highly skilled job in Seattle, described in vivid detail his bout with meprobamate addiction and his attempts to maintain his supply. He had been a heavy drinker and had found, to his delight, that he could take meprobamate and not feel any more hangovers. "This was a revelation," he said, "that the hangovers were so diminished. I did notice instead of drinking more I came to rely more heavily on meprobamate in doses of perhaps 400 milligrams to overcome tremors which I formerly attributed to drinking. I was not aware that I was building a bodily resistance to this meprobamate and that normally prescribed amounts were insufficient." He said the need for meprobamate over the next few months "increased alarmingly" and he found he could not go off the drug for two days without feeling tremors, a sign of withdrawal and physical addiction. He reached the point of taking ten or twelve tablets a day. "I realized dimly that I was hooked on the stuff," he said. He was failing at work and following the classic pattern of the drug addict. He was devoting more and more time to maintaining his supply of the drug. His scheme was legal. He would file a prescription with one pharmacy and get it filled. He would pick a chain store. When that pill supply ran out, he would bring the empty bottle to another store in the chain where, he said, "they were only too happy to refill it." He made a full circuit of all the stores in the chain and carefully rotated his purchases to avoid suspicion at any one of them. He eventually lined up twenty different stores to maintain his habit.

He also made a cross-country trip, he said, and discovered he could walk into any doctor's office with a complaint of some kind, and they would write him a prescription for meprobamate. He said he never had to alter or forge a single prescription to keep up his drug supply; in fact, he said a prescription written in 1959 was refilled a week before the hearings—more than seven years after the doctor had written it. This was the process of "legal" diversion—repeated all over the country—which would never show up in any diversion accounting.

Dr. Carl Essig, the quiet researcher whose tranquilizer findings had kicked up the storm, also testified and brought with him a gruesome film of dogs going through meprobamate withdrawal. Many of the dogs died from convulsions during the withdrawal. Dr. Lemere had also testified to having witnessed convulsions in humans during meprobamate withdrawal. All this from a "minor" tranquilizer. Also testifying was Dr. Jerome Jaffe, then professor of psychiatry and pharmacology at the Albert Einstein College of Medicine in New York (later to be director of the federal Special Action Office for Drug Abuse Prevention); Dr. Jaffe was and is widely regarded as one of the most brilliant minds in drug abuse research. He testified that a "considerable proportion" of people on barbiturates would shift to meprobamate if the barbiturate supply were curtailed or cut off, although he said the abuse liability of meprobamate was lower than barbiturates. His testimony included information about the three components that determine a drug's abuse potential. First, a drug needs to give a "feeling" the user wants to repeat; the feeling may be euphoria, release of inhibitions, or simply something pleasurable. Second, it must induce a withdrawal syndrome when given in large doses and abruptly stopped. Third, it must suppress the withdrawal effects of a drug which is known to be addictive, such as barbiturates. Any one of these criteria would suggest a potential for abuse, Jaffe said, and meprobamate fulfilled all three. This is what separates drugs of abuse from drugs like aspirin, or other kinds of tranquilizers which do not induce a feeling of pleasure. "When someone is intoxicated on barbiturates he has a typical cylindrical pattern, slurred speech, euphoria, incoordination, nystagmus, elevation of seizure threshold, and generally a certain amount of sedation," Jaffe said. "This is very similar to what one sees with a high dose of meprobamate. I find it difficult indeed in examining patients to distinguish between two patients, one of whom is intoxicated on barbiturates, the other of whom is intoxicated with meprobamate." Also presented at the hearing were various journal articles suggesting that meprobamate was no more effective than a placebo in reducing anxiety.

To provide yet another dimension in the backdrop of these hearings, in January of 1966, just as the FDA was moving to control meprobamate, Carter-Wallace had pleaded no contest to a charge of false and misleading advertising for an ad on Pree MT. It is a combination of meprobamate and hydrochlorothiazide (a diuretic) and it is prescribed for premenstrual tension, high blood pressure, and other problems. Carter-Wallace had run the ad in four successive issues of the *Journal of the American Medical Association* in June of 1964. It had been the first criminal action brought by the FDA against a drug company under the Kefauver-Harris Drug Act of 1962. The FDA had charged that Wallace Labs had excluded mention in the ad of side effects and contraindications (specific medical indications that suggest a drug should not be prescribed). The ad had said flatly: "Contraindications: None known." The truth was that some had been known as early as 1960 and were so listed in the package inserts for Pree MT. Patients on the drug required careful watching for signs of a very serious blood disorder. Somehow this had escaped the vigilant attention of the AMA *Journal.* Carter-Wallace—after changing its original plea of innocent to no contest—had been fined $1,000 on each of two counts in a federal court in Trenton, New Jersey; this was the maximum fine for such a misdemeanor.*

---

*The best account of this case appears in the afterword to Chapter Four in Morton Mintz's excellent book, *By Prescription Only,* 1967, Beacon Press.

All these earlier events, added now to the testimonies of Drs. Essig, Lemere, and Jaffe, were making Carter-Wallace and meprobamate look very bad. Although the press coverage was not extensive, it was substantial enough to tarnish the image that the company had spent millions to create. Coverage had waned at the Washington hearing after much of the bad news, and Carter-Wallace feared presentation of its case would not attract the kind of coverage needed to offset all that had gone before it. So they came up with an idea. Now that they were putting forth their case and they could make the good news flow abundantly, why not revive press interest by changing the site of the hearings? So the company asked the FDA to shift the hearings to New Orleans, ostensibly to make it convenient for their witnesses. However, "some of their witnesses came from the Midwest," FDA attorney Byerley recalls, "and it was never clear to me why going to New Orleans was so much easier than going to Washington." Hearing Examiner Brennan acceded to Carter-Wallace's request and for a few days the hearings were held in the damp heat of New Orleans. Carter-Wallace put a number of doctors on the stand who testified their patients had had no negative experiences with meprobamate. Dr. Edward Annis, a Miami physician, testified that he had prescribed meprobamate for ten years to hundreds of patients, with no serious problems. He said putting meprobamate under the DACA law would be "harmful" and would cause "guilt by association" when classified with the "goofballs" and "pep pills." Interestingly, in 1963 and 1964, Dr. Annis was president of the American Medical Association. These same two years, Carter-Wallace was the single biggest advertiser in the *Journal of the American Medical Association,* which is the biggest money-making publication for the AMA. Carter-Wallace did succeed with its New Orleans gambit, as it received many favorable press stories.

The star witness for Carter-Wallace's entire case was Dr. Frank Berger. His creation of meprobamate had turned the sleepy little company into a pharmaceutical wonderhouse overnight and Berger was tenaciously trying to keep his legend alive. Berger disputed the whole FDA case and much evidence that had piled up against meprobamate over the past ten years. He said the only type of person who would abuse meprobamate would be a "psychopath"; according to him meprobamate produced no euphoria, "no kick," as he called it. He was struck, he said, by the very low number of dependence problems with meprobamate and told of the many "unsolicited" letters he had received from patients who took meprobamate for years without any problems, even though this was never the point of the hearings. Berger estimated that 500 million prescriptions for meprobamate had been written since he had developed it. He said meprobamate had a highly selective action on the brain and could not be compared with barbiturates. Berger was correct and proper on the stand, bristling at times under Byerley's questions but usually maintaining his composure. He said the reason for abuse of meprobamate was the same as abuse of aspirin, Coca-Cola, or anything else. "There are certain abnormal individuals who will abuse almost anything and some of them abuse meprobamate . . . ." "Were all six million alcoholics abnormal or psychopathic?" Byerley asked. Berger wriggled out of that by claiming there was no adequate definition of alcoholism. Berger was asked by Carter-Wallace's attorney what would happen if meprobamate went under the DACA regulations. Berger forecast catastrophic results. People who needed meprobamate might be fearful of taking it; doctors would be less inclined to prescribe it. "They may just assume," Berger said, "that because meprobamate and other tranquilizers are the subject of government hearings there must be something wrong with these drugs, and thus make the physician disinclined to prescribe them, or prescribe barbiturates in their place." That could mean, Berger allowed, an additional 2,000 deaths a year from barbiturate overdoses—at least. Berger would not budge from his ardent defense of meprobamate.

"My own impression of why Carter-Wallace fought so hard," Byerley recalled later, "is not because of Wallace's corporate officers. The real reason was Berger. Meprobamate was like his baby, his only child. He would not believe anything bad about it. The net impression I got was that I was attacking him personally. That I had said his child was a mass murderer and he couldn't accept it."

But there was even more to it than that, as became evident with Byerley's next line of attack. He attempted to demonstrate Berger's financial stake in meprobamate. He probed gingerly at first, then asked Berger about the patent, which had been issued to him in 1955. Did he still hold it? Berger bolted. No longer was he the pleasant, affable scientist. He demanded his personal lawyer. "I have the right to consult with him before [answering], and I don't think this is relevant. What are you trying to do here now?" Berger demanded. Byerley said he was trying to establish "credibility and financial interest." Carter-Wallace's lawyer argued that the line of questioning was irrelevant. Examiner Brennan said it was relevant but that Dr. Berger did not have to answer. Berger wanted the financial questions skipped but Byerley was trying to get as much on the record as he could, to show that Berger was speaking with a financial and not a scientific interest.

Berger said he didn't like the "implication" of Byerley's questions and the underlying assumption that Berger would "disregard the truth just because I *may* have an interest in the well-being of Wallace Laboratories."

Byerley came at him from another angle. "Doctor, can you tell us, year by year, the amount of money that has been paid to you under any licensing agreement?" he asked.

Berger turned down the question flat. "I consider the implication of the question improper, and refuse to answer," Dr. Berger replied. That was the end of it.

If Byerley had searched back into the Kefauver drug hearings of 1960 he would have discovered why Berger was so recalcitrant. By acquiring records from the Securities and Exchange Commission, the Kefauver subcommittee had been able to detail Berger's economic stake in meprobamate. Berger had told Kefauver he was making more than $26,000 a year, hardly a pauper's wage, *before* he came to Carter-Wallace. Part of the reason for going to Wallace and leaving his private practice and university position had been to make more money, he said. After developing and patenting meprobamate, Berger had sold the patent to Carter-Wallace. "What I get depends on the sale of the product," Berger had stated at that time. In 1958 Berger made $295,755 off the sales of meprobamate, plus his salary of $35,000 a year. In 1959 his royalties from meprobamate reached $344,000, in addition to an $80,000 annual salary. As the late Senator Kefauver remarked: "I see. This should be an incentive for young people to be scientists and discover something." In those two years of 1958 and 1959, Berger had earned $639,755 from the sale of meprobamate. At the time of the hearings in 1966, Berger had undoubtedly become a multimillionaire from his discovery. Besides attacking his "baby," Byerley and the FDA were also attacking Berger's bank account. "If we helped or saved one person by the controls we were trying to put on meprobamate," Byerley remarked later, "it was all worth it." For Frank Berger and Carter-Wallace, it apparently wasn't.

The hearings ended September 16, 1966, after about 60 witnesses and 142 exhibits were introduced into evidence. On January 13, 1967, a year after the original FDA order, Examiner Brennan found meprobamate to be a depressant drug within the meaning of the DACA law. He recommended that FDA Commissioner Dr. James Goddard control meprobamate under the law. More delay. Dr. Goddard heard oral arguments from both parties in July of 1967 and reviewed more memoranda. He also read the transcript. Finally, on December 6, 1967, nearly two full years after the initial issuing of the order, he directed meprobamate come under the DACA controls. Naturally, Carter-Wallace appealed to the federal courts. More delay. More profits. More problems for the public health.

12: Librium and Valium Go To Trial

"... she began to hallucinate, with auditory hallucinations. She described hearing French horns and orchestral sounds."

A DOCTOR DESCRIBING HIS WIFE'S
LIBRIUM EXPERIENCE

THE hearing for Librium and Valium began on August 8, 1966, in the government's attempt to include these drugs in the DACA law. Librium had been marketed for six years and Valium for three. It was not enough time, as one FDA attorney remarked, for all their "anomalies" to surface and provide a strong case for the FDA. The focus in this hearing would be aimed more at potential abuse than actual abuse. Trying Roche Labs' case in this mock court was Thomas Finney, Jr., the same Washington lawyer who had worked to shape the law on Capitol Hill. He was assisted by a number of other lawyers. The government's case was tried by James Phelps, then a zealous young attorney for the FDA, and T. Gorman Reilly, another young FDA lawyer. The ground rules in this hearing were the same as the meprobamate hearing. The examiner's decision would not be binding. The FDA commissioner could either accept or ignore it.

The hearing examiner was Edgar Buttle, with his deep,

sonorous voice, white hair, and calm, grandfatherly manner. Besides twenty-seven years of trial experience, his major qualification was his degree in chemistry. Buttle also had a long history of involvement with the drug industry. His father had been a former president of Sterling Drug, Inc., of New York, maker of Bayer aspirin and other products, and both Buttle and his father were friendly with Elmer Bobst, who for several years had headed Roche Labs. In the 1950s Buttle himself had owned a small chemical company and produced chemical intermediates which were supplied to Sterling Drug. He later had gone out of business because of competition from German chemical firms which could sell the same intermediates in this country cheaper than Buttle's company could make them. His attitude toward the drug industry was and still is sanguine. He believes we live in a "chemically oriented society" but he fingers the advertising agencies as the "real culprits" for this, not the drug companies who hire them. "I explained my background to both sides before we proceeded and they accepted me," Buttle recalls; "there were no problems."

A problem for the government that had arisen with the meprobamate hearings was appearing again in this case. "We really had to scratch around to get witnesses," FDA counsel Reilly recalls. "We had the evidence but we were combating a hell of a lot of money Roche was putting into this case." Finney, for example, was earning at least $100 an hour for his legal fees. That was a lot of money, but *every day* he kept Librium and Valium out of the controls, Roche was making an additional $15,000 to $20,000 in sales.

The hearings began in the basement of the HEW North. Buttle sat in the front center behind what looked like a lunch table. Behind him was a dirty window that was barely translucent. Roche Labs was lucky; the lay press was busy covering the meprobamate hearing and barely covered this one. Only a representative for the drug industry trade press's F-D-C

Reports, commonly called the "Pink Sheet" because of its color, attended regularly.

Phelps made the government's opening statement. He said the hearing would be heavy with scientific overtones but "we should all remember that this case has more than theoretical applications. The dangers we will demonstrate, are dangers which can ruin or mar the lives of people—victims and the people around them—and can even kill people."

Finney spoke next. The real objection, he said, was the "misclassification" that would come by controlling Librium and Valium in the same way as barbiturates and amphetamines. "This incorrect impression will interfere with the prescribing of these drugs by the medical profession and the use of these drugs by patients for whom they are prescribed." Or to put it another way, it would hurt our sales. Finney concluded by saying that he was there to inform and persuade, and hoped FDA would be open-minded. "We hope that we are equally open-minded, that we are also here, if the evidence justifies it, to be persuaded," he said.

And so it began. Dr. Leo Hollister, chief of staff at the Veterans' Administration Hospital at Palo Alto, California, testified about Librium's potential for physical addiction. In 1960 Dr. Hollister had administered very high doses of Librium to thirty-six mental patients. The doses ranged from 100 to 600 milligrams, or about ten to twenty times a normal therapeutic dose. Then Hollister had abruptly stopped the Librium with eleven patients after they had been on the high doses for two to six months. Ten of them had signs of physical withdrawal; two suffered convulsions, one of whom had no history of convulsions; six of the eleven became depressed and psychosis was aggravated in five. Said Hollister: "I think in general it would resemble withdrawal from alcohol, barbiturates, or meprobamate, with the major distinguishing feature being the timing." He said Librium withdrawal was delayed for forty-eight hours but then it appeared "somewhat subtly and insidiously." Even Hollister admitted the doses were "monumental" but that was not the basic issue, although Finney and Roche tried to make it the sole issue. Dr. Harris Isbell, one of the best known and respected drug addiction researchers, talked next about drug dosages. He testified that most people who take prescribed drugs handle them well. But, he said, there is a small number of them "who keep on trying to get more relief, raise their doses, and sooner or later get into a dosage range that would create dependence." This is the point. Drug abusers do not take therapeutic doses, they do not follow their doctor's instructions. Some take "monumental" doses on their own and can become physically addicted to Librium. There are recorded cases of barbiturate addicts taking 5,000 milligrams at a time. This is about fifty times the recommended dose.

Roche contended no significant misuse would occur because Librium and Valium do not create euphoria and would not induce people to keep taking it for a pleasurable effect. This was disputed. An FDA witness said it acted as a "mood elevator" and in one of Roche's own medical exhibits a patient described the effect of Librium as "walking on air." Librium and other tranquilizers go by the street name of "floaters" because of this effect. They don't zap the mind like a shot of heroin or speed, but the effect is often very pleasant. Hence their widespread use.

Dr. John Lofft, a psychiatrist in private practice in Washington, D.C., who even Roche Labs conceded had wide experience with Librium, testified next, and related the following case history.

His patient was a woman, the mother of a Washington, D.C., policeman, whom he was treating for alcoholism. One day her son called to report that his mother appeared drunk but he said a complete search of her home turned up no liquor bottles. Dr. Lofft went to her home where he found her "staggering; she literally fell into my arms."

"There was an open bottle of Librium, capsules strewn about the place," Dr. Lofft testified. "The bottle was half empty. Instructions were for one, four times daily." Dr. Lofft said the woman denied drinking and yet she appeared to be drunk. Her speech was slurred and Dr. Lofft was convinced that she must have taken something other than the Librium, apparently believing such a "mild" drug would not have such untoward effects. She had taken nothing else. She was admitted to a hospital and in twenty-four hours her condition cleared up. Dr. Lofft said Librium appeared to "produce amnesia so that the woman could not control her dosage."

The temporary amnesia, or "fog effect," was also brought out in the meprobamate hearing. A person takes a tranquilizer or a barbiturate, and a few minutes later forgets how many he took or even if he has taken any at all. He takes another and another, until he is essentially drunk on the drug.

A poignant case history came from Dr. Edward Uzee, a New Orleans psychiatrist, who described in detail his wife's involvement with Librium. In 1963 she gave birth to a premature daughter; because of the circumstances of that birth his wife became anxious and also developed some minor physical reactions. Both Dr. Uzee and his wife were seeing an analyst at the time and his wife's doctor prescribed ten milligrams of Librium three or four times a day. She took it and said it helped dramatically. Soon she began increasing the dosage at bedtime to two and then three capsules. Dr. Uzee assured his wife that this was all right, apparently accepting much of the early, company-arranged data on Librium that suggested it was problem-free. His wife said she was increasing her dosage because "it didn't give her the same effect as when she started taking it." This is an indication of physical tolerance—one of the signs of physical addiction. Dr. Uzee said her supply came from a Roche detail man at Charity Hospital in New Orleans. She soon upped her dosage to four or five twenty-five-milligram capsules a day. Dr. Uzee and his wife's doctor both continued to give it their tacit blessing. In July 1964, after his wife had been on Librium for more than a year, she required surgery and Dr. Uzee was now concerned because of the high doses of Librium she had been taking. He consulted another doctor at the hospital, and was told there were instances of Librium withdrawals in medical literature. Dr. Uzee was caught in a bind. Because of the impending operation, it was a bad time to cut off his wife's dosage or even to lessen it. So she maintained her Librium intake up until the time she was admitted. Then, said Dr. Uzee:

"She went into the hospital, was operated on, and had no Librium at all, for the first time in a year or so. Two days post-operatively she began to hallucinate, with auditory hallucinations. She described hearing French horns and orchestral sounds.

"It was my feeling this was due to withdrawal of Librium. I went out and got some twenty-five-milligram capsules and gave her one. She stopped hallucinating within hours after we started the drug again."

"What does that show?" Phelps asked for the FDA.

"I think it corroborates that there was a withdrawal effect there," Dr. Uzee answered. By giving her Librium at the hospital, he prevented further withdrawal reactions.

His wife since tapered off Librium and now does not take it at all.

Examiner Buttle asked a series of questions to determine if Dr. Uzee could back up his contention. Could it have been another drug at the hospital? Could it have been the anesthesia? Dr. Uzee said no. She had been through operations before and never experienced "any adverse reactions whatsoever," to any kind of drug.

Another witness at the hearing, Dr. Neville Murray, a psychiatrist and neurologist from San Antonio, Texas, described a high number of auto accidents involving patients on Librium. He said one of the persons got two speeding tickets after twenty years of commercial driving without a ticket. Another backed his car into a tree at thirty miles an hour. Dr. Murray contended that impaired judgment or a feeling of great security may have been responsible for these accidents. He had written to the editor of the *Journal of the American Medical*

Association about it and said the accidents appeared to be caused by the "liberating of aggressive, euphoric or under-lying self-destructive tendencies." In his FDA testimony, Dr. Murray said the driver who got the two speeding tickets be-came "enraged" when he believed he was given an improper receipt, a rather strange way to react on tranquilizers.

Dr. Murray testified at length about this Librium phenom-enon, called "paradoxical" rage. A thirty-year-old Latin American woman who had not been sleeping well for several days had become very agitated. She took 100 milligrams of Librium and then drank a glass of beer, which Dr. Murray said increased the effect of the Librium. Very shortly, the woman became enraged and went to her closet to get a gun. She called a baby sitter for her four children. She fired the gun in front of the baby sitter, apparently to impress her with the seriousness of her mission. She then walked six or seven blocks to the home of her sister-in-law, where her estranged husband was then living. She demanded to see him and fired the gun into the floor to force her sister-in-law to fetch him. Her husband came out and she fired the gun once more, either into the floor or at him, Dr. Murray is uncertain. In either case, she missed. The police soon arrived and disarmed the woman, and then took her to jail. Later that night her father bailed her out. He also took away her Librium. The next morning she went to a medical clinic where she was prescribed more. Dr. Murray suggested more study was needed on this bizarre rage reaction. He suspected, he said, that the tranquilizer released underlying hostility and suicidal tendencies in some people. The abating of the anxiety in-creased the hostility, much like alcohol or barbiturates make some people violent.*

---

*A study published in the June 1968 issue of the *General Archives of Psychiatry,* and based on a battery of widely accepted psychological test-ing methods, concluded that the "specific action" of Librium in some people increased assaultiveness and hostility and could lead to "rage reaction."

Roche Labs and Finney disputed Dr. Murray's testimony by noting he had billed Roche $8,172.07 for consultation fees and travel when he reported the Librium-related auto accidents. Finney suggested Murray was acting out of vengeance for not having been paid this money. Murray replied that the bill for consultation was a "rather crude" safeguard against lawsuits stemming from the auto accidents. He said he never had any hope Roche would pay it but he billed the company anyway, for purposes of legal protection, on the advice of his attorney. When the two-year statute of limitations on the filing of lawsuits expired, he withdrew his bill for consultation and asked Roche to reimburse only his travel expenses. Dr. Murray said his experience with Roche "became one of considerable distress to me"; Roche had also turned down his request for relabeling Librium to warn of the danger of paradoxical rage.

Finney took many legal tacks. He contended that Librium and Valium are very selective and act primarily on the limbic system of the brain, not on the cortex as barbiturates do. In the House Commerce Committee report on the DACA law, but not in the law itself, the word *similar* appears. Finney suggested this meant that a drug could be controlled by FDA only if it could be shown to have an effect "similar" to barbiturates. "That was the legislative intent," he said. "I was walking the hall of Congress when this bill was passed. I know what the legislative intent is," Finney pronounced, one of the FDA lawyers recalls. It had the ring, but not quite the authority, of God speaking to Job. It also did not answer the problem. If a person intoxicated on Librium or Valium and another person intoxicated on barbiturates act the same, what difference does it make what the primary action of the drug is? The effects on the person, the society, and the public health are equally bad.

Evidence was heard on Valium, but generally the FDA based its case against Valium primarily on the fact that it is so chemically similar to Librium that proof against one is proof against both. No widespread black market diversion of the drugs was shown but a user did testify on the multiple prescription ploy, much the same as in the meprobamate hearing. Tranquilizers are not diverted by wholesale thefts as were the amphetamines and barbiturates. Its real diversion is through multiple prescriptions.

Finney charged again and again that the evidence against Librium and Valium was not "substantial," somehow hoping, as one lawyer said, that the words "potential for abuse" would drop out of the law. In fact, Finney had almost accomplished this on Capitol Hill. He asked the government to "forthrightly" list the number of cases of abuse and called the cases of abuse presented by the FDA "anecdotal," "almost completely undocumented," "ambiguous," and "inconclusive." He called the FDA regulatory attempts "bounty hunting," and termed the conclusions in Dr. Murray's testimony on the auto accidents an "Orwellian pronouncement." "I got the feeling at times," says a member of the FDA legal team, "that Finney had almost an emotional involvement in the case. He really got carried away. I remember him as a real namby-pamby. He got outraged at little things. If we gave him a bad Xerox copy of a report he'd say the government was throwing trash at him. He had a real case of coffee nerves and was chain-smoking. He was really tied up in knots. It looked like he was mistaking himself for Roche Labs at times and that he took it as some sort of crusade. Maybe it had something to do with the fee he was paid."

Finney, however, did the better legal job. He argued his case more precisely and more persuasively than the younger and more inexperienced FDA lawyers argued theirs. "I don't know of a thing Mr. Finney could have done that he didn't do," Examiner Buttle recalled later. The hearing ended November 18, 1966, after more than 5,000 pages of testimony. The only thing Finney had against him was the evidence. On April 7, 1967, after digesting the testimony, legal briefs, and oral arguments, Examiner Buttle ruled for the government.

His recommendation to control Librium and Valium under the DACA law went to the desk of FDA Commissioner Goddard.

Goddard was busy with other and more pressing problems. Reviewing hearings was low on his agenda. He would need to read the entire transcripts of both the meprobamate hearing and the Librium and Valium hearing. It would take time, and every additional day meant an extra $15,000 to $20,000 in sales for Roche Labs.

13: More Bureaucratic Barriers

He's the only lawyer I know who can lose and win at the same time.

AN FDA LAWYER DESCRIBING TOM FINNEY

FDA Commissioner Goddard ordered meprobamate regulated under the DACA controls in December 1967, and Carter-Wallace immediately appealed. When Goddard got around to reviewing the Librium and Valium case, however, bureaucratic paralysis set in at the FDA. It worked to Roche Laboratories' advantage as surely as would any favorable ruling. The 1963 Prettyman Commission report contained a recommendation which had long been advocated in many quarters, even as far back as the 1949 Hoover Commission report. The recommendation was to combine federal drug abuse enforcement under one agency. Enforcement had been fragmented in the Federal Bureau of Narcotics (FBN) (under the Treasury Department), and the Bureau of Drug Abuse Control (under the FDA). The Prettyman Commission recommended they be combined under the single jurisdiction of the Justice Department.

From time to time the idea had arisen to place all federal

drug abuse enforcement under the FBI and Director J. Edgar Hoover. However, when reorganization was seriously considered in 1967, Hoover apparently decided he did not want it. A former government official who knows the history of attempts to place drug enforcement under the FBI says: "Hoover did not want a jurisdiction that would give his bureau problems. He liked the statistics his men compiled, and he often bragged that an FBI agent had never been bribed. Well, he was probably right. The FBI concentrates on recovering stolen cars that go across state lines and putting kids in prison for stealing them. That's easy work and the recoveries and arrests look good on paper. Who's going to bribe anybody over stolen cars? But in narcotics trafficking a lot of money is at stake and bribe attempts would be made and are made. Hoover didn't want any part of this."

Joseph Califano, a special assistant to President Johnson, remembers contacting Hoover on at least one occasion concerning reorganization. "At first Hoover was not for reorganization at all. He did not want a drug enforcement agency in the Justice Department and he did not want drug enforcement with the FBI," Califano recalls. "He gave two reasons. One, the FBN agents were not of FBI quality and, two, there was a lot of corruption in the narcotics agency that needed to be cleaned out before he could accept it. We didn't press the issue with him, and in return he did not oppose the reorganization so long as the FBI would not be involved. We discussed the possibility that in three or four years the functions would shift to the FBI and Hoover and he seemed to accept that."

Although the FBI would have been the logical choice because of its high professional standards and its incomparable laboratory work, Hoover's opposition prevented the FBI from taking over the drug enforcement job. So, on February 7, 1968, President Johnson recommended that the two drug enforcement agencies of Treasury and the FDA combine under one roof at the Justice Department. It would be called the

Federal Bureau of Narcotics and Dangerous Drugs (BNDD).
There was resistance at Treasury and some on Capitol Hill
but in April of 1968, Congress approved the reorganization
and BNDD became official. John Ingersoll, a member of the
Justice Department for only a few months, was selected by
Attorney General Ramsey Clark to head the new agency.
John Finlattor, who had headed the FDA's Bureau of Drug
Abuse Control, and Henry Giordano, who had headed the
Federal Bureau of Narcotics, came over as assistants. (Gior-
dano bitterly resented not being chosen for the top spot and
soon departed.)

"It was a time of complete inaction on Librium and Valium," a BNDD counsel says of this period. "The FDA didn't
want to do anything, and why should they? They were not
going to enforce it anyway. So Goddard never finalized the
order." Librium and Valium just kept falling into the cracks.
Goddard recalls: "I talked with Ramsey Clark about two
issues when the drug abuse controls were transferred from
FDA to Justice. One thing I mentioned was that kids had been
telling me that narcotics agents were selling drugs. We looked
into it and found it was true. I told Ramsey he should take a
very careful look at the agent situation." Clark did and found
a lot of corruption involving former FBN agents who had
transferred to the FDA drug enforcement bureau. Many resignations were accepted and indictments were handed down to
many of these agents. "The second thing I told him," Goddard says, "was that it was not fair that I make a decision on
Librium and Valium before the transfer to Justice. I thought
some of the psychiatrists at the hearing had established that
the drugs had a potential for abuse, but I thought the evidence on street abuse was weak. One of the problems, of
course, was that both Librium and Valium were relatively
new, much newer than meprobamate. So I procrastinated
so BNDD could have time to develop evidence of street abuse.
My general feeling is that almost all substances can be abused
and I see no reason why Librium and Valium cannot be

abused." Goddard's reservations about the evidence of street abuse were not shared by many lawyers acquainted with the requirements of the 1965 DACA law.

With the enforcement functions now shifted to BNDD, there were a number of obstacles in the path of quick action. The new agency was organizing itself, hiring a staff, setting objectives. Because of this, the regulation of Librium and Valium was ignored for another full year, good for another $10 million in sales for Roche Laboratories.

In May of 1969, BNDD Director Ingersoll finally ordered that they be federally controlled. Naturally, Finney filed objections on behalf of Roche, thereby prompting still another delay. BNDD scheduled another hearing, both to update the evidence and to build a stronger case of street abuse.

But there was even more delay. Another full year went by until April 1970, when the BNDD hearing on Librium and Valium finally began. Meanwhile, in 1970 a study at the Los Angeles County-University of Southern California Medical Center implicated Librium and Valium in widespread drug misuse. The study found Librium and Valium, along with meprobamate, Seconal, chloral hydrate and Darvon, were the drugs most often prescribed in "excessive quantities." A follow-up study was conducted on these drugs, confirming the earlier finding. Librium and Valium, along with Darvon and phenobarbital, accounted for 90 percent of all "excessive quantity" prescriptions. One patient was prescribed 800 Librium capsules. Another got 600 Valium tablets in one prescription, both far more than should be responsibly prescribed. Another patient was prescribed 200 Valium tablets from one doctor and on the same day was prescribed 200 more from another doctor.

Librium and Valium sales had reached about $200 million a year by 1970, or about 40 percent of the total U.S. tranquilizer market, now glutted with some 700 varieties of tranquilizers and tranquilizer combinations. Roche's Nutley operation was taking in 40 percent of the entire Hoffmann-

LaRoche worldwide earnings of $1.2 billion in 1970. *Fortune* Magazine, which is very careful and very accurate in these areas, estimated that Roche's u.s. operation in 1970 made $200 million in profits, or about eight times what the secretive Swiss managers said it earned. *Fortune's* article in fact was titled: "The Secret Life of Hoffmann-LaRoche." Librium had become the best-selling prescription drug in the United States during the latter part of the 1960s until it was displaced by Valium in 1969, then Librium dropped to second place, the best testimony yet to the power of promotion and advertising. Total worldwide sales of these two drugs by 1970 came to $2 billion from the time they were introduced. Clearly, the drug industry was busy during this period, even if the mechanisms for governmental control were at a standstill.

The 1970 BNDD hearing brought out little new information. An audit of ten Miami drugstores by the Florida Board of Pharmacy found a shortage of more than 100,000 Librium pills in a period of a year. Roche said this was because of a problem with Cuban doctors. Michael Sonnenreich, then deputy chief counsel at BNDD, presented the BNDD case at the hearing. Edgar Buttle was again the hearing examiner and Finney defended Roche. Regular drug users testified at this hearing that they used Librium and Valium as downers to come off speed and LSD trips; one said he used Librium 50 times for that purpose. An eighteen-year-old high school student said she was introduced to Librium by her mother, who gave it to her "whenever I got upset." BNDD tried to show that these drugs were used in conjunction with illegal drugs. Users said Librium took the "terror and horror" out of bad LSD trips, a therapeutic use that had apparently escaped Roche's promotional department. The hearing went on intermittently for fourteen days and ended June 15, 1970. On November 16, 1970, Examiner Buttle once more ruled for the government, saying the two drugs had a "substantial" potential for abuse.

So Roche lost again, or did it? When James Phelps, the FDA counsel in the first hearing, found out Finney and Roche had lost another hearing, Phelps wrote Finney a letter. "I congratulated Tom for losing another hearing. I told him that should mean Librium and Valium would not be controlled for another century. He's the only lawyer I know who can lose and win at the same time." The BNDD would issue the order to control the drugs and Roche would appeal to the federal courts nearly five years having passed since the government had first attempted to control these drugs. But as these administrative hearings were being held, a parallel attempt was being waged in the Senate to control Librium and Valium legislatively, and Roche Laboratories was prompting a very bitter and expensive lobby fight in response.

14: Dodd Strikes Back

> *". . . If we shut off the black market in these drugs,*
> *the manufacturer will ultimately lose the profit from*
> *these original sales; but I think the health of this*
> *nation is worth that loss."*
>
> SENATOR DODD, ON THE SENATE FLOOR

"I remember his telling us that he would be the first censured senator ever to get a major bill passed," recalls a former staff aide to Senator Dodd. "He wanted to vindicate himself and he thought the new drug bill would do it." There was little that could vindicate Dodd following his censure in June of 1967. The evidence had been overwhelming. He admitted diverting campaign funds of more than $100,000 to his personal use and by a vote of 97 to 2, Dodd became the first U.S. Senator ever censured for financial misconduct. Newspaper editorials demanded his resignation. His name became synonymous with political corruption. The press back home in Connecticut had become almost universally unfriendly and his support in the state Democratic party was evaporating, leaving his renomination in 1970 in grave doubt. In the Senate, where Dodd had always been a loner anyway, he was now more alone, avoided like a contagious disease. Even the lobbyists no longer seemed to want to see him.

The 1968 elections brought in President Nixon and a new Congress on the wings of the law and order issue; the Congress that convened in January of 1969 would go down in history as the "law and order Congress." Dodd began investigating new patterns of drug abuse. His Juvenile Delinquency Subcommittee staff was gathering arrest data which showed predictably that drug arrests were soaring in most major u.s. cities. It had emerged, since the time of Dodd's earlier investigations, from a number of localized drug abuse problem areas to a full-blown national crisis.

Dodd's staff was now preparing a comprehensive drug bill that would radically revise the penalties for drug violations. The major features would end the repressive minimum penalties, reduce the marihuana penalties, and coordinate the control of narcotic and drug abuse laws under the Bureau of Narcotics and Dangerous Drugs (BNDD). If passed, the bill would give sweeping new enforcement powers to BNDD and the Justice Department.

In the eyes of the drug industry, the most sensitive section of the bill was the Controlled Substances Act. This was a classification system for all drugs which would determine their uses and their dangers, and then would regulate them accordingly. Dodd's bill had three such categories, called schedules. Within schedule one, the most tightly controlled of the three, were hard narcotics such as heroin, cocaine, and other drugs having no recognized medical use and a high potential for abuse. Most of the drugs in schedule one were either banned or were subject to the strictest of controls. In schedule two were drugs with a high potential for abuse but with recognized medical uses. These drugs would require very strict records, the licensing of manufacturers, production quotas and tighter regulation of imports and exports. Included in this schedule were amphetamines, barbiturates and other stimulants and depressants, including meprobamate and Librium and Valium. Schedule three included drugs with a low potential for abuse and having accepted medical uses, such as cough syrup containing codeine.

Essentially, by listing corporate drugs in schedule two, the Dodd bill was telling a drug company how many pills it could produce and how much profit it could make from them. Quotas would be established based on estimated national needs, and in many cases the production quotas would certainly be far less than the number of pills already being produced and marketed. This would insure industry opposition from any one of a number of companies involved.

On April 18, 1969, Dodd introduced his drug bill in the Senate, under the title of "Omnibus Narcotic and Dangerous Drug Control and Addict Rehabilitation Act of 1969." The first major reaction came from BNDD: a loud scream. Michael Sonnenreich, the deputy chief counsel at BNDD, was working on the Administration's drug bill at the time, and the Dodd bill seemed suspiciously similar to one of his own drafts, which had not yet been introduced in Congress. He called Dodd's office in an angry huff. Who stole my bill? he demanded. He calmed down enough to generously allow that he didn't want to "hang anyone by the thumbs," but he remained vexed. Sonnenreich, a bright and openly ambitious young lawyer, was caught in a bind. He was faced with the apparent theft of his bill, but by the Subcommittee whose support the Administration might need for passage of its upcoming law and order drug bill. In the end he decided to tread lightly and not push further. BNDD Chief Counsel Donald Miller also called Dodd's office to complain about the pirating of the bill, and said whoever took it from BNDD was in for trouble, a generous understatement.

Was the bill really stolen? Dodd's Subcommittee staff people maintain to this day that the similarities were natural and almost predictable. Both were revisions of an existing drug law; both based their drug classification generally on the international psychotropic drug convention, and both bills sought to transfer a large portion of drug regulation power from HEW to BNDD. Sonnenreich now only says the Dodd bill and his draft were "incredibly close." All of the reasons for the similarity remain unclear.

The second major reaction to Dodd's drug bill came from the drug industry trade press. The industry-supported trade paper, the "Pink Sheet," called Dodd's bill "more a political move" than a "substantial contribution." The "Pink Sheet" dismissed it by saying the Administration bill, not the Dodd bill, would get Congress's attention.

The Administration bill drafted by Sonnenreich originally included by name Librium, Valium and meprobamate for control. But at a panel discussion in April at the BNDD Pharmaceutical Manufacturers and Wholesalers Leadership Conference, the BNDD publicly admitted to industry representatives that lobby opposition to naming these drugs in the bill would delay it. Therefore, Librium, Valium and meprobamate were dropped from the bill. Carter-Wallace and Roche were delighted; they had won with only the threat of a fight. Meprobamate was in the federal courts and Roche was still awaiting the second BNDD hearing on Librium and Valium. The president of the American Pharmaceutical Association (the pharmacists' society whose lobby often works with the drug lobby) later admitted his staff, along with representatives of the drug industry and officials of the Justice Department and BNDD, attended "several" conferences regarding the bill during its drafting stages. The pharmacists' society wanted pharmacists exempted from the inventory and inspection provisions.

In July 1969 President Nixon sent Congress his drug bill, along with the message that a "new urgency and concentrated national policy is needed at the federal level to begin to cope with this growing menace to the general welfare of the United States." The late Senator Everett Dirksen of Illinois and Senator Roman Hruska of Nebraska, both Republicans and unflinching advocates of the drug industry and virtually every Administration policy, introduced the bill in the Senate. The Dirksen-Hruska tandem had thrown up every roadblock conceivable a few years earlier to block passage of the Kefauver-Harris drug bill. But now their stance seemed to have shifted position. The Administration's drug bill resembled the Dodd bill in major respects, except for certain crucial differences. In the drug classification section, called the controlled substances section as in the Dodd bill, the Administration had included four drug schedules instead of three. In schedule three of the Administration bill were barbiturates and amphetamines. But schedule three of the Administration bill, in fact, provided the same controls as the 1965 DACA law. There were no separate record requirements for these drugs, unlimited production was still allowed, all the controls that had proved so completely ineffective in preventing abuse and illegal traffic were maintained intact.

Dodd wanted his subcommittee to be able to consider both bills. He could then blend them and still get the major credit for enactment. He would be, in his own mind, vindicated. But there was wrangling over who would get the Administration bill and Dodd's major competition was Senator John McClellan's Criminal Laws Subcommittee, a part of the Judiciary Committee. McClellan, as ranking majority member of the Committee, had more power than Dodd and he also had the support of Hruska and Dirksen who knew McClellan could be relied on to bully the small time operators and not the drug industry. Dodd got the bill, even though the Judiciary Committee, through which it was routed, was headed by Senator James Eastland, an ardent supporter of the Nixon Administration. "A policy decision was made downtown (at the Justice Department) to give Dodd's subcommittee the bill," according to an official who was familiar with the negotiations. "It came through Eastland who gave his consent, and Dodd got both bills." Why? Dodd got them because in his hands the Administration could exert the kind of leverage it wanted. Still looming over Dodd's head were possible criminal charges stemming from his personal use of campaign funds. He could be charged with tax evasion, fraud, or a number of other crimes, any one of which would have certainly brought his political career to an abrupt end. There was also the possibility of a civil suit from the Internal

Revenue Service (IRS) to collect back taxes on the campaign funds. The implicit pressure would always be there and, if ever needed, it could be made explicit to force Dodd back into line with the Administration. Although Dodd's political career seemed mortally wounded to everybody but Dodd himself, he clung tenaciously to the idea that he would be reelected and vindicated. He wasn't just saying it for public consumption; he believed it. Tucked somewhere in his mind he knew he would resurrect himself. What better issue to use than drug abuse? He had been in there early; no one could accuse him of jumping on a bandwagon. He would see this one through. If it meant doing things according to the Administration's demands, he would do that but he would get some credit.

John W. Dean III, then with the Justice Department and later with the White House staff, was the chief Administration lobbyist. Dean—later to be linked with the Watergate incident—would shepherd the bill through Congress, protecting the Administration's and the drug industry's interests and guarding against congressional encroachment. The Administration bill, like the Dodd bill, sought a broad shift of decision-making power in the field of drug abuse and enforcement from HEW to the Justice Department and BNDD. Since many decisions in drug abuse are medical, the bills were arousing strong opposition from HEW. Opposition was also heard from various members of Congress. On this major issue of HEW versus Justice, Dodd would be expected to support the Administration right down the line. It would be an important fight that would draw attention away from the quieter struggles between the drug industry and Congress.

One of the first approaches to Dodd's subcommittee came from Mike Sonnenreich of the BNDD. He would be BNDD's key lobbyist on the bill, serving his bureau as John Dean would serve the Administration. "Sonnenreich had almost completely written the Administration bill," recalls Carl Perian of the Dodd subcommittee. "He told me the Administration wanted the bill fast and they knew they were going to have trouble with it from the lobbyists. That was the reason they didn't put amphetamines and barbiturates in their schedule two under quotas. Sonnenreich asked Dodd to eliminate production quotas during the hearings and the floor debate so we could run the bill through and get it signed into law. It sounded reasonable to me because the major focus as far as I was concerned was to change the archaic penalty structure for drug crimes. But we only agreed to change the controls on amphetamines on the basis of a promise from Attorney General Mitchell that these drugs would come under strict controls administratively after the bill became law." Dodd bought the deal. He wanted a bill.

Although the Administration asked Dodd through a memo from John Dean to drop Librium and Valium from the bill, he didn't. The Administration was not adamant. If it had been, Dodd would likely have acceded to the request. Perian especially wanted to keep them in their bill; he was still smoldering over the 1964 episode when he caught Finney and Roche torpedoing their drug bill of that year. To him, it was more than a personal matter; he thought it was criminal. "Roche knew for certain by the time of this later bill that a lot of people were abusing their drugs," Perian says. "I regard everything they did to keep them out of regulation as unethical."

Finney monitored the progress of the drug bills for Roche. The specter of controlling Librium and Valium in the bill was to be avoided at all costs. If Congress finally passed the bill with them included, there could be no more appeals or delays. They would be controlled and regulated by BNDD, subject to record-keeping requirements, prescription refill limits, and inventories. If they remained in Dodd's scheduling scheme (which seemed doubtful since the Administration was pushing to keep all major corporate drugs away from quota requirements), production ceilings might even be established. Finney visited Perian to find out what was going

on. It was not a warm welcome in Perian's office. Finney
had brought a retinue of his people, and Perian had a
couple of secretaries and an investigator there. There were
suggestions that Finney's and Roche's motives were not all
that pure and that maybe, just maybe, money was the real
issue. It got testy and Finney left without finding out much
of anything except that the subcommittee was determined to
control Librium and Valium in the new bill. Perian did not
then, nor does he now, disguise his loathing of Finney: "He's
just a blatant, tough advocate of the strong and powerful."
Finney, who remembers that meeting with Perian, says of
it: "I normally don't make mortal enemies on the Hill. I
must have done something to piss them off." Although
Finney remained active for Roche, he no longer visited
Perian. Doing so was like raising a red flag.

Dodd scheduled hearings in September 1969 in the Old
Senate Office Building. Both bills were to be considered.
Dodd read a long opening statement in which he called drug
abuse a "major crisis in our times." "But," he said, "it is a
crisis that we can overcome. We must." Dodd sat at the center of the committee table, flanked by Roman Hruska and
Edward Kennedy. Perian was there, too. At one point during
the hearing Dodd reluctantly admitted the failure of the
1965 DACA law, saying that despite its passage, billions of
legal pills were still diverted into the black market.

The first witnesses were Attorney General John Mitchell,
BNDD Director John Ingersoll and Sonnenreich. Mitchell
went into a detailed explanation of the Administration bill.
He said it was "extremely necessary" that swift action be
taken by Congress. He said that amphetamines were "subject
to increasing abuse" but that they had wide medical uses—
a tactic used to prevent tighter controls. Ingersoll, a round-
faced man who answers questions in brief monotone sentences, said there was "lax security and record-keeping" with
these drugs. He also said a BNDD study showed *92 percent* of
the amphetamines and barbiturates found in the illicit market

were of *legitimate* origin. Still, the Administration had put these drugs under the same controls that had not worked in the three years they had been in effect. Dodd did not pursue this contradiction. At Perian's urging, Dodd asked Mitchell why Librium, Valium and meprobamate were not included in the bill. "These are surely dangerous drugs," Dodd said. "I know they have therapeutic value. I am well aware of that. But I think these three are in a category of drugs that are widely abused." Mitchell conceded this was an area in which he and the companies were "currently at odds." Ingersoll said an effort was now underway at BNDD to control these three tranquilizers. He said the meprobamate case had moved swiftly, relatively speaking, and was already in the courts. BNDD was moving administratively toward the control of Librium and Valium.

"I tried four years ago to get those drugs included. The effort was defeated and I think the industry was very active, very successful. They did a lot of lobbying around here. I don't suggest that that is the reason nothing has been done about them, but the fact is nothing has been done," Dodd said. Dodd invited Roche Laboratories to the hearing and it accepted. Its representatives were scheduled to testify two weeks after the hearing opened.

But before appearing, Roche's people tried one more tactic to soften the approaching blow. The day before they were to testify, Peter Rodino, a Democratic congressman from New Jersey, brought Ellis Anderson, vice-president and general counsel from Roche, and Dr. John Burns, Roche's vice-president of research, to visit the Juvenile Delinquency Subcommittee. Finney discreetly did not attend. Dodd made only a token appearance and asked the Roche people to speak with his staff. Rodino made it clear to Perian and Gene Gleason, the Subcommittee press director, that he was only acting as a middleman, a kind of host, and was seeking no favors. Anderson and Burns were there to be friendly, to show they were nice guys and to put themselves on the good side of the Subcommittee. Anderson is an extremely tall and lanky man with light hair and an angular, Scandinavian face. A thoroughgoing company man, Anderson made a pitch for Roche: we are not trying to hinder you, but to help, was his message to Perian. We want a good law and we want to cooperate with Congress and your subcommittee and you can depend on us to do everything we can to assist you. At one point in their meeting Gleason, who can come on with a fierce and intimidating look, asked Anderson why he was talking to them. Why are you here? What do you really want? He tried to extract from Anderson an admission that it was, after all, just a question of profits. Gleason thought if he could get Anderson to admit this in private, it might slip out in the public hearing. Anderson didn't yield. He smiled, held his temper as best he could, and didn't react to Gleason's hostile questions. He said BNDD's proposed regulation of Librium and Valium (the hearing had not yet been held) would not stand up and he asked Perian not to be misled by it. The meeting ended and nothing more happened. Only Dodd seemed upset by what had transpired. On the way to the hearing the next day, he told Perian he overheard some of what went on and he was annoyed at Gleason for giving Anderson such a rough time. He said it was impolite. His attitude would change.

The hearing began. Enter once more Ellis Anderson. Unsuccessful in his private meeting with the subcommittee staff, Anderson had taken an added precaution. An old friend, Senator Birch Bayh of Indiana, a member of the Dodd subcommittee, would give Anderson an effusive introduction. Bayh had not attended the hearings, nor had he shown any interest in them. But he came now, especially to give Anderson a glowing send-off. Bayh admitted he did not know what Anderson was going to say, but he hoped the Subcommittee would accept it on its merits. He said he first met Anderson when Anderson was city attorney in Indianapolis under Senator Vance Hartke, who was then mayor. "He was born in Hoosierland, received his bachelor of arts degree from Indiana University and doctor of laws degree from that law school, which puts us both as members of the alumni of that alma mater," Bayh said in a burst of Hoosier chauvinism. He regarded it as a "privilege" to introduce Anderson, Bayh said, "inasmuch as I have known him for a number of years." Anderson glowed. When Bayh finished, Anderson said: "If I might, I might add to the kind remarks of Senator Bayh; he said I was once a Hoosier. I have to say once a Hoosier, always a Hoosier, Senator Bayh."

"You had better bet on that," Senator Bayh answered. Only the soft humming of "Back Home Again in Indiana" was missing. Bayh then left the hearing room, explaining that he had other commitments.

It began well. Anderson read a long statement, written mostly by Finney. It agreed the new law to control mood drugs and narcotics was fine "so long as appropriate distinctions are maintained between these two very different classes of substances." Dodd interrupted Anderson before he had finished his statement with the point that the segregation of the different classes is provided in the bill. "You think that the public will associate non-narcotics with narcotic problems if they are in the same schedule? Why, we can correct that easily by labeling the containers, can't we?" Anderson agreed but explained that he was worried about the interweaving of all the drugs in the regulatory scheme. Anderson had criticized Dodd's bill, which would have set off Dodd in any case. But more annoying than that to Dodd was Anderson's attitude; he was haughty, arrogant, at times talking to Dodd like teacher to pupil. Dodd was ordinarily thin-skinned, but he was all the more vulnerable after his censure. He began to seethe. "What are you afraid of? Guilt by association? That is a good old statement," Dodd said. Perian was passing notes to Dodd, containing questions to ask, points to mention.

Anderson backed off slightly. He said it was not so much the schedule of drugs that worried him but more the fact that many countries look to the United States for its lead in regulatory schemes, and some of those countries "are not capable of making the sophisticated distinctions" that the United States can make. Did he have in mind such backward countries as Germany, France, Sweden, Japan, or Great Britain? Anderson accused the Dodd bill of suggesting that mood drugs like Librium and Valium and narcotics were all the same. Dodd let him read on. Anderson even provoked a couple of laughs in the hearing room which Dodd did not appreciate. Roche's side brought out the argument that it was "unjustified and unwise" to list drugs like Librium and Valium as inherently dangerous, that it would increase patient anxiety and make the doctor's job tougher. Dodd said there was nothing fixed or permanent about the schedules. Drugs could be moved into a tighter or less restrictive schedule as the evidence permitted.

Anderson pointedly reminded Dodd that Roche had stood in the forefront of support for the 1965 DACA law—a revisionist view of history Dodd couldn't swallow. "What a simple piece of legislation it was," Dodd said, "and yet you people at Roche so violently opposed it."

"I want to stress again, as I said earlier," Anderson answered testily, "our current president, our then executive vice-president, and vice-president for research testified in support of that legislation."

Then you think there should be controls over amphetamines and barbiturates, is that your position?" Dodd asked. "I have really no position on that," Anderson answered, slipping the punch. Dodd waded in again. He asked Anderson about his assertion that Librium and Valium have a "remarkable safety record." Don't you need warnings on these drugs? Dodd asked. Of course, Anderson snapped, but all prescription drugs need warnings. Dodd jabbed some more, Anderson bobbed and weaved and jabbed back, getting angrier as he went. "You get some of the same problems with these drugs that you get with respect to barbiturates,

don't you?" No, Anderson shot back, we do not believe they
are the same. The FDA hearings on Librium and Valium
never happened. Dodd submitted a Librium advertisement
in which the required warning said in part "withdrawal
symptoms (including convulsions), following discontinua-
tion of the drug and similar to those seen with barbiturates
have been reported."

Then the other Roche representative, Dr. John Burns,
read a statement calling for separate and distinct classes of
drugs. Dr. Burns held another position as well: he was
chairman of the Committee on Problems of Drug Safety for
the National Academy of Sciences National Research Council. The council is a quasi-official agency which serves as a
major consultant for the FDA on such things as drug policy.
It also provides the industry with one more influential inroad
into the government's decision-making process. Burns went
on to say that the choice of the word "remarkable" to describe
Librium's safety was used in comparison to other drugs.

Dodd kept coming, and Anderson grew angrier. At one
point, Dr. Burns turned in anguish toward the audience.
"He had the look on his face of a man who was asking
himself 'what the hell am I doing here?' " says an observer
in the hearing room. He knew Anderson was taking the
wrong approach. Anderson was simply losing his cool. Dodd
asked Anderson about diversion. He said a BNDD audit of
several New York City drugstores revealed shortages of up to
50 percent of Librium and Valium. Anderson commended
BNDD for discovering this. Dodd cited 2,200 cases of injuries
from Librium and Valium and 36 cases of suicides, and then
asked Anderson what he thought should be done. Anderson
showed the face-saving quality of elusiveness; he shifted the
focus to BNDD and said they were proceeding administratively. Finally, Dodd got to the heart of the issue. "Let me
ask you a general question: Why do you worry about putting
this drug under control? Wouldn't you feel better about it
as the producers? You say, okay, there is a substantial body of

competent opinion which thinks there is a real danger here. Okay, let's put it under control. What is that going to do to your business?" Dodd asked. "Is that what you are worrying about? What is it about—"

Anderson interrupted. The "body of factual evidence does not establish the need" for controls, he said. "There is this new evidence that I have just heard for the first time. There is, as the chairman knows, a proceeding pending before the department to regulate—"

Now Dodd cut *him* off. He was taut. "I told you I don't care to get into the proceeding," he shot back. Anderson never did answer Dodd's question.

Dodd had asked Anderson and Roche Laboratories the publicly unanswerable question: Why, in the face of a national crisis of drug abuse, after the FDA hearing examiner ruled against you, after many experts and case histories have documented that your drugs have a potential for abuse and are abused, why do you refuse to choose a safer course in the name of the public health? Of course, it will cost you money in sales losses. But even if you steadfastly believe your drugs are safe, don't you agree that the many competent experts who contend your drugs are abused might have a point? Can they all be fools? Can they all be mistaken? And what about the "new evidence" Anderson spoke of? Evidence of diversion, abuse and misuse had come out at the FDA hearing years before.

Yes, we are concerned, Roche said out of one side of its corporate mouth; but no we won't do anything about it, it said out of the other.

When Dodd finished with Ellis Anderson that afternoon he was, in the words of an aide, "sweating and almost trembling, he was so mad. He couldn't stand that big Swede [Anderson] looking down his nose at him that way." Anderson's arrogance and anger had belittled Dodd. His attitude provided more incentive than anything else in launching Dodd's crusade against Librium and Valium. Meanwhile, back in Nutley, Anderson was roundly chastised. Why hadn't he controlled himself? Why had he attacked Dodd? His performance may have had another, farther-reaching result. About a year and a half later, Dr. V. D. Mattia, Roche's president, died of a heart ailment. Anderson had been one of those in line for the presidency, but he didn't get it and it filtered out that one of the reasons was his performance that day in front of Dodd.

Dodd concluded his drug hearings on October 20, 1969. The drug bill, a combination of the Administration bill and Dodd's bill, went to his full subcommittee for action, and was then sent to the full Judiciary Committee despite the strong reservations of some of the most liberal subcommittee members about the law and order aspects of the bill. A number of them objected to the "no knock" provision in the bill, which gave narcotics agents the right to enter without knocking if they had a warrant. Also, the shift of so much drug enforcement power from HEW to Justice and BNDD deeply troubled many members of Congress. These were the open issues, appearing in the press and removing all attention from the less visible battles with the drug industry. At the end of October the bill went to Eastland's Judiciary Committee. Senator Eastland, who runs the committee with all the democratic fair-handedness of a plantation owner running his plantation, scheduled several secret committee sessions to consider the bill. During one Saturday session Eastland had a television set brought in so the committee members could watch the football game while they considered matters of public policy. Disruptions caused by the "March Against Death" war protest caused a minor delay. The bill before Eastland's Judiciary Committee was basically Dodd's bill with some changes inspired by the Administration. The fact that Dodd's bill—which was tougher on the drug industry and easier on the street offenders than the Administration bill—had gotten this far was a distinct surprise to the drug industry, which had expected it to be discarded long ago in favor of the Administration bill. Because Dodd tailored parts of his bill to Administration wishes, he did not face strong opposition from the Administration. He had dropped quotas and stricter record-keeping on amphetamines and barbiturates, as well as Librium, Valium and meprobamate, and the administration then did not fully oppose the inclusion of the tranquilizers, although it was not happy with what Dodd did. Dodd broadened his bill to four drug classification schedules, a change desired by the drug industry, and BNDD. The PMA specifically wanted four schedules for the "perfecting" of the Dodd bill, and they also wanted full hearings and judicial review—plus a five-year delay—before a drug could be shifted into a more tightly controlled schedule.

Dodd's bill emphasized law enforcement, but not with the same heavy hand as the Administration bill. It eliminated mandatory minimum sentences while the Administration bill maintained them. A seller of marihuana could still get a five-year minimum sentence with parole or probation. Dodd, Perian, and some other subcommittee staff members did some careful lobbying on their own before the Judiciary Committee voted on it. They spoke with members of the Judiciary Committee about the bill, were generally helpful and solicitous, and worked to establish their point of view within the committee. It helped considerably that Dodd was also a member of this committee, so he had entree, unlike his previous experience with Lister Hill's Labor and Public Welfare Committee.

While Dodd's subcommittee occupied itself with getting the bill through the Judiciary Committee, Ellis Anderson, the big Swede from Roche Labs, was again talking with his old Hoosier friend Birch Bayh to ask a small favor of him. What Anderson had lost in his public confrontation with Dodd he was determined to atone for in private, so he was using his friendship with Bayh to change the bill. This form of lobbying is subtlest, most effective, and usually the least traceable kind. In the name of friendship and Hoosiership, could Bayh, Anderson asked, introduce a minor amendment to the Dodd bill during one of those secret sessions of the Judiciary Committee? It would simply remove Librium and Valium from the bill. No one would know about it. Bayh is a skilled politician and in most instances his instincts are commendable. He is a friendly man, given to Rotary Club handshakes and warm smiles, so when the big Swede made his pitch Bayh accepted. Anything for a fellow Hoosier. Bayh had paid no attention to the Dodd bill and had in fact been absent from the important Subcommittee vote on it prior to its transfer to the Judiciary Committee. During one of Eastland's sessions about the bill, Bayh brought up the amendment for Roche. Eastland, his cigar twirling in his mouth, leapt on Bayh before he even finished speaking. What is this, he demanded of Bayh, coming in here this late with some new idea? Bayh was surprised at the vehemence of the attack. He hemmed and hawed sheepishly. Dodd broke in to mention the hundreds of documented cases of Librium and Valium abuse. Senator Hugh Scott (R.—Penn.) asked Dodd if Librium was that "killer drug" he'd heard about. Dodd assured him it was. "Let's vote on it right now," demanded Eastland, and Bayh was caught in a beartrap. Bayh protested that it hadn't been discussed. Another senator said it had been discussed. Bayh, embarrassed and hopelessly outgunned, backed off and withdrew the amendment. He never really got to offer it. A Justice Department lawyer who witnessed the confrontation said of it later: "Bayh didn't know a damn thing about what he was doing. He just did it because of his friendship with Anderson and he got burned." But it was a nice try for Roche Labs and the big Swede.

After that session members of the subcommittee staff went into the corridors outside the Judiciary meeting room. "We saw the boys from Roche were there," Perian recalls. "I'm not sure how many were around, but they were there outside the committee room, waiting for the word. There was Travis Steward, the Roche Washington lobbyist, and a couple others. When they found out what happened to Bayh they seemed kind of depressed but they said 'Well, the war isn't over yet.' And it wasn't."

Dodd maintained his steadfast support of the Administration's desire to shift power from HEW to BNDD and it was rewarded. On December 23, 1969, after the Judiciary Committee finished its consideration of the drug bill, Attorney General Mitchell told Dodd in a letter that he would not be prosecuted on any criminal charges in connection with his censure. No prosecution was warranted, Mitchell said. The letter said the decision was reached after a two-year investigation by the Justice Department and the Internal Revenue Service (IRS). This did not end all possibilities of criminal action against Dodd. The Justice Department could always claim later "new evidence" had come to their attention and the case could be reopened. It also did not foreclose the possibility of a civil suit by IRS. Dodd publicly claimed he had been cleared of any "wrong-doing" according to Mitchell's letter and again said the money was a "gift" to him from his political supporters.

Following the Congressional Christmas recess the Dodd drug bill was reported to the Senate floor. In late January of 1970 the debate began. The issues of drug penalties, the marihuana commission, the "no knock" authority, and the new powers for the BNDD dominated the attention of the Senate, the press, and the public. Perian and Dodd knew that Roche would lobby primarily on the House side to keep Librium and Valium out of the bill, and as the Senate neared a decision there was no evidence Roche would fight in the Senate to keep its drugs out. The meprobamate case was still in federal court and was close to final action, so Carter-Wallace merely sent a statement to the Senate saying that if meprobamate had to be included at all it should be in the category of "low potential for abuse," and not under "high potential for abuse" as the Dodd bill had classified it. But Carter-Wallace preferred that meprobamate not be included at all. "In view of such pending court action," their statement said, "we urge the Committee to defer any action as to meprobamate until the court has rendered its decision."

Dodd's opening remarks in the floor debate took dead aim at the drug industry and its role in drug abuse. "Multi-hundred million dollar advertising budgets—frequently the most costly ingredient in the price of a pill—have, pill by pill, coaxed and seduced post-World War II generations into the 'freaked out' drug culture. . . . Detail men employed by the drug companies propagandize harried and harassed doctors into pushing their special brand of palliative. Free samples in the doctor's office are as common nowadays as inflated fees." Our love affair with drugs, Dodd continued, was not an "accidental development."

The main area of contention during the Senate debate came from Senator Harold Hughes, a Democrat from Iowa, who wanted to shift much of the drug control power away from Justice and BNDD, and back to HEW. Hughes' Subcommittee on Alcoholism and Narcotics had held hearings over a nine-month period and Hughes, a stubborn man in any case, was adamant in his desire to prevent drug abuse from becoming only a law enforcement issue. Many Republicans and conservative Democrats opposed him. That was the Administration line: keep the power away from HEW and put it into the new, tough elite drug agency where things could be done and where they would be under Mitchell's thumb. Dodd did the Administration's bidding and opposed Hughes, and the two men debated numerous times, although never heatedly. In the end, Hughes lost. His amendment was not adopted. At about 5:30 P.M. on January 29th, the Dodd bill passed the Senate by a voice vote. No nays were heard. The bill was pretty much what the Administration wanted.

BNDD and the Justice Department assumed power over drug enforcement. No quotas or tight restrictions of any kind were placed on amphetamines and barbiturates. Librium and Valium and meprobamate were listed in the same schedule as amphetamines and barbiturates, meaning they only had to keep unsegregated records and have a refill limitation. But at least now they were listed. There were no floor arguments to stiffen the controls over amphetamines or barbiturates, despite the evidence that the existing controls did not work.

Although no one even remotely challenged the inclusion of Librium and Valium during the floor debate, Perian and Dodd decided to put something on the record anyway. In a highly unusual statement, Dodd warned the House of Representatives, which would now consider the drug bill, to beware of Roche Laboratories. In the House, Dodd said, Roche would make "serious and strenuous efforts to have these two drugs deleted from the final House version." The Roche lobbyists had virtually admitted this to Perian earlier when they warned him the war wasn't over. Dodd accused Roche of deploying more lobbyists to fight for their drugs than he had staff members on his Subcommittee; he accused Finney's law firm of having been paid fees from Roche Laboratories amounting to three times the total Subcommittee staff budget for the year 1969; he inserted into the record a BNDD audit showing a shortage of 753,434 doses of Librium and Valium from fifty-six pharmacies in six states. "We have an epidemic of tranquilizer deaths directly accountable to Librium and Valium. And I mean just that, an epidemic," Dodd contended. He went on to say there was no reason to protect Roche's position in supplying both the druggists and the black market with these drugs. "Of course, if we shut off the black market in these drugs, the manufacturer will ultimately lose the profit from those original sales; but I think the health of this nation is worth that loss."

Dodd concluded by again focusing the battle on the drug industry, and not the marihuana or heroin peddlers. It is the industry, he said, that has undertaken "such a successful campaign to make these stimulants and depressants attractive to our young people . . . who pop them into their mouths much as earlier generations popped lollipops into their mouths."

The Dodd drug bill went to the House of Representatives. Once there, it got nowhere due to a constitutional problem. Because the Dodd bill involved marihuana and narcotics, and because these drugs have traditionally been controlled under tax laws, the Dodd bill necessarily involved taxation. According to the Constitution, any bill involving taxation must originate in the House. It was feared that if Dodd's bill were to be passed in the House and signed into law, it could later be challenged on Constitutional grounds since it originated in the Senate. The House would therefore only consider the Administration bill, which would originate in the House. The Dodd drug bill never left the House Speaker's desk. It was not entirely wasted, however; Dodd had compiled an extensive record that the Senate would later consider when the Administration bill came back. Dodd intended to see to it that the record would not be forgotten.

Bitter wrangling went on in the House regarding the question of which committee had jurisdiction over the Administration drug bill. It was finally split between Wilbur Mills's Ways and Means Committee, where the tax and revenue sections would be considered, and the House Commerce Committee where the other sections would be considered. The House, however, was destined to see more battles over this issue. A few of its members were developing their own ideas about tightening the controls over amphetamines.

15: Pepper's Crime Committee

One can never be sure how a market does fluctuate.
A SPOKESMAN FOR SMITH KLINE & FRENCH

CLAUDE Pepper is a Democratic congressman from Florida's eleventh district. He is a short, craggy-faced man with the accent and courtly graces of a gentleman of the deep South. Born in 1900, he was having difficulty hearing by the age of sixty-nine, but his mental acuity and intelligence were and still are undiminished by age. His unusual political career now spans five decades, during which some of both the best and the worst aspects of American politics have been played out.

Pepper was born and raised on a farm near Dudleyville, Alabama. He was graduated sixth in his class from Harvard Law School in 1924. After Harvard, Pepper taught at the University of Arkansas, where one of his students was J. William Fulbright, now chairman of the Senate Foreign Relations Committee. Pepper later moved to Tallahassee, Florida, where he opened a law practice and first entered politics. His first exposure was brief. As a twenty-eight-year-old freshman in the Florida State Legislature, Pepper refused to support a censure motion in the legislature against the first lady, Mrs. Herbert Hoover, whose crime had been to invite a black member of Congress to the White House. Pepper was not reelected to a second term but he remained active in Florida state politics. In 1936 he was appointed to fill a vacancy in the U.S. Senate. If Pepper was liberal for the rest of the country, he was radical for most of the South. He was a consistent supporter of FDR's New Deal program and, as a member of the Senate Committee on Labor and Public Welfare, he took an active interest in health legislation. During his freshman year in the Senate, Pepper co-sponsored a bill creating the National Cancer Institute. During World War II he was chairman of the Subcommittee on Wartime Health and Education, and he took that opportunity to expand government-supported medical research and to lay some groundwork for a medicare program. Pepper also had one other consuming interest in the Senate: foreign relations. He was an early advocate of intervention in World War II against Hitler and generally supported an interventionist foreign policy in the era of isolation. After World War II Pepper spoke out against the developing cold war and laid much of the blame on President Truman and Secretary of State Dean Acheson. At one point he was photographed chatting with Joseph Stalin during a visit to the Soviet Union, a picture which would prove to cost him dearly.

In 1946 he was chief sponsor of the bill to create the National Institute of Mental Health and in 1948 he was chief sponsor of a bill for the National Heart Institution. By 1950 Pepper was two years away from the chairmanship of either the Committee on Labor and Public Welfare, where he would exert great control over national health legislation, or the Foreign Relations Committee, where he would be the major congressional voice on foreign policy. But he also had an election in 1950.

Running against Pepper in the Democratic primary was

George Smathers, a congressman and a Pepper protégé. Smathers in fact had been an aide on Pepper's Senate staff. In the one-party South, the primary winner would be the next senator. Pepper lost that primary election in what is still considered to be one of the dirtiest major political campaigns ever waged.

Because Pepper advocated government medical programs he was hotly opposed by the medical politicians of organized medicine. Smathers had a built-in organization working for him. Doctors all over Florida worked against Pepper. When Smathers came to a town to campaign the doctors would work to get the crowds out and enthusiasm up. When Pepper came in they would work to turn the crowds away and, failing that, they would plant a few embarrassing questions in the audience. The Joe McCarthy era was at its frenzied peak and Pepper's picture with Stalin was widely distributed, giving him a red taint. A pamphlet was also distributed. It was called "The Record of Red Pepper." Smathers did everything but call Pepper a communist. "I thank God I wear the orange and blue of the University of Florida and not the *crimson* of Harvard . . . ," Smathers would say. "I'm not a classmate of Alger Hiss." Surrounded with such a poisonous political climate, Pepper lost and to this day he has not recovered from it. He calls it "the most vicious campaign in the twentieth century." But more than the loss of his Senate seat and his power, the psychic wound to Pepper has been profound. He has never since been fully able to trust subordinates nor to take the risks he once took.

Pepper retired to private life after the 1950 defeat and reopened his law practice. In 1958 he tried to unseat the late Senator Spessard Holland and was defeated. In 1962 he tried for the House from the Eleventh District and won handily. In this way he became the only member of Congress in this century who served first in the Senate and later in the House. Pepper has since 1962 won handily in his district, but he is one of about fifty congressmen who still maintain a private law practice. Although he gives it little time, it remains a source of possible conflict of interest. But Pepper won't give it up; he cannot forget that stunning defeat in 1950 when he was left with no job and no money.

Having been a long-time proponent of medicare, in 1965 Pepper helped enact the medicare bill against the all-out opposition of the AMA. In 1967 he received the prestigious Albert Lasker Public Service Award for his service to medical legislation throughout the years, and with it went a $10,000 honorarium.

In 1969, partly through Pepper's own efforts, the Democratically controlled House of Representatives created the Select Committee on Crime on "Law Day," May 1; it was a move meant both to placate a public aroused and angered by crime in the streets and to answer the "soft on crime" label the Republicans had pinned on Democrats in the fall election. A select committee differs from a standing committee in that it is usually constituted only for the two-year Congressional term in which it is created. Each succeeding Congress must renew it if it is to continue. Second, it does not have the legislative power of a standing committee. Pepper was close to then House Speaker John McCormack and the present majority whip, Thomas "Tip" O'Neill, and because he first urged formation of the Crime Committee and was friendly with the House leadership, he was named chairman. The Crime Committee was created to investigate crime and then to draw up legislation and work with the appropriate standing committee to enact it.

Named to the Committee with Pepper were Martha Griffiths of Michigan, Robert Nix of Pennsylvania, and Jerome Waldie of California, all Democrats; and Albert Watson of South Carolina, Charles Wiggins of California and Robert Denney of Nebraska, Republicans. Richard Kurrus was named by Pepper to be chief counsel. An acrid and tough-minded Harvard Law School graduate, Kurrus' extensive experience was mostly in maritime law, but he knew how Capitol Hill operated. So he began to chart the course for the Crime Committee. Pepper and Kurrus visited Attorney General John Mitchell as a courtesy and to ask for his cooperation. Mitchell promised his department's cooperation in any areas the Committee investigated but said he couldn't promise any help from the Federal Bureau of Investigation (FBI). Puffing calmly on his pipe, he told an astonished Pepper and Kurrus he considered J. Edgar Hoover to be the "greatest obstacle to law enforcement in the United States."

Kurrus spoke next with Robert Morgenthau, the highly respected U.S. Attorney for the Southern District of New York. Morgenthau promised the Committee could have access to his office's files. A short while later Morgenthau had to renege; John W. Dean III, then a deputy assistant attorney general, told him not to make the files available. The Republicans feared the Crime Committee would use the files to embarrass them.

The Committee membership made one more acquisition. Larry Reida, a member of Congressman Denney's staff, joined it as the associate chief counsel. He was in fact the Republican minority counsel. A young, square-shouldered midwesterner, Reida is a conservative Republican with consummate political skills.

As the Committee sought its way, it began to turn its attention increasingly to drugs. Hearings were held in Washington, D.C., Boston, and Omaha, and the direct link between drugs and crime became preeminent. Hearings on marihuana were held in Boston and Omaha and in August tentative plans were made to go to the West Coast for more drug hearings. Amphetamine abuse was a full-scale epidemic in the Bay area, with the supply coming from legitimate channels and the many clandestine labs springing up all over.

Larry Reida, who had led the initial foray to San Francisco, was one of the staunchest supporters for staging the hearings there. "In San Francisco there were a couple of incidents that got to me. One involved seven or eight kids shooting up with speed and then turning on a girl in the group and killing her like a pack of dogs." The hearings were set for October 1969.

Prior to going there, the Committee subpoenaed the records of all the drug companies that distributed amphetamines in the West and Southwest, where the problem of amphetamine abuse was known to be greatest. It was an attempt to determine if any correlation existed between the amount of drugs going into this region and the abuse of the drug. Smith Kline & French, Abbott Labs, Eli Lilly, and many smaller houses all submitted their records as was required under the DACA law. But as also required under that law, the records did not have to be segregated. The committee staff ended up with boxes and boxes of invoices. Amphetamine shipment records were mixed among cotton and aspirin records and every other product the company made. Often the drugs appeared with other items on the same invoices, some of them being six pages long. Every page had to be examined in order to find what could turn out to be only one entry for a few hundred amphetamines. And these were only the records of the wholesalers and manufacturers. Julian Granger, Arnold Shulman and Deb Hastings of the committee staff, along with three staff people assigned from the Government Accounting Office (an investigative agency responsible to the Congress) worked full-time for four or five weeks to sort out the amphetamine shipments. "It was an impossible task really," Reida recalls. "Here we were, working full-time with a lot of people, and we didn't even finish going through all the records. You can imagine one FDA inspector out there in the field going through that. As far as I'm concerned, that 1965 law was inoperable."

But what did become obvious from the records was that a disproportionate number of amphetamines were being shipped into the West and Southwest by the drug companies. One small company, Bates Labs in Chicago, had shipped

1.5 million amphetamine pills in a period of eight months to a drug distributor in Tijuana. The Crime Committee, with assistance from BNDD, investigated and found that no such drug distributor, warehouse, or drugstore existed at that address. If taken literally, the address to which Bates was sending all those amphetamines was the eleventh hole of the Tijuana Country Club golf course. Obviously they were falling into the hands of the black market for illegal sales. BNDD intercepted a shipment and Bates Labs was confronted with the evidence. Because the laws were unclear, it was questionable whether Bates Labs had even broken the law. If they had, the maximum penalty would have been a $1,000 fine for each count of sending the pills to unauthorized persons. Bates Labs was not charged with anything but the company later told the Crime Committee that it was ceasing its amphetamine production.

The year 1968 had been called the "year of speed" and many sensational incidents captured national headlines. Linda Fitzpatrick, the daughter of a wealthy, suburban Connecticut family, and her friend Groovy were found dead, their heads smashed in a basement in the East Village of New York. They ran with the "speed" crowd. Charles Whitman, the sniper who killed fifteen people and wounded twenty-nine others from his perch atop the University of Texas tower in 1966, was later discovered to have been an amphetamine user. The rock group "Canned Heat" recorded a popular song called "Amphetamine Annie" which told of the physical decline and paranoia of an amphetamine user. Alan Christie Wilson, a co-founder of the group and a collaborator on that song, died in September 1970 at the age of twenty-seven from a barbiturate overdose. Speed had changed a movement of flower children in Haight-Ashbury in San Francisco into a vicious subculture perpetually on the knife-edge of violence. Many of the flower children fled. A young amphetamine user named Susan describes her experience: "I got extremely violent," she remembers. "I had all kinds of hallucinations—spiders, bugs, and one time I thought everything had been changed around in my room on me." Now twenty-two, thin, almost frail, with short red hair and a delicate, freckled face, Susan remembers walking through the East Village with a knife in her boot. "If I had to get the drugs I would. I would even get my knife out and go at people with it, for no reason. These people were just walking along the street but I thought they were coming at me. I went on to other drugs, heroin for one. Heroin I had to have but the thing I wanted most was speed. I have never wanted anything in my life so badly."

Susan was the product of a comfortable suburban home. Her drug habit began with her mother's barbiturate supply in the family medicine cabinet. She soon began gulping them down. She took up with a boy friend at a military base who could replenish her barbiturate supply by stealing them from the base. She traded him sex for barbs. She split from her family, slid into a full drug habit and drifted into the drug subculture. Somehow, in the desperation of her experience, she lifted herself out and has spent a long while at a drug rehabilitation center outside Washington, D.C. Her only drug habit now is smoking. She has still not reconciled with her family. Her days and nights of speed runs and paranoia are ended but bitter memories linger: "I have friends who are in mental hospitals now because of speed," she says. "They'll never be the same. It's a crime what it did to them. I mean a crime."

The drug subculture alerted itself to the hazards of speed. From the East Village to Haight-Ashbury the slogans "Speed Kills" and "Meth is Death" appeared on posters and in underground papers. The poet Allen Ginsberg also issued a warning in his "Declaration Against the Use of Speed." Some young people in the underground at least were showing more concern over the hazards than the drug industry. Abuse spread. A national survey in 1966–67 of 1,314 college students revealed a third of them experimented with amphetamines, and on all but one campus students who admitted using amphetamines outnumbered those who used marihuana. In San Mateo County near San Francisco, a survey of high school students in 1969 showed 20.8 percent of them experimented with amphetamines, an increase of more than 4 percent over the previous year. At the time of the Crime Committee hearing, the California Rehabilitation Center in Coronado published a report saying 4,000 people in the San Francisco area were shooting speed regularly. All patients at that center reported having begun with legal pills. This is part of what Claude Pepper's Crime Committee began looking into.

There were disputes within the Committee. Albert Watson, the South Carolina Republican described by one staff member as being "a political Neanderthal," wanted to jump on drug users and crime in the streets, and ignore virtually everything else—including the drug industry's role in the crisis. Another staff dispute threatened to seriously undercut the San Francisco hearings. Pepper had brought in Joseph Nellis, a participant in the Kefauver crime investigations of the early 1950s, to act as special counsel. Nellis, who was in private practice, had known Pepper for a number of years. In organizing the West Coast hearings Nellis and Chief Counsel Kurrus argued over who was running the show. Pepper intervened but did not fully settle the dispute. Each man finally went his separate way and concentrated on a different area for the hearing but the antagonism between them did not subside.

The hearings began on October 23 in a large, richly paneled room of the Federal Office Building in San Francisco. The room was often packed with onlookers who sometimes had to be quieted by the marshals during the hearing. The Committee heard what at first seemed to be a replay of the Dodd hearings a few years earlier but multiplied in intensity by ten. Everything was worse. The 1965 DACA law

obviously did nothing to stem the problem. California Lieu-
tenant Governor Ed Reinecke described to the Crime Committee a rap session he had had with a group of teen-agers.
"They told me it was easier—much easier—for them to buy
speed than beer. The reason was simple," Reinecke said.
"There are such great quantities of all kinds of vicious,
dangerous drugs made by bona fide manufacturers and in
backroom laboratories. The availability of amphetamines,
desoxyephedrine, and barbiturates is not the fault of law
enforcement. Local, state, and federal agents and the police
are doing a masterful job in apprehending the users. Our
problem lies with the lack of control on the distribution of
both dangerous drugs and the chemical components of synthetic drugs." Reinecke asked for "badly needed new federal
regulations" to stop the explosion in juvenile drug arrests.
He noted an increase of 175 percent in these arrests in 1968
over 1967, and the projections were for a doubling of the
number of arrests in 1969 over 1968. Reinecke assured the
Committee he was "no foe" of private industry or of the
drug manufacturers but he was demanding tighter control
over virtually every phase of dangerous drug distribution. He
mentioned that drug shipments to Mexico were well in excess
of what could be legitimately needed in that country, and
said if a national quota on amphetamines could be set for
Mexico, one could be set for this country. To set production
limits on legally produced, non-narcotic drugs was a radical
notion in the drug industry's thinking, and it was beginning
to develop a keen interest in the hearings. A number of the
companies' Washington lobbyists appeared in the hearing
room to take it all in and quietly prepare a defense for when
they got back in Washington.

Amphetamine distribution records proved beyond a doubt
that a disproportionate number of legal amphetamines were
going into the West and Southwest, so they became the basis
for the questioning of company representatives. Smith Kline
& French (whose sales in 1969 of about $20 to $25 million

for its amphetamine product line made it the largest amphetamine producer in the country), sent as its emissary
Donald K. Fletcher, a former Texas state policeman who
had been hired by Smith Kline & French in 1961. A friendly,
pleasant man, large and stocky with long sideburns and a
crewcut, Fletcher looked like a football guard. Fletcher's
role at Smith Kline & French was and still is a dual one.
His title of manager of distribution protection suggests he is
charged with monitoring Smith Kline & French products in
the distribution chain but his more important role is public
relations, "the house narc," as he has been described. "He
was hired as congressional pressure was beginning to build to
control amphetamines," a former Smith Kline & French
executive said. "Fletcher was to keep the heat off." Fletcher's
role involves more than the cultivation and placation of
government inquisitors such as the Crime Committee. It is
also up to him to cultivate and placate local and state police
authorities. He has become a police lobbyist of sorts. He
visits police, bringing along a supply of Smith Kline & French
pamphlets on the drug abuse problem. Under his direction
Smith Kline & French set up a police laboratory—since disbanded—to aid police in drug identification. He speaks at
schools and colleges about drug abuse, but his major contact
has been with police, and over the years he has built up a
considerable constituency among the local drug enforcement
authorities. After all, he is one of them. He makes personal
visits and by his presence convinces the police of his company's good intentions. He stages police seminars and drug
enforcement symposiums and has generally worked himself
into the good graces of many local authorities. Why? A BNDD
lawyer acquainted with Fletcher's operation once said of it:
"It worked a lot of different ways. If there were any question
about Smith Kline & French products getting diverted or
abused, the police chief would say it was the kids making
the stuff that was the problem, not the drug company. Don
Fletcher is his friend and he won't tell on his friend."

Fletcher works out of the home office in Philadelphia and puffs with pride about the company's quality control and the care with which Smith Kline & French products are manufactured. As Fletcher explains it, he came to Smith Kline & French "to provide the industry with expertise in the drug abuse problem." During his years as a Texas state policeman he experienced firsthand some of the law enforcement problems, he says. Smith Kline & French has about 200 drug distributors of its own and another 200 are served through a major wholesaler, McKesson-Robbins. Smith Kline & French closely monitors the drug distribution system, Fletcher says, and follows up reports that its drugs have been seized in the black market. Fletcher claims Smith Kline & French has suffered through the years because Benzedrine and Dexedrine have become almost generic names for all amphetamines in general. In a seizure, amphetamines are simply called "bennies," he says, and Smith Kline & French is made to look bad. Neither Fletcher nor the other people who run Smith Kline & French and the other major drug companies are greedy, venal, nor insensitive people intent on undermining the nation's health. But they are smart and successful businessmen and therein lies the conflict. Good business can often result in bad medicine. They make profits from the sales of drugs. The more sales, the more profits and the more secure their jobs, the better off the company, and the happier the stockholders. It is the business cycle. When under scrutiny from the federal government they fight back to avoid losing the competitive edge. The vast majority of the diversions occurred beyond the immediate control of the company, and by then the company had already made its profit. But what actually created diversion was the massive overproduction of the drugs. The production came from many companies—large and small—and it created a situation where legitimate medical needs could not absorb all the pills. So illegitimate needs did. Public health ran a distant second place against the urge to protect the company's position in the industry. This was the case for virtually all of the major manufacturers of mood drugs.

Fletcher's policing duties at Smith Kline & French are elusive. He has nothing to do with plant security nor does he check on wholesalers to determine their legitimacy. His job seems almost exclusively to make friends with police and project Smith Kline & French's image of having an interest in public welfare by speaking out against drug abuse. Recites Fletcher: "Do I attempt to project my company in a favorable light? Sure I do. But do I go into enforcement and education? Sure I do. If that's a public relations (PR) effort when you speak well of your company, fine. Then I'm glad to be considered a PR man." Fletcher denies that amphetamines are the major drug problem. "Alcohol is," he says, and adds that his company has done all it can to prevent the abuse of amphetamines.

A member of a competing drug company, but not a producer of amphetamines, says of Fletcher's role: "I really think Fletcher's work helped delay tight controls on amphetamines for a number of years."

Fletcher sat before the Crime Committee in October 1969 and testified on behalf of Smith Kline & French. He said Smith Kline & French is one of the ten largest prescription drug houses in the country, and employs more than 9,000 people worldwide. About 5,600 of the employees work in the U.S. company. Smith Kline & French owns and operates twenty-two foreign subsidiaries, including an amphetamine-producing plant in Mexico City. He told the Crime Committee he had personally conducted an investigation along the Mexican-U.S. border to determine the amount of Smith Kline & French pills falling into the black market. His conclusion: "Although I found the Smith Kline & French product was almost never seen in the illicit market, it was possible to have a *few bottles* coming out of drugstores back into California and Texas." [Author's italics]

This directly contradicted certain testimony heard a few

days earlier by the Pepper committee from an admitted drug peddler, who told of a specific purchase in Mexico of 300,000 Benzedrine tablets (a Smith Kline & French amphetamine) for illegal sale in the U.S. The peddler also told of the ease with which these pills could be smuggled into the United States for illegal sale. At first Fletcher denied the pills could have been Smith Kline & French products. He was then told by Joseph Nellis, the special counsel who interrogated Fletcher, that the BNDD reported that as of June 30, 1969, it had seized several large amounts of Dexedrine, Benzedrine, Dexamyl, and Dexamyl No. 2—all Smith Kline & French amphetamine products—at the Mexican-U.S. border. Fletcher thanked Nellis and the Committee for supplying him with that information and again suggested he or anybody else could go to Mexico to buy a "few bottles" of pills made by Smith Kline & French or anyone else.

In his low, husky voice, Nellis asked about the big gap in the pill-to-people ratio, which demonstrated graphically that people in Southern California were gulping more pills per person than people in other regions. In an eighteen-month period the committee found that people in Arizona, Nevada, and Southern California were shipped twice as many pills per person as people in Texas. This was from statistics of only three firms, Smith Kline & French among them. Did this suggest something to Smith Kline & French? Nellis displayed a chart prepared by the Crime Committee staff showing this disproportionate pill-per-person ratio and then asked: "Now, do you have any thoughts as to the nature of production or overproduction? Why are we producing so many millions of these dangerous substances? It appears to us, at least, so many millions more than the consumer can possibly use. Would you address yourself to that?"

"I would be very happy to address myself to this point as best as possible," Fletcher answered. He contended again that Smith Kline & French products were only minimally represented in drug seizures and the illegal market. His public relations efforts began to show signs of strain.

Nellis persisted: "Is there some special reason, then, why in the Southern California area contiguous to the Mexican border, and I make no invidious inference whatever, why the ratio is almost twice—in fact it *is* just about twice—what it is in Texas?"

Fletcher responded: "You know, I really do not know. All I do know is that we are using here figures of January 1, 1968, to June 30, 1968." Then he explained lamely that one "can never be sure how a market does fluctuate."

Nellis came to another instance where the drug company's suspicion should have been aroused. In Monterrey, Mexico, located about 150 miles south of the u.s. border and having a population of less than one million, were located seven drug wholesalers. Fletcher was asked about Smith Kline & French's business there because the charts showed that Smith Kline & French and other companies shipped nearly four times as many pills—both barbiturates and amphetamines—as there were people. Fletcher, who apparently does not think well on his feet, said he had not examined that city's drug shipments for the hearing because it was so far inland and was not considered a border town. Therefore, he said, he could not "come up with an explanation." In other words, "Give us time, we'll think of something."

The Crime Committee had also examined the records of the Eli Lilly International Corporation. Lilly is based in Indianapolis and is the country's largest marketer of barbiturates. William Clutter, a Lilly vice-president, was questioned by Nellis and members of the Crime Committee. Pepper, Waldie, Watson, Wiggins and Denney, all committee members, were there. Clutter contended that antitrust laws actually prohibited Lilly or any other drug company from refusing to sell to a wholesaler as long as his sales were "legal." Said Clutter: "The Sherman Act provides that it is illegal to enter into any combination or conspiracy or agreement of any kind to limit the sales of the product to another person." The industry knew the antitrust law well, since many of their sales and licensing agreements between one another had repeatedly violated it. But Clutter now gave a self-serving interpretation of it by saying, in effect, that if Lilly or any other company was suspicious of the legality or motives of one of its wholesalers but could not prove it was not properly safeguarding its supply of drugs, Lilly could not stop selling to the wholesaler. The company would be helpless; it could not violate the antitrust laws. Lawyers on the Crime Committee thought this was stretching the interpretation of the antitrust law beyond its intended limits, and they agreed unanimously that, faced with such a critical problem as drug abuse, Eli Lilly or any other company could have easily obtained an antitrust waiver from the Justice Department to allow it to halt sales to a suspect wholesaler. "The Crime Committee would have even interceded with the attorney general to get the waiver," says one committee counsel, "and there would have been no difficulty getting it." They had no industry takers.

The attitude expressed by Smith Kline & French and Eli Lilly, when stripped of its qualifiers, was that the responsibility of the drug companies ends with the "legal" sale at the loading docks. Once the pills were sold to a distributor or a private doctor the profit was assured and the responsibility ended. Fletcher talked of Smith Kline & French's efforts to track down diversion of its drugs, but somehow he alone among drug investigators seemed unable to find Smith Kline & French drugs in the black market. The Committee also heard from illicit manufacturers, many of whom were supplied their chemicals from legitimate chemical manufacturers. The barbiturate problem was not as widespread or as serious, the Committee determined, and there was the added consideration that barbiturates have a far wider range of legitimate medical uses than do amphetamines. Minority Counsel Reida, whose instinctive dislike of federal control over private industry was being sorely tested, was troubled by the idea that it had been up to the Crime Committee to point out to the drug companies the disproportionate number of their pills which were flooding Southern California. "Shouldn't the astronomical per capita pill consumption have put them on notice that something was happening in these areas? Why was it that someone else always has to put them on notice and point out the problem to them?" The Committee would now move to put the brakes on the flow of speed. Nothing could stop the problem because it was completely beyond control; but something could be done to lessen its wide impact and Reida would take a prominent role.

16: More Evidence Mounts on Amphetamines

The law will become a laughingstock.
DR. LEO HOLLISTER, A DRUG RESEARCHER

AFTER the October hearing in San Francisco the Crime Committee scheduled a one-day hearing in Washington. Although the Committee was having problems stirring up press interest, the drug industry was very alert to its activities. At one point, Joseph Nellis, the Committee's special counsel who questioned many industry witnesses in the hearing, received a call from an old friend and former college classmate, who was now a vice-president for a major amphetamine manufacturer. "This man is still a friend of mine and I don't want to identify him in any way. I simply don't want to jeopardize his livelihood," Nellis explains. "He called me at my home one night after the hearings and he told me I was making a lot of needless enemies. He implied that I wouldn't get any drug industry business in my private law practice. I played along and kept saying I really didn't understand why he was calling because he was speaking in such an indirect way. I told him if there were any falsities at the hearing I would be glad to rectify them. I never had any drug industry business before or since so there was no problem there. I never had another call from him."

On November 19, 1969, the Crime Committee held its Washington hearing. By this time Dodd had already concluded his drug bill hearings in the Senate and was ushering his bill through his Subcommittee and the Judiciary Committee. On the House side, Pepper had invited several recognized medical experts to testify on the legitimate medical uses of amphetamines. The industry was then making the solid claim that amphetamines were useful for at least eleven major medical uses:

1) Weight control
2) Narcolepsy
3) Treatment of mild depression
4) Hyperkinetic disorders in children
5) Treatment of Parkinson's disease
6) Prevention and treatment of surgical shock
7) Relief from fatigue in individuals with deteriorated psychomotor performance
8) Enhancement of action of pain-killing drugs
9) Antagonism of the actions of depressant drugs (e.g., barbiturates and alcohol)
10) Inducement of insomnia and counteraction of fatigue in persons occasionally required to perform mental or physical tasks of long duration.
11) Maintenance of blood pressure during surgery.

This was a far lower number than the thirty-nine uses concocted a few years earlier, but many responsible doctors even regarded several of these eleven uses as questionable and some as an outright danger to a patient's well-being. Amphetamines had been cautioned against thirty years earlier for relief of fatigue, and their use in weight control and depression was coming under heavy criticism. At the hearing, Dr. George Edison, chairman of the board of trustees of the

Community Drug Crisis Center at the University of Utah, told the Pepper committee: "Amphetamines provide one of the major ironies of the whole field of drug abuse. We continue to insist that they are good drugs when used under medical supervision but their greatest use turns out to be frivolous, illegal, and highly destructive to the user." Dr. Edison remarked that no abused drug has as "wide a spectrum of hazards" as does amphetamine, and he then pointed out another irony. "The interesting thing," he said, "is that in the last ten years the quantity of these drugs [being] produced and consumed has proliferated, while the list of legitimate medical indications has shrunk. In my opinion, and in the opinion of a number of other physicians, the list of legitimate indications has now shrunk virtually to zero."

A major reason for the shrinking number of uses, Dr. Edison explained, has been the advent of better drugs for many of the cases in which amphetamines had previously been used. They are not only ineffective in weight control but are "quite unsafe" because of their addictive potential. Ritalin, the amphetamine-type stimulant, was most often prescribed for hyperkinetic children and in fact even today about half of Ritalin's $13 million in u.s. sales is for hyperkinesis. This use of amphetamines, however, was then and still is coming in for serious questioning. Hyperkinetic children are compulsively active in school. They are disruptive and often unteachable although they are usually of normal or above normal intelligence. Rather than pepping up such children even more, stimulants were observed as early as 1937 to create a "paradoxical" or calming effect. As other uses of amphetamines declined, this one picked up and was promoted by the drug industry. No one seems to be able to adequately describe the cause of hyperkinesis; only its effect is evident. Often no abnormal finding of any kind can be detected by doctors, a fact which has led to the strong suspicion that hyperkinesis is more often than not a social problem defined by exasperated teachers and school

principals. The child may be bored or come from an unhappy home, and so becomes disruptive in school. Some
children seem to operate better with the drug. But some
young children develop a dependence on it or become ter-
ribly disturbed. One eight-year-old child on fifteen milligrams of Dexedrine a day began hallucinating and developed
feelings of persecution. A Canadian study revealed a two-
and-a-half-year-old child on the drug who was so severely
disturbed he "screamed for several hours until he fell asleep,
exhausted." The most impartial experiments, done without
the researcher's knowledge of which child was getting what
pill, have shown in many cases it was not the effect of the
amphetamine but rather the *expectation* of the drug's effect
that seemed to calm the child in his own eyes and in the
eyes of his teacher. Placebos were mixed with the real drug
and teachers noted improvement in 88 percent of the children treated with Ritalin. But they also said 67 percent of
the children given placebos improved. Today some 300,000
children between the ages of five and twelve are receiving
"behavior modification" drugs. The message is clear: if the
child is unhappy or disruptive, don't seek the source of the
problem either in the home or in the school; just try to
change the child's behavior with drugs.

The Crime Committee wanted to find out how many
amphetamines we were producing, and how many the country needed for medical purposes. Claude Pepper called on
Dr. Sidney Cohen, the director of the division of narcotic
addiction and drug abuse for the National Institute of
Mental Health, who said the pills were useful in the "rare
instances" of narcolepsy, a rare sleeping disorder, and the
truly hyperkinetic child. The number of pills actually needed,
then, would be "in the thousands," Cohen said.

Pepper asked how many were being produced in 1969.
Between eight and ten *billion* answered Cohen. The Committee had done some figuring on its own. By calculating
the amount of bulk material produced, adding the exports

and including Ritalin and Preludin, it calculated also that eight billion were produced—that is, an overproduction of about seven and a half billion.

Another key witness was Dr. John Griffith, the same Dr. Griffith who reported on the underground amphetamine traffic in Oklahoma City in 1963. An assistant professor of psychiatry at Vanderbilt University when he testified, Griffith is outspoken by the standards of reticence in his profession. His expertise in amphetamines is unquestionable. He dismissed the need for amphetamines for obesity, saying the hazards far outweigh the benefits. He calculated 8 percent of the prescriptions written in the country were for amphetamines, and that probably about nine million adults in this country had become exposed to amphetamines. "Addiction to amphetamines also occurs," Dr. Griffith said. "The older medical literature suggested that this was not so; however, direct observations of amphetamine addicts now make it clear that amphetamine addiction is *more* widespread, *more* incapacitating, *more* dangerous and socially disrupting than narcotic addiction." He estimated that drug houses often realize very small profits from each pill. "Because of this small profit margin," he said, "companies simply cannot afford to scrutinize their sales."

Dr. Griffith went on to talk about his personal experience with the drug. "It is easy to dismiss the amphetamine addict as a criminal or useless derelict of society. The Committee should recognize, however, that many were once useful professional people of great promise. For example, the first case I observed—1960—was a young psychiatrist who had been confined in a locked ward. The second, an award-winning Air Force tanker pilot."

Another witness spoke. Dr. David Lewis, a young doctor at Harvard Medical School, said his surveys of speed-users revealed that 90 percent of them began with legitimately produced oral pills found in their home medicine cabinets.

Should amphetamines be banned? Dr. Griffith said the

amphetamine-barbiturate and amphetamine-tranquilizer combination drugs should be. They have no place in medicine, he said. But the real message the doctors communicated to the Committee was the urgent need to do something about it—control them more efficiently and bring the production more in line with the need.

The Crime Committee was its own victim. There was no medical doctor on the staff and because the emphasis had been on "speed," the predominant feeling among the committee members was that the banning of speed would go a long way toward solving the amphetamine problem. The Committee believed, partly due to drug industry propaganda which spoke of speed as some alien chemical, and partly due to the words of witnesses in San Francisco, that speed meant just methamphetamine shot up by needle. This is the most potent form of amphetamine and it was what the kids were shooting up during that time. Pepper and some committee co-sponsors drafted the chief bill, which called for tighter restrictions on amphetamines and a complete ban on methamphetamines. It also put tight restrictions on the chemical precursors of methamphetamine in order to hold down clandestine laboratories, and hopefully would cut down on the enormous diversion of amphetamines—still amounting to billions annually. In December of 1969 the bill was submitted and was referred to the Subcommittee on Public Health. The Crime Committee was undergoing some internal upheavals at that time. Richard Kurrus, the chief counsel, resigned. He was annoyed at what he regarded as Nellis' intrusion during the San Francisco investigation and Pepper's unwillingness to solve it. He also had a major case pending in his private law firm which he felt obliged to handle. Shortly after, Nellis also left to return to his private law practice. Minority Counsel Reida became the glue holding the Committee together.

Reida and other members of the Committee and staff continued to immerse themselves in amphetamine studies and to examine alternative legislative approaches. They invited drug industry representatives to submit proposals for ending the street abuse of amphetamines. So, in late 1969 and early 1970 there were several meetings between members of the Pharmaceutical Manufacturers Association and the Committee. Bruce Brennan, PMA vice-president and general counsel, visited the Committee with lobbyists from Eli Lilly and Smith Kline & French in tow. They all gave the appearance of full cooperation. None of them opposed the ban on methamphetamines. They told the staff they were amazed at the high diversion rate of the drugs and pledged to help solve it. The companies and PMA then came up with their own suggestions to plug the very same loopholes which they had put there in the first place. "They appeared to want to help," Reida recalls. "I was a bit cynical, about half cynical and half believer. I'd been on the Hill for a while and had dealt with lobbyists before." While the drug lobby was stalling on coming up with a draft bill to stem amphetamine diversion, the Crime Committee staff was reaching the correct conclusion that banning methamphetamine would not end speed abuse since an addict would switch to another amphetamine if he could not get meth. Finally, at the end of February, the industry submitted a draft bill to the Committee with the promise that it would end diversion. But the bill was unworkable; it left power in the hands of state pharmacy boards and local authorities, the same agencies who openly admitted they were unable to cope with diversion.

The Committee's bill to ban methamphetamine was still pending and Pepper was scheduled to testify before the Public Health and Welfare Subcommittee in support of it. Just before that was to happen, Reida was approached by Mike Sichel, the Washington lobbyist for Abbott Laboratories, the country's largest manufacturer of methamphetamine, a product then worth about $7.6 million a year in sales to

Abbott. It was sold under the trade names Desoxyn and Desbutal. The methamphetamine ban would stop Abbott's products completely. Sichel is a pragmatic man and rather frank as lobbyists go. He argued with Reida that banning methamphetamine would not solve the problem of speed abuse because users could turn to any other amphetamine. Besides, banning methamphetamine was discrimination against one company when the responsibility was with many. Actually, Reida had already changed his mind on the ban since the bill had been submitted. "I had come to the conclusion that all of the amphetamines were equally as bad. It's just that meth happened to be the drug of choice and is easy to make in clandestine labs. But if you dried that up the users would go to something else. With Pepper's authorization I went to Jesse Steinfeld, the surgeon general, and put this to him. He said he could not go so far as to say all amphetamines were equally as bad but he did write a letter to the effect that methamphetamine and dextroamphetamine had the same potential for abuse. We were in a real bind because Pepper was scheduled to testify before the Health Subcommittee at ten o'clock the next morning on our bill to ban meth." Sichel wanted badly to see Pepper to explain Abbott Labs' case, and Reida arranged a meeting the next morning at nine. In the meantime, Reida had gotten the letter from Dr. Steinfeld to show to Pepper in order to convince him to drop the ban on methamphetamine. The meeting occurred, and Sichel made an offer. If Pepper dropped the ban, Abbott in turn promised to give full support to the Crime Committee in getting tight but equal controls on all amphetamines. Pepper mulled it over, asked a few questions, and finally accepted it. As Pepper said later, "it was a reasonable offer and a fair one." Pepper did not act out of kindness to Abbott. The drug lobby is a tough and usually united group and is rarely split. The opportunity to divide and conquer was rarely available. "It would give the

Crime Committee a better chance at putting all ampheta-mines under tighter restrictions, which was now our objec-tive," Reida said of the Abbott Labs offer.

"After talking with Sichel and Abbott," Reida recalled later, "it became clear to me why these other companies were not fighting us on our methamphetamine ban. Smith Kline & French was selling millions of dollars a year of its amphetamine products and they had nothing to lose and much to gain if meth were banned. They would hurt a competitor and help themselves." Besides Smith Kline & French, which is both a bulk and a pill producer, many other companies stood to gain from the meth ban.

Pepper came before the Public Health and Welfare Sub-committee only moments after leaving Sichel in his office and accepting the offer of support from Abbott Laboratories. Pepper's bill which was co-sponsored by three other com-mittee members, called for strict production quotas on all amphetamines, strict and separate record-keeping, a pre-scription refill limit of three in three months, licensing of all manufacturers and dispensers of amphetamine, and a flat ban on methamphetamine. Other members of the Crime Committee had also submitted bills. Congressmen Denney and Wiggins had drafted versions which did not seek the meth ban.

John Jarman, a Democrat from Oklahoma, was the chair-man of the Subcommittee, but Paul Rogers, a far more forceful personality, presided that morning. He has since become the chairman. Rogers and Pepper are both from Florida but that is where the similarities end. Pepper is a staunch liberal; his clothes usually look rumpled on his short, squat body; he believes the House is his foster home and he feels out of place there. The Senate is his real home. Pepper is a crusader, a fighter in many doomed causes, whereas Rogers prefers the sure thing; he is a man of quick and decisive gestures and statements. He is very conservative and his political instincts are with business and industry. In

1969 he won a 94 percent rating from the Americans for Constitutional Action, a conservative political group. Rogers is tall and has distinguished gray temples; he strides purposefully through the corridors of the House, where he is a recognized power. He is from West Palm Beach and has held his seat in Congress since 1955 when his father, who was the district's congressman, died suddenly and Rogers won in a special election. Since then he has emerged as the single most influential man in Congress on matters of health. Rogers and Pepper do not especially like one another.

Rogers' subcommittee had before it that day the Administration drug bill, which President Nixon had sent to Congress in July of 1969 and which Dodd had considered along with his own bill in his Senate hearings. Pepper hoped to attach his bill to it or get the contents of his bill into the law. Rogers introduced Pepper as his "good friend and colleague," and so Pepper began. First, he recited many of the amphetamine abuse findings of his Crime Committee. He then told Rogers that he wanted to modify part of his statement and withdrew his call for a ban on methamphetamine in favor of tighter restrictions on all amphetamines. He mentioned the discussion with Sichel from Abbott Labs and told of Abbott's promise to "take the lead in the enactment and support of legislation which would establish production quotas for all amphetamines."

So Pepper's agreement now passed to the Rogers-Jarman subcommittee. Would they opt for strict controls on all amphetamines, as Pepper requested? In the Administration bill now being considered by the Subcommittee, amphetamines were a schedule three drug; in other words, the same unsuccessful controls that had been employed by the DACA for three years would be continued. The kinds of controls now proposed by the Pepper Committee would place amphetamines in schedule two of that bill, thereby providing controls similar to those for narcotics. The congressional battle over amphetamines would now focus on which schedule they would be placed in and would be highly influenced by how much Abbott Labs would fight to get them all in there.

It was soon apparent that, although Pepper was paid congressional courtesies, his testimony and the Crime Committee's investigation of amphetamines would be disregarded. The real tip-off, as to the attitude of the Rogers-Jarman subcommittee, the group which would hold the real power over the bill in the House, came with the testimony of Donald Fletcher, the Smith Kline & French security manager. A few months earlier he had been reduced to admitting he could not account for the huge amphetamine distribution imbalance in many areas when he was questioned by the Crime Committee. Now he was before a friendly subcommittee, and being accorded a politeness that bordered on obsequiousness. He commented on the present drug bill by saying it was a fine bill with its lack of restrictions on amphetamines, and he told of Smith Kline & French's own all-out efforts to stop drug abuse. Finally he concluded and Chairman Jarman's congratulations rang in his ears: "Certainly Smith Kline & French is to be commended for the constructive and vigorous, and the hard-hitting role that you have played in the fight against drug abuse." That was about as tough as the interrogation ever got. Amphetamines would remain in schedule three as long as the Rogers-Jarman Subcommittee was in charge of the bill. If those controls permitted a few billion pills to be diverted, abused and to destroy lives, so be it. But the question remained: Why was the Rogers-Jarman Subcommittee reluctant to tighten the clamps on amphetamines? One more subtle but very significant factor must be taken into account in understanding the entire picture.

Philip Jehle (pronounced Yalie) is a large, jolly jellyfish of a man who goes laughing and backslapping his way through the corridors, offices and committee rooms of Congress. His dark hair sweeps up in a wave that sits back on a receding hairline. He wears conservative suits and peers through dark-rimmed glasses. Laughter comes easily, and at such times his eyes crinkle up in paroxysms of delight. Jehle appears to be a happy man. He is also Smith Kline & French's chief Washington lobbyist. Smith Kline & French had a $20 to $25 million investment in amphetamine sales in 1969 and the company intended to protect it against interference by an old crusader like Claude Pepper, with his notions of quotas and licensing and tight prescription limits. Jehle is a lawyer and was until 1959 a staff member of the Senate Select Committee on Small Business, where he gained an intimate knowledge of Capitol Hill and many members of Congress. He later served as the Washington lobbyist for the National Association of Retail Druggists. In 1965, in fact, as their lobbyist he tried unsuccessfully to exempt pharmacists from the record-keeping requirements of the DACA law. He then came to Smith Kline & French and has been diligently protecting the company's corporate interests since then.

Jehle's genius—and as a lobbyist he indeed has a genius— is his warm, gregarious manner coupled with a beautifully tuned and often subtle political instinct. He feels a genuine interest in people, and on Capitol Hill and in the regulatory agencies where he occasionally prowls even his enemies concede that he is a nice guy. He does not wear a black cape or hand out bags of money; he is a friendly persuader, both cuddlesome and cunning at the same time.

Phil Jehle operates on the basis of friendship, his most dependable and salable commodity. He plays golf with the staff members and politicians in Congress and is a member of the congressional golf club. When they go out to dinner together Jehle picks up the tab. Parties are staged, gifts and campaign contributions given. Congressmen come to Jehle's house for dinner. Almost everybody calls him Phil. Ancher Nelsen is a Republican congressman from Minnesota who lives alone and enjoys company. So Jehle invites Nelsen to his house for dinner and a pleasant evening with his family. Ancher Nelsen is a fine and honorable old man who would probably never do anything dishonest. But Phil Jehle is his friend, and helping out a friend isn't dishonest. Nelsen, incidentally, also happens to be the ranking Republican on the Public Health and Welfare Subcommittee (whose name has since been changed to Public Health and Environment), one of the most important subcommittees in Congress as far as the drug industry is concerned.

"I think Phil Jehle is the most effective guy in the whole drug industry on Capitol Hill," says a former Crime Committee staff member. "He's not a fixer or a creep. He's a very good politician. He doesn't come on as some insidious guy. He loves you to death. He's really a people lover and he doesn't just put it on to get a favor—it's really him. He grows on you like a wart. He's so effective because he's not obtrusive. He never tried to put the arm on me or try to sell me in that sense. He comes in and talks to you. He can bullshit about anything, football games, you name it. He's very disarming, and he's also too damn big to throw out of the office. Phil is the soft-sell. He is the perfect lobbyist for the 1970s. Tommy the Cork is good for a lot of the older members but Phil is the best for now." Jehle's mode of operation is simple: make friends with the policy-makers so when they come to making a policy that might affect your company, they won't want to hurt your feelings.

A former staff member of Rogers' Subcommittee says of Jehle: "He is pretty influential with the members because of the kind of person Phil is. I'm no longer on the Hill and where I am I can't do a damn thing for Phil or Smith Kline & French. But Phil sent me a ticket to the superbowl just because he's a nice guy. He had no real reason to do that." No reason? "Well, I may have helped him out by giving him information once in a while." Information is what Jehle often seeks. Where is the bill now? What is the status of the drugs my company makes? Anybody on the subcommittee making any funny noises about tighter controls? Anyone from Pepper's staff over there visiting?

Neither Jehle nor the drug lobby in general surfaces very

often in enemy waters; their methods tend more toward the ulterior: a committee chairman who won't give a hearing on a drug bill, or a floor speech against some regulation of the drug industry from a member of Congress whose constituency is not directly involved. Jehle works through a nucleus of about thirty men on Capitol Hill. They are his friends. Hubert Humphrey, John Sparkman, and Roman Hruska are among his Senate friends; Ancher Nelsen and Paul Rogers are among his key House friends. The wheels of Congress are oiled in many ways and campaign contributions are an important lubricant. Most drug companies and the industry itself favor their friends at election time. Their contributions are often untraceable because they are made in cash, or the Congressman or Senator will ask to have the contribution routed through his party's national committee, which in turn routes it back to him in the party's name. That way no large contribution from one source appears on his campaign finance statement. It makes a sad joke of the campaign disclosure laws.

However, not everyone who comes in contact with Jehle regards him as warm, lovable old Phil. Says a former FDA Commissioner: "Phil Jehle is a very smooth fellow. You have to watch him every step of the way. Phil used to call me. 'Commissioner,' he'd say, 'sure is a beautiful day and it would be a lovely night to take a cruise down the Potomac. Congressman Rogers is going. Wouldn't you like to join us?' Well, I'd just tell Phil that I was very busy and would have to work late. Sorry, can't make it."

Another congressional staff member who knows Jehle mutters that if Jehle ever had a serious drug abuse problem with one of his kids he would know the full consequences of his jolly friendships and his company's hunger for profit.

One of Jehle's closest and most important friends in Congress is Paul Rogers; "Mr. Health," they call him. All major health and drug legislation in Congress will usually find its way to Rogers' Subcommittee. Here is where the lunches, golf dates, and hail-fellow-well-met camaraderie pay off for Jehle and Smith Kline & French—and where the public loses. Jehle and Rogers do not have a simple lobbyist-politician relationship. It is a friendship. And it was this friend whom Jehle visited when Claude Pepper and his Crime Committee were making disquieting noises about putting tight restrictions on amphetamines. Jehle had gone to San Francisco to observe the hearings and had visited the Crime Committee staff. He knew for a long time what they were up to. So he asked Rogers for help. Not only does he have access to Rogers' office, he may even have a key. "You have to understand how it works," says someone privy to the relationship between Jehle and Rogers. "When Pepper was putting in his amphetamine bill Phil just went to Rogers and asked him to help him out. He goes to Rogers as a friend and asks for a hand. Rogers and Pepper don't like one another anyway so Rogers and other subcommittee members who are close to Phil help out. It's nothing dark and mysterious. It's friendship. Sure, there are some campaign contributions along the way that help things out, but Phil is successful because he has cultivated these guys so long that they like him and agree with him. It's that simple." Jehle's technique is the blending of friendship with influence. It is power, but only in the loosest sense. So Jehle works on what is available, and he is a master at it. His friendship becomes influence so subtly that the people he is working on often can't recognize it when it happens to them.

Jehle speaks. His voice flows like oil, warm and reassuring. "I've got five kids myself," he says with a controlled convulsion; "I know what it's like." We're all in this world together, so let's be friends. "I'll tell you one thing," he once said privately, "working for Smith Kline & French has gotten me from a small apartment in southeast Washington to a nice home in Potomac." Laughter follows. It explains a lot about motive. Potomac is one of Washington's plushest suburbs. At lunches with friends and foes alike, Jehle will swap funny stories, exchange tidbits of information, and even tell a funny story about Roman Hruska, the congenial defender of the drug industry. Hruska's impassioned defense of the industry even embarrasses the industry at times, Phil says, and you have to calm Roman down. At a lunch with Benjamin Gordon, the staff economist on Gaylord Nelson's Subcommittee on Monopoly, and a sharp critic of many drug industry practices, Gordon might begin to stare Jehle down. "What happens to a society that indulges itself in so much drug-taking?" Gordon asks, hypothetically of course. Phil gulps a bit. Well, he says, it "weakens the moral fiber." Then he catches himself: "But you'll never see anything of that kind from Smith Kline & French." Jehle pays for the lunch and extracts a couple of small pieces of unimportant information from Gordon. It makes the lunch a worthwhile investment for Jehle.

What about all those amphetamines pumping out of Smith Kline & French and other companies? Jehle brushes aside the eight *billion* figure given by the Pepper committee as being a wild exaggeration. The figure, he explains, is closer to three and a half or four billion. "You're going to hear that we (Smith Kline & French) opposed Pepper. Well, we plead guilty to that," Jehle says. The reason was not self-interest, Jehle explains. "Why, they never held legislative hearings. If Pepper had really wanted that amphetamine amendment he should have gone to Paul Rogers and talked with him." But Pepper did talk with Paul Rogers and he did want to tighten control of amphetamines, Gordon argues. Well, Jehle explains, the Pepper hearings "did not justify" the tight restrictions he was demanding. "Our drugs were not abused. Dexedrine and other drugs were not falling into illegal hands. I'm proud of what we've done. Remember, we spearheaded the 1965 law." Lightning does not strike.

Jehle is very circumspect about his relationships with men in Congress. "I've survived in this town for a long time by keeping my mouth shut," he says. He claims he doesn't have influence; he merely talks with the members of Congress, presents his company's side, and prays to God they will listen to him.

Paul Rogers is equally tight-lipped. "Oh, I suppose a few of the lobby people visited the Subcommittee. They were around but we didn't pay any attention to those people," he says with a wave of the hand. "We did our own work." Phil Jehle, Rogers suggests, is just one more of those lobbyists who keep coming around to make those transparent, self-serving pitches to which the congressman pays no mind. But why, it can be argued, with the documentation compiled against them, were amphetamines not tightly controlled when the Subcommittee was considering the drug bill? "The Administration opposed it and our medical people who testified felt they should be in schedule three, not schedule two," Rogers says. But many medical experts wanted them tightly controlled in schedule two in light of overwhelming evidence of their hazards and abuse. "Well," Mr. Health explains, "you can always find a few who will disagree." One searches for Rogers' "medical people." Even the AMA, no bellwether in recognizing the hazards of amphetamines, seriously questioned the placement of amphetamines in schedule three instead of two in its testimony before Rogers. Another of the "medical people" Rogers must have forgotten was Dr. Leo Hollister. A recognized drug expert and associate chief of staff at the Veterans' Administration Hospital in Palo Alto, California, Dr. Hollister spoke about the scheduling arrangements in the bill, saying that amphetamines should be controlled in schedule two of the law. If not, he said in a letter to the Rogers subcommittee, "the law will become a laughingstock." And Phil Jehle alone would be laughing.

17: Amphetamines Escape Again

They have made a choice between protecting the profits of the drug industry and protecting the children of this nation. Their decision to favor the profits over the children is a cruel decision, the consequences of which will be suffered by thousands of our young people.

REPRESENTATIVE JEROME WALDIE

MEMBERS of the Rogers-Jarman Health Subcommittee treated representatives of the drug industry warmly during their hearings. If a prickly question were asked, it was not followed by another prickly question. Peter Kyros, a Maine Democrat, asked Bruce Brennan of the PMA whether television drug advertising should also warn people not to use drugs excessively. "Should we have that kind of self-policing thing from the drug industry?" Kyros wanted to know. Brennan gave this answer:

"I think this is probably not warranted because it would have the additional effect of giving concern to people over very useful commodities. In other words, a physician is telling his patients, 'make sure you take these drugs.' The patient goes home and hears on television you had better watch out if you are taking any drugs. It is a quite different thing from smoking, which is strictly a luxury and a pleasure. There is a very useful side to any medicant and to give people pause as to whether or not they should take that medication, particularly those ones we are talking about, which are only given on prescription, I think the negative effect would outweigh any sociological benefit of keeping people from using drugs."

Kyros did not seem fully satisfied but he pursued his line of questioning only weakly. When he finished he said to the PMA witnesses: "Thank you very much, I appreciate your testimony and candor in here this morning."

The Health Subcommittee completed its hearings on March 3, 1970, and amphetamines remained in schedule three. There was no hope of moving them to schedule two before the bill reached the House floor. Dodd's Senate drug bill contained a similar control of amphetamines. But the Pepper Crime Committee, which conducted the most detailed investigation of amphetamines in the history of Congress, had developed most of its results *after* Dodd's hearings on his omnibus drug bill. The refusal of the Rogers-Jarman Health Subcommittee to put them under strict controls was a blatant disregard for the public health. The House Commerce Committee, which has jurisdiction over the Health Subcommittee and the bill, also did not change the status of amphetamines when it considered the bill. Both were aware of the Crime Committee's evidence and had heard Pepper describe it. Both the Subcommittee and the full Commerce Committee had seen the failure of those same DACA controls which they were now willing to continue. Pepper's Crime Committee had played according to the rules of the House. It investigated a source of crime; it drafted legislation and gave it to the proper legislative committee. But the information and legislation were ignored. The new objective of the Crime Committee now became clear: when the full drug bill reached the House floor for a vote, an amendment would be offered to move amphetamines into schedule two. Then they would be controlled like they should have been for the past decade. But besides having to buck House opposition, an awareness was growing in the spring of 1970 that the Nixon Administration opposed tight amphetamine controls. Some kind of deal apparently had been struck, members of the Crime Committee believed, during all those "conferences" between the industry and the Administration, and the "conferences" were still continuing. "We surmised," Pepper said later, "that the Administration had decided to do nothing that would offend the drug industry."

On April 1 the Crime Committee hired a new chief counsel, Paul Perito, fresh from the U.S. Attorney's Office in the Southern District of New York, where he served as a federal prosecutor. Perito and Minority Counsel Reida together would provide the crucial leadership for the staff and guidance for committee members. The two men are opposites. Perito is a Bostonian and a liberal Democrat. He is always moving—running to a meeting or checking a detail or making a phone call. He was known as the "hyperkinetic kid." Perito is the son of an appliance dealer who had little formal education but who brought his son up to treasure the life of the mind, and indeed, Perito was an exceptional student. He was graduated first in his class from Tufts University, then won a traveling fellowship to Europe, and later returned to enter Harvard Law School, from which he was graduated with honors. A prominent Boston corporate law firm hired him, but he became bored and in a year and a half left to join the U.S. Attorney's office, which selects only the top law school graduates. He served there four years and tried twenty cases, including the prosecution of Roy Cohn, and discovered he wanted to remain in public service.

Reida, by contrast, is the son of an Iowa dairy operator. He is conservative and to his knowledge no one in his family has ever voted for anyone other than a Republican. He entered Iowa State University—light-years away from the Ivy League—to become a dairy operator, only to discover he already knew more about dairies than he could be taught. So he transferred to the University of Iowa where he later entered law school. After graduation, he entered private law practice in Lincoln, Nebraska. Unlike Perito, Reida is very deliberate. He possesses an extraordinary memory with almost total recall of times, events, dates and conversations. Like Perito, he was very successful in private practice but was also very bored. "The idea of buying a big house and two cars just wasn't my idea of living the good life," Reida says. "I believe, as corny as it may sound, that a man is judged by the impact he makes in the time in which he lives. To me the way to make an impact is in politics." He began in politics by working for Congressman Denney in Nebraska and came to Washington as his aide. He later joined the Crime Committee as minority counsel. If either Reida or Perito, then both in their early thirties, had remained in private practice both would undoubtedly be very comfortable, if not wealthy. But neither did and neither is.

Both men possess intuitive political instincts but at the time Perito joined the Crime Committee Reida was the teacher and Perito the student in this art. Reida still finds federal regulation "repugnant to my philosophy," but his deepening investigation into amphetamine abuse and the culpability of the drug industry in it steeled him to the belief that both these drugs and the industry demanded closer federal regulation; the industry simply was not policing itself. "I'm sure if you gave Larry [Reida] and me a list of a hundred topics, we'd disagree on ninety-five of them. But on this issue we thought identically," Perito remarked later.

During the spring and summer of 1970 the Crime Committee began its own lobbying to build momentum for its amphetamine amendment when the drug bill reached the House floor. A whip system was set up among Crime Committee members with Pepper, Waldie and Wiggins being the most active. They buttonholed fellow congressmen, gave their side, spoke of the necessity for tight control of amphetamines, and asked for commitments. Sometimes the fellow congressmen requested time to study the question, sometimes they gave commitments. Only about a dozen Republicans favored it but more than a hundred Democrats said they would support it. Meanwhile, the drug companies were working just as diligently in the opposite direction. "Representatives from the drug industry were in my office often," Congressman Waldie remembers, "and I presume in many other congressmen's offices, to persuade us that the science in the field was such that tight controls were not required. They tried to convince us that they had great controls over their drugs and additional government controls were not needed." Larry Reida remembers: "There were a lot of counterarguments. One of them was if you put tight controls on legal amphetamines you would encourage clandestine labs to increase. Our answer was if something is bad, the government can't condone it by allowing it to continue. You move in to try at least to slow it down. If illegal speed labs spring up there are already adequate laws to deal with that. There weren't adequate laws to deal with legal speed. You just can't sit back on something like that and wait for the country's guts to get torn up."

It was evident that the Nixon Administration did not want tighter controls on amphetamines. What was still uncertain was whether this was merely a tactic to assure swifter passage of the drug bill or a commitment to the drug industry. How strongly would the Administration actually resist the Crime Committee's efforts? A letter from BNDD Director Ingersoll was circulated through Congress; it said the amphetamine controls were "under considerable review" by BNDD and the Bureau might place them in schedule two by an administrative procedure *after* the law was passed. This essentially gave any member of Congress an excuse to vote against the Crime Committee's amendment and still appear to favor tough controls. Many members took advantage of it, saying amphetamine controls should be "left up to the experts" at BNDD. As a result, the Crime Committee was seriously undercut. Pepper and the other members of the Committee said in their private arguments with members that the administrative route could take years. Witness how long the meprobamate and Librium and Valium hearings took, they argued. But the real point stressed by the Crime Committee was that amphetamine abuse was a clear and present danger. Why wait even a few months for controls? Congressional action would be immediate and unappealable.

The FDA belatedly in August 1970 recommended amphetamines for only three medical uses: obesity, narcolepsy and hyperkinesis. Although this recommendation was not binding on doctors, it gave additional credence to the Crime Committee's course.

Staff members of the Crime Committee spoke before women's groups, fed information to the press, and encouraged editorials. *U.S. News and World Report,* a conservative newsweekly, ran an article in late December of 1969 entitled: "Two Doctors Warn Against the Abuse of Amphetamines," which excerpted some of the strongest testimony before the Crime Committee. Public awareness was slowly being aroused.

As Chief Counsel Perito became more immersed in amphetamine abuse literature he began to associate the clues to amphetamine addiction and paranoia with the symptoms experienced by a friend of his before his death in January 1969. This friend was Mark Shaw, a well-known New York fashion photographer and also the personal photographer for President Kennedy, whom Shaw had met while on assignment for *Life* magazine in 1960.

"I first met Mark at a party in New York when I was with the U.S. Attorney's office there," Perito remembers. "I have an interest in photography and I remember we talked for quite a while that first meeting. We saw each other from time to time after that and soon we became very close friends. Mark was a beautiful man. Very sensitive, very soft-spoken, and very gentle." Their friendship grew closer and Perito at one time even dated Shaw's ex-wife, actress Pat Suzuki. Although divorced, Shaw and Miss Suzuki maintained a good relationship and saw one another socially. But Perito began to notice a gradual personality change in Shaw that seemed to be worsening. Shaw became suspicious of people and started calling them at all hours of the night to complain about some triviality. "Those last months were very sad," Perito remembers. "Mark had really become paranoid. I tried to help him and told him flat out that he needed psychiatric help but finally it became so bad I had to keep some distance from him because I was then a prosecutor with the u.s. Attorney's office and there could be problems." Perito did not know the causes of Shaw's personality change although in retrospect he now recognizes some hints. "He was going to Dr. Max Jacobson at the time and I found it rather strange that he was seeing him every day, sometimes more than once. He also seemed to hold him in some awe, which I found rather strange. But as he got worse he would say that Jacobson was holding out on him and that he wasn't giving him his medicine," Perito remembers. "It became very bizarre."

On the night of January 26, 1969, Mark Shaw died at his Kips Bay apartment at the age of 47. The cause of death was initially listed as a heart attack. Perito was among the first to be called by Shaw's former wife. "I didn't believe Mark had died of a heart attack at the time. I first suspected it was suicide. But I became convinced as I learned more about amphetamines that Mark had a classic case of amphetamine psychosis. His behavior fit in almost every detail." An autopsy later confirmed Perito's suspicions. Shaw's internal organs were loaded with methamphetamine residue and the cause of death was finally determined to be "acute and chronic intravenous amphetamine poisoning," by a New York medical examiner. This was not made public at the time.

Dr. Jacobson, who was Mark Shaw's doctor, is a highly sophisticated Viennese. His office is located on the fashionable upper East Side of New York. Besides Mark Shaw, he had a large clientele of the famous and powerful. Among his patients were President and Mrs. Kennedy, movie director Cecil B. DeMille, singer Eddie Fisher, playwright Tennessee Williams, writer Truman Capote and, to Perito's surprise, Congressman and Mrs. Claude Pepper. Pepper had been treated for a serious case of eczema by Dr. Jacobson and Mrs. Pepper had also been a patient. They both held him in some awe, as did many of his patients. Based on several conversations Perito had had with Jacobson's New York patients, he had privately come to the conclusion that Jacobson was administering an intravenous amphetamine mixture to his patients, including Mark Shaw. And because of the effects he witnessed on Shaw, Perito developed a strong emotional involvement in the amphetamine investigations. In June of 1970, while the House action on the amphetamine amendment and the drug bill was pending, the Crime Committee held heroin hearings in New York. Without consulting the staff or other committee members Pepper had invited Dr. Jacobson to testify on his alleged heroin cure. He wanted to give a good friend a public platform. Pepper and many of Jacobson's other patients were apparently unaware that he was administering some kind of amphetamine mixture in his treatment. Most assumed he injected his own vitamin mixture into his patients.

When Perito found out Pepper wanted Jacobson to testify before the Crime Committee he was astounded, because Jacobson was not a recognized expert and because of his questionable practices, he argued Pepper into withdrawing the invitation. The night before the final day of the New York hearings, however, Pepper, Mrs. Pepper and Jacobson dined out together, and Pepper left that dinner firmly convinced he should recall the doctor to testify. He phoned Perito at his hotel room late that night to tell him Jacobson would testify. Perito argued that Jacobson had no expertise in heroin treatment and he recalled his experience with Mark Shaw. Why was Pepper inviting this man? Perito demanded.

Finally Pepper said it was irrevocable. Jacobson would appear. Perito told him he would not be responsible for the consequences of Jacobson's appearance and he would inform the members of the Committee of his deep reservations about Jacobson.˙ "I told Claude that was my obligation," Perito says. He phoned the other members that night.

The next day, as scheduled, Jacobson appeared, where he was lauded by Pepper. Several committee members left when the doctor testified. Jacobson was grateful for Pepper's introduction and offered inconsequential testimony.

Two and a half months later, in mid-September, as the House vote on the drug bill was nearing, Perito was in casual conversation with writer Peter Maas of *New York Magazine*. Maas mentioned that another writer, Susan Wood, was about to finish an article on a few New York doctors who injected their patients with amphetamine. She had also compiled a list of some of their famous patients and she would at least imply they had received amphetamine injections. "I really became panicked when I heard that," Perito recalls. "If it came out just before the amendment vote that Claude Pepper might have gotten amphetamine injections it would shatter all the work we had done and probably end our chance for the amendment. I knew Claude had seen Dr. Jacobson and there was no reason for me to think the good doctor had changed his formula. It would have been all the drug companies needed to destroy us." Although Pepper's relationship with Jacobson became public during the heroin hearings, the fact that Jacobson administered doses of amphetamine to some of his patients was not public knowledge. If the link were made, the Crime Committee's amphetamine investigation was probably doomed. Something had to be done.

A meeting was called on the evening of September 16 in Pepper's House office, attended by Perito, Larry Reida and Pepper. Perito and Reida explained the implications of the *New York Magazine* article. Pepper heard them out. Although he was concerned, he did not appear overly worried because he still held the highest respect for Jacobson and could not imagine his having done anything unethical or hazardous to his patients. He also did not believe the doctor shot amphetamine into his patients. Nonetheless, he authorized Perito to go to New York to see what could be done about the *New York Magazine* article. "When I left I thought the article was imminent and I knew if the writer had done her research Claude's name would be mentioned," Perito says. Miss Wood, an excellent reporter and writer, had indeed done her research. She knew Pepper was among Dr. Jacobson's patients and she believed Dr. Jacobson was injecting some patients with amphetamine although she had not established that Pepper had received any such injections. The story was already in galley proofs when Perito arrived; Pepper's name was mentioned in the article. Perito explained: "I said to Susan that if she really wanted to do something about the amphetamine problem I hoped she would not mention Claude by name in the article. This fact, if printed, could ruin our entire investigation and make all the work we'd done meaningless and end any chance at controlling amphetamines. I tried to convince her that one line in her story would not add all that much to it but would really end our work. Susan is a sincere and compassionate journalist, and when I left that day she seemed to lean toward the idea that Claude's name would not appear in the article. She was also worried about some of the libel implications of the article." As it turned out the article did not appear until the following February. It could still have crippled Pepper's amphetamine investigation but his name was omitted. The article referred only to "a congressman." Some names were mentioned but for reasons of libel, the names of the doctors were also omitted and went under the general title of Dr. Feelgood.

Perito returned to Washington after his frenetic trip to New York and his meeting with Susan Wood. The following

Thursday, September 24, only a week after Perito first learned of the magazine article, the drug bill was scheduled to reach the House floor. The lobbying and counter-lobbying on the amphetamine amendment had intensified. It was known to the Crime Committee members that John Dean III, the chief Administration lobbyist, was lobbying against their position. The drug industry was also busy. Representatives from Smith Kline & French, CIBA, makers of Ritalin, and Geigy, makers of Preludin, were lobbying hard. An unsigned memo fell into the hands of a member of the Crime Committee which said the imposition of quotas on amphetamines "would simply stimulate underground production," and it contended the Pepper plan would "create an administrative burden overwhelming in its complexity and prohibitive in cost to both government and industry."

The bill had reached the House floor and the vote would come in the afternoon of September 24. That morning the full Crime Committee met in executive session to plan strategy. The critical decision revolved around what kind of amendment to offer. Reida and Perito reported their findings, as did other staff members and committee members. The general feeling was that a ban on methamphetamines alone would pass, but the chance of a wider amendment covering all the amphetamines was highly doubtful. From a publicity standpoint it was very tempting to settle for the meth ban; the Crime Committee could say it had been responsible for stopping speed. But the Committee knew the only way to control amphetamine abuse was through a quota system on all of them. The source of the problem, overproduction, had to be attacked frontally. Nothing else would succeed. In that spirit, the Crime Committee unanimously decided to go for the full amendment to put all amphetamines, including Ritalin and Preludin, into schedule two of the drug bill. The battle lines were clearly drawn.

Opposing the Crime Committee would be the Nixon Administration, the drug companies, members of the Jarman-

Rogers subcommittee, and the full House Commerce Committee. The prospects were not good. The earlier promise of support from Abbott Laboratories had apparently been forgotten, although Abbott maintained that it still supported the Committee. "A lot of the other drug houses had been leaning on Abbott during the summer and they had been turning a bit mushy on us," Reida recalls. "At the time of the vote we really were not sure what Abbott would do."

As in the Senate, much of the debate on the drug bill revolved around the power balance between BNDD and HEW. A strong lobbying effort by members of the academic and scientific communities had been partially successful in restoring some authority to HEW. The activities of the Crime Committee were not nearly as well-known. Early during the floor discussion of the bill Pepper offered the amendment. Pepper, whose thick Southern accent can at times rise to eloquence, put his argument squarely to the House members and said there should be no delay in getting the amphetamines under a quota system. "Why do we say that, Mr. Chairman and members of the Committee?" he said, speaking directly to Jarman and his Committee, who had control of the bill on the floor; "Because it is undisputed that today the manufacturers of these drugs are turning out eight *billion* of them a year to the people of this country, many of them into the hands, and the bodies, and the brains of the young people of this country. Eight billion! This is the equivalent, assuming our population to be 200 million, of forty of these 'speed' pills a year for every man, woman, and child in the United States." Pepper cited the testimony from his Committee which said 50 percent of these eight billion pills were diverted onto the black market every year.* Pepper then introduced into the record a newspaper article indicating that speed users were turning to heroin as an antidote to bring them down.

---

*Later, more careful estimates suggested the diversion figure was probably closer to 20 percent, still an enormous percentage. It also did not take into account multiple prescription diversions.

Pepper was immediately supported by Congressman Waldie who, along with Congressman Wiggins, had been the stalwart members of the Crime Committee. Opposition surfaced in strange places. In a completely unexpected maneuver, John Kyl, Republican from Iowa, argued against Pepper. Kyl was not a member of the Rogers-Jarman subcommittee nor was he a member of the House Commerce Committee, nor was there a major drug company located in Iowa. Kyl had not been heard from before on the issue. He argued that passage of the Pepper amendment would establish a black market amphetamine trade with an "impure product." It sounded much like the argument in the drug industry memo that had circulated earlier. Kyl went to visual aids. He brought out an exhibit prepared by an unnamed drug company. He said it showed 150 different pills involved in drug abuse, and therefore no law would solve drug abuse. Rather, Kyl said, it was all a matter of individual "psychological problems."

A crucial argument against the Pepper amendment came from Congressman Tim Lee Carter, a member of the Jarman-Rogers subcommittee and a Republican from Kentucky. His opposition was all the more damaging because Carter is a medical doctor and a member of the AMA, and his words on medical issues carry great weight in the House. Carter argued for not restricting Ritalin and Preludin, saying that to include them with amphetamines was a mistake. Carter termed Ritalin a "rather innocuous drug," and said of Preludin: "It is effective and lacks unpleasant side effects." According to him, it was "beyond the realm of reason" to classify these two drugs in schedule two. Carter had offered a complete distortion of the best medical evidence on the dangers of these two drugs. He was responding in part to a well orchestrated letter-writing campaign by parents of hyperkinetic children treated with Ritalin. They wrote that the rescheduling of Ritalin would cause them undue hardship because of the strict curtailment of prescription refills in schedule two. The letters were similar enough to suggest to

Crime Committee members at the time that it was part of a program by CIBA Corporation detail men and their doctor customers. "If the Pepper amendment is adopted, a great hardship would be placed on many individuals," Carter said. Carter threw in one more argument: if the Pepper amendment passed it would mean a total of *6,100* drugs would move into schedule two. Carter wanted all to ponder the immensity and unfairness of that. "Of all the things thrown at us," a member of the Crime Committee later remarked, "I regarded that argument as the only unethical one. It was completely spurious. They counted the same drug if it had different amounts of amphetamines, they threw in drugs that had been off the market for twenty years. Every conceivable drug connected with an amphetamine was included. If you added it all up there'd be a few hundred drugs at most that would be affected by our amendment."

Waldie ranked with Pepper as the most liberal member of the Crime Committee. He sat and listened to much of the debate on the floor and then rose to speak. He mentioned the wide variances in the number of drugs that would be included and then said pointedly, for Dr. Tim Lee Carter to hear: "As a matter of fact, the only opposition to this amendment has come from the manufacturers of amphetamines." Waldie then talked of the hypocrisy of what the House was doing. "In my view, as many of you readily know, the House has responded in some instances to the problem of crime by overreacting. But where the House has acted and acted strongly it has always been in relation to crime on the streets. Now that we are talking about crime that involves a corporation and its profits, that seems to me to be just as difficult a problem for America and ought to receive just as sincere and immediate concern in this House as does the rest of crime in America."

"What Jerry did that day takes a lot of courage," a committee staff member said later. "You don't lightly go before the House of Representatives and tell some of the members they are acting for the drug industry."

Waldie said on the floor that he was "depressed" to find the Nixon Administration opposed to the Pepper amendment. "They have made a choice between protecting the profits of the drug industry and protecting the children of this nation. Their decision to favor the profits over the children is a cruel decision, the consequences of which will be suffered by thousands of our young people."

Paul Rogers stayed in the background for most of the debate; the members of his Subcommittee were doing the job for the drug industry. He said his Committee had "tightened up" the distribution of amphetamines; he didn't explain how. According to him, BNDD should retain the power of decision on amphetamine control and he stated flatly: "The amendment is not needed."

In the House gallery were Phil Jehle of Smith Kline & French and Mike Sichel of Abbott Labs. An unanswered question still lurked: What was Abbott's position? What about the solemn vow of support made to Claude Pepper seven months earlier? Robert McClory, a Republican from the Chicago area, rose to speak against the Pepper amendment. McClory's district includes North Chicago, the home of Abbott Laboratories. McClory made it abundantly clear he was speaking on behalf of Abbott Labs by explaining "there are large pharmaceutical manufacturing interests centered in my congressional district." Into the record McClory inserted an advertisement for Abbott: "Abbott Laboratories has named its campus-like complex of modern structures and open-space land 'Abbott Park.' Abbott's slogan is 'health care worldwide.' " That done, McClory, an amiable man, said he had an "intimate knowledge of the high principles which characterize" the business activities of Abbott. But what about the promise to Pepper? While he congratulated the fine work of the Crime Committee, McClory said: "I have not been able to ascertain that any of Abbott Laboratories' products have found their way into the wrong hands." Then he said: "In our zeal to reduce drug abuse, including abuse of legitimate drugs, it is my hope that we will not impose undue burdens or take punitive and economically unfair steps adversely affecting the highly successful and extremely valuable pharmaceutical industries which contribute so much to the health and welfare of mankind in a great variety of ways." If the speech were not written in the public relations department of Abbott Labs, it could have been. "We asked Abbott about their promised support and they maintained they were being true-blue and iron-bright. When we mentioned McClory's statements they replied this was not a breach of faith by them. This was simply a congressman expressing his own personal views," Reida later recalled.

William Springer, an Illinois Republican and ranking minority member of the House Commerce Committee, argued against Pepper's amendment on what can only be considered jurisdictional grounds. He seemed to be saying that Pepper and the Crime Committee had no right to butt in. The Pepper Committee, said Springer, "has to do with crime. . . . It does not have to do with medicine or any part of medicine." He spoke of the long considerations by the Health Subcommittee and the full Commerce Committee which led to its amphetamine decision. "There is no problem here of economics having to do with any drug industry. If this amendment prevails, it would not have any effect of any consequence upon the drug industry," he said.

The debate drew to a close. Robert Giamo, a Connecticut Democrat, offered a succinct statement supporting Pepper. It was one of the best. Said Giamo: "Why is this gross overproduction necessary, Mr. Chairman? Why are these excesses justified? Why should we allow the legitimate drug manufacturers to indirectly supply the organized criminals and pushers by producing more drugs than are necessary? When profits are made while people suffer, what difference does it make where the profits go?"

Then came the vote. The type of vote on Pepper's amendment would be crucial. The chair called for a voice vote. The nays had it, the chair ruled. The amendment had lost. The Crime Committee wanted to force a record vote, believing they would win if they got one. No congressman would have voted for "speed" publically, or at least not enough of them to defeat the amendment, thought the Committee. The rules of the House are very circumscribed concerning record votes. The only way one could be called for the Pepper amendment would be for the ranking minority member of the House Commerce Committee to agree to it. That was Springer, and he was opposed. No record vote could be taken. Pepper would try for the next best thing, a teller vote. Under the rules of the House at that time a teller vote gave only a final tally. But the members must walk down the aisles and make their vote and there was the hope that even this might swing it to the Pepper amendment since disclosure of their vote to their colleagues might push enough members to Pepper's side. So Pepper tried twice for tellers, but he was refused both times. He had made his request too late; he should have asked prior to the yea and nay vote. "It was a mistake," a member of the Committee said later. But as Pepper was making his request, Congressman Craig Hosmer, a moderate Republican from California, asked for a division. Hosmer had come around to the Crime Committee's view during the pre-vote lobbying by the Committee. A division is the simplest concession the Crime Committee could have won in forcing the members to own up to their votes. Those in favor were to stand. Those opposed would stand and at least they would be seen, but a division was not granted—arbitrarily, some Committee members believe—and this ended any chance of flushing out the House opposition. The amphetamine amendment nurtured by the Crime Committee for several months went down to defeat without a single member of the House of Representatives able to be held publicly accountable for it.

Later that same day, the Comprehensive Drug Abuse Prevention and Control Act of 1970, complete with its "no knock" warrant provision, passed the House by a vote of 341 to six and went on to the Senate.

18: A Second Chance

*If you ever sat in on a House-Senate Conference,
you'd move to another country.*

A CONGRESSIONAL STAFF MEMBER WHO

HAS SAT IN ON MANY

THE defeat of the Pepper amendment was inter-
woven with the internecine jealousies of the House, the
lobbying of the drug industry, and the subterranean opposition of the Nixon Administration. The rivalry between
Pepper's Crime Committee on the one hand, and the Health
Subcommittee and full Commerce Committee on the other
hand, was a major factor. These latter standing committees
traditionally handle health bills, and their members guard
their prerogatives zealously. No upstart committee like
Pepper's was going to easily usurp their territory. Congressman Waldie later speculated that Rogers, Jarman and
others "were responding to representations from the drug
industry which they accepted as being true, that their drugs
were not required to be included under that control." Of
the Administration he says: "I don't know if the Administration made a deal, but it is my feeling that they had responded
to the importunings of the drug industry. What those im-

portunings were and what the parameters of the agreement were I don't know. All I know is the result."

The disappointment of the Crime Committee members was considerable but it was most keenly felt by staff members, particularly Larry Reida, who had labored for more than a year to investigate and control amphetamines, and Paul Perito, who had a personal involvement. Reida's workdays frequently ran to fourteen and sixteen hours, spent in performing his Committee functions and learning more about amphetamines. "My feeling after we lost the House vote was of course extreme disappointment," Reida says. Members of the Crime Committee felt they had been unfairly treated on the floor. The denial of the teller vote and the suggestion that the Committee really had no right to offer the amendment left a bad taste. There were no more alternatives on the House side. The drug bill was passed to the Senate, but House rules prevent attachment of nongermane amendments to its bills. No other drug or crime bill was pending so there was no hope of another shot on the House side. Reida was tenacious. He was unwilling to give up a year's work on the basis of the House vote and he wanted another try to reach a final conclusion, one way or the other. He asked for authorization from Chairman Pepper and Wiggins, the ranking Republican, to see what could be done on the Senate side. They agreed, and it began one of the most unusual episodes in the ten years of amphetamine politics. It would also finally force the Administration opposition into the open.

Reida went to the Senate with the intent of convincing a senator to attach the amphetamine amendment to some kind of noncontroversial bill. Unlike the House, the Senate allows nongermane amendments to be attached to its bills. Reida's first idea was to attach it to a pending veterans bill. As a necessary courtesy, he asked permission from Congressman Olin Teague, chairman of the House Veterans Committee, who refused Reida's request; he feared it could jeopardize its passage. As Reida looked for ways to get the amendment passed, he was joined by Julian Granger of Senator Harold Hughes' Subcommittee on Alcoholism and Narcotics. Granger had originally been a Crime Committee staff member, and he and Reida remained friends.

As they mulled over the situation, the drug control bill just passed by the House was making an uncommonly speedy journey to the Senate. The Administration was pushing hard to pass it before the November elections and the Senate was persuaded not to hold additional hearings; the earlier Dodd drug hearings would suffice. The Senate in turn raced the bill toward a vote before election. This was Reida's chance. This would be the best vehicle for the amphetamine amendment. At that time Reida was in a personal bind. He had put in an exhausting, and at times a frustrating, year and a half with the Crime Committee, and he planned to leave at the end of the year to become legislative counsel for the Interstate Commerce Commission (ICC). Senator Roman Hruska, a fellow Nebraskan, was his sponsor for that post. Hruska was also a key Administration spokesman for the drug bill, as well as a floor manager, and he was an avid supporter of the drug industry as well. There loomed the very real possibility that if Reida tried for the amphetamine amendment in the Senate, it could jeopardize his ICC job and his political future. By this time, however, Reida's intense involvement with amphetamine control overshadowed his personal stake in the matter, so he decided to move ahead with the amendment. "Whenever it came down to those tough choices, Larry just made the choice he had to make," Perito later commented.

Reida and Granger began the search for a Senator who would sponsor the amphetamine amendment during Senate consideration of the Administration drug bill. It would be identical to the Pepper amendment. Perito and other Crime Committee staffers were also looking for a candidate for the amendment. Dodd was the clear choice because of his long-standing interest in drug abuse. And so Dodd was asked. He appreciated the idea, he said, but he needed time to think it over. He would have to make some phone calls. Who he called is uncertain but more than likely he checked with the Administration, which still had any number of criminal or civil suits hanging over his head. Dodd, whose election was a month away, called back a while later to say he simply could not take on the amphetamine amendment. It was apparently too risky for him.

Granger then asked Senator Hughes, another logical choice because of his interest in drug addiction. Hughes said he supported the amendment but he was too busy with his own drug rehabilitation amendment, which he hoped to attach to the drug bill. Granger and Reida literally began walking the halls of the Senate in search of a taker. Senator Joseph Tydings, a Democrat from Maryland, declined when asked, but said he would support the amendment. Gaylord Nelson, a Wisconsin Democrat who was heading a lengthy investigation into the drug industry, was out of town and could not be reached quickly. Senator Jacob Javits, a liberal New York Republican, said he was opposed to it. New York had too many drug companies. Perito also continued to look. Time was growing short. It was now predicted the drug bill would be voted on within a very few days, maybe in a day or two. A member of the Crime Committee staff, Andy Radding, dated the daughter of Senator and Mrs. Thomas McIntyre; McIntyre is a New Hampshire Democrat. Radding knew Mrs. McIntyre and called to persuade her to persuade the senator to take on the amphetamine amendment. While that was happening Reida and Granger's search came to a happy end—they found a taker in an almost unknown junior senator from Missouri, Thomas Eagleton. Two years later everyone would know about him, and his medical history. A bright, intense, articulate man, Eagleton was given a quick course in amphetamines for a full afternoon and he was incredulous at the overproduction. Reida told him what the Crime Committee had done and what they wanted out of the amendment. Nancy Chasen, a young legislative aide of Eagleton's, began digging into the subject and helping to inform Eagleton. The Senate vote would probably come the next day or the day after. The Pepper hearings impressed Eagleton, as did the evidence of the vast overproduction of amphetamines. It was a simple case, Eagleton said later, "where they were produced in the millions and millions, and there was a legitimate medical need for only a small quantity. That's the reason I decided to go with the amendment."

There were several things favoring the passage of the amendment in the Senate. Eagleton is a gifted and eloquent debater and can also assimilate complex information very quickly. Also, the drug lobby traditionally has had less influence in the Senate than the House. And finally, for the first time, the drug companies were caught napping. Confident that the House defeat was the end of the amphetamine amendment, Phil Jehle of Smith Kline & French and other lobbyists relaxed. Not until the Eagleton amendment was about to spring did they catch on. The "no knock" controversy and the division of power between BNDD and HEW were still receiving all the attention. Amphetamines remained quietly in the background.

"I remember spotting Phil Jehle and Wally Johnson of the Administration in the Senate cafeteria on the afternoon of the vote. Only then had they finally realized what had happened and they were stunned. It was as if they couldn't figure out how this all developed," Granger remembers fondly.

It was now October 7, 1970, the day of the Senate vote and only two weeks after the House killed the Pepper amendment. That night President Nixon was delivering a speech on Vietnam, and many Senate Republicans would be at the White House for a briefing and to watch the speech. It would be an ideal time to offer the amendment. As the drug bill was debated, Eagleton rose to offer his amphetamine amendment. It was about 7:30 P.M. and only a handful of Senators were present. His amendment was identical to Pepper's House amendment in requiring narcotic-like controls on amphetamines. Because Eagleton was still unsure of some of his information, he invited Larry Reida to join him on the Senate floor. Perito watched from the gallery, along with the now alerted lobbyists. Reida was dressed in a red shirt and did not go unnoticed. "I really have to give Larry credit," Granger says; "he showed tremendous courage. His shirt was blazing red and he stood out like a sore thumb on the Senate floor, sitting there next to Eagleton. Larry's job with the ICC was already lined up, Hruska was his sponsor and Hruska had to know what was going on. He was only a few feet away from him." The element of surprise had been maintained to the last possible moment. Hruska, who was an Administration floor manager for the bill, was not fully prepared to battle the amphetamine amendment.

Eagleton spoke. He made an eloquent case and in the opinion of many there that night a crucial one. "I think a lot of senators came to the floor and were converted on the spot because of Eagleton's presentation," a witness recalls. Eagleton cited statistics of abuse and diversion, and he noted in 1968 that 80 percent of the amphetamines seized by the BNDD—the same bureau that unofficially opposed the amendment—were of legitimate origin. "And most disturbing of all," Eagleton said, "the use of speed is on the increase, even down to the grade-school level."

Hruska began to regroup. He argued that the Eagleton amendment would affect 4,000 to 6,000 drugs in the amphetamine family. He explained the Administration was reviewing the amphetamine situation and then stated flatly the Administration's position: "The Administration is opposed to this amendment for a very solid reason," Hruska said twisting the facts as he went. "All the people who are producing or distributing between 4,000 and 6,000 items will be thrown into the same category as this particularly harmful drug—'speed'—which is the methamphetamine to which reference has been made." The Republicans began to seep back in, but so did the Democrats. The Senate floor was filling. Senator McIntyre, who had been contacted earlier by the Crime Committee, supported the Eagleton amendment. He spoke of the "many examples of the horror" of amphetamine abuse. Like Eagleton, he pointed out that malnutrition, paranoia, infections, and brain damage were among them. Hruska stalled for time. He said the amendment was a "very important and serious change" in the drug bill and it needed time for discussion.

Dodd rose to speak. Dodd had earlier fought at Hruska's side against Senator Hughes' rehabilitation amendment, which passed this time, and Dodd supported the Administration in virtually every detail. "When Dodd got up we had no idea which way he would go," Perito recalls. Dodd stunned everybody. He supported Eagleton. He said amphetamine has medical uses but a "great capacity" for harm. "Because it has, I believe it should be strictly controlled. That is my case. That is all there is to it." When Dodd finished a shocked Senator John Pastore (D.—R.I.) inquired: "Mr. President, do I correctly understand the Senator from Connecticut to say that he is for the amendment?" Dodd said simply: "Yes, I am." "I want to thank the Senator from Connecticut," Pastore said.

"When Dodd went with us I looked down at Larry from the gallery. He glanced up with a big smile on his face," Perito recalls of that moment.

Having finally committed himself, Dodd began to argue against Hruska. Dodd suggested putting tight controls on amphetamines just to be on the safe side. It was reversible; the companies could petition and request they be put into the lesser schedule if the evidence later warranted it. Hruska retorted that many of the drugs to be rescheduled were not harmful. Dodd answered that, if the drugs are not harmful,

the people will not suffer: "Only the big, powerful manufacturers of these pills may find a reduction in their profit.
The people will not be harmed."

"I am not interested in whether it would be harmful to
the manufacturers," Hruska answered.

"Of course. But the little people of the country should
be protected. Let us put the controls on and find out more
about it. If there is evidence that they are not damaging to
people, then we can remedy the situation," Dodd concluded.

Perito watched intently from the gallery. "You know, I
know Dodd's son, Jeremy; I was appalled about what Dodd
had done with his campaign funds and I had told his son
that. I'm still basically a prosecutor. But that night on the
floor Dodd did something very courageous. It took a lot to
do it. The Administration had things over him which could
have destroyed him. But Dodd had carved out something
for himself in drug abuse and he wasn't going to let go.
I think this was the one area where he had his self-respect
and he wasn't going to back off, regardless of the personal
consequences to himself."

There was a recess during the floor debate as Hruska and
the drug lobbyists mustered more support. Eagleton was
debating and Reida was supplying him information as the
vote drew near. Eagleton named the four major amphetamine makers: Smith Kline & French and the three bulk
producers, Hexagon Labs, Roehr Chemicals and Arenol
Products, all of New York. There were other companies
involved but Eagleton did not list them that night. Finally
the vote came. This time it would be a record vote. The
names were called out. The yeas were carrying it with
Democrats and scattered Republican support. The final vote
was forty to sixteen—the Eagleton amendment had passed.
The Senate had voted to put tight controls on speed. Every
vote against it had been Republican. Reida and Eagleton
were jubilant. After more than a year of plugging, Reida
had staged a political coup and won. Mike Sichel, the

lobbyist for Abbott Labs, had watched from the gallery. When it was over he came down and grudgingly congratulated Reida, as one professional to another. As the senators filed out that night at about 9 P.M. Perito walked up to Dodd and thanked him. "I told him he had done a very courageous thing. He put his arm on my shoulder and said, 'there are some things you just have to do.' "

Reida recalls a later meeting with Dodd that same night. "We were out celebrating at the Carroll Arms, having drinks and some dinner, when I noticed Dodd over in a corner. I had thought he was kind of a schlock with the censure and all, but that night I went up to him and shook his hand and said, 'Thank you, Senator.' "

It is still not completely understood why the Administration had opposed putting tight controls on amphetamines. The industry denies any suggestion of a deal, of course. Donald Fletcher of Smith Kline & French says simply: "There was no deal of any kind. People don't make those kinds of promises. I think you are overestimating our power."

Michael Sonnenreich of BNDD, the architect of the drug bill, says: "The Administration didn't oppose putting amphetamines into schedule two." But why did Hruska say it did? "That was something that happened in Congress," Sonnenreich tries to explain.

Says Perito: "My instincts are as a prosecutor, and as a prosecutor you draw a lot from inferences from people's actions. My inference from what the Administration was doing was simply that it was doing much more than seemed necessary to get the bill enacted. It simply did not want tight controls on amphetamines."

Earlier that night on the Senate floor Dodd also made a final try to include Librium and Valium in the drug bill, because the House had not included them in the drug bill it sent to the Senate. This had been due to a superbly run lobby campaign by Roche. In order to fully understand the implications of this, it is necessary to move backward in time to early 1970, when Roche Labs had hired Arnold and Porter, one of Washington's most influential law firms, to lobby on its behalf. Joseph Califano, the former assistant to President Johnson and at one time his most trusted aide, worked for Arnold and Porter, and Roche specifically asked for his services. Califano accepted. Tom Finney was tied up with the BNDD hearing on Librium and Valium so Califano became his pinch-hitter.

Califano had been engaged in many Administration lobby struggles on Capitol Hill and he knew his way around. He visited Rogers and the staff of the Health Subcommittee. Roche wanted to add another schedule to the four drug classification schedules in the drug bill. The extra schedule would include Librium and Valium and other minor tranquilizers, and would separate them from amphetamines and barbiturates, thereby removing the stigma. Rogers was the key to success and Califano knew it. Califano made his pitch and Rogers bought it. He added another schedule to the bill during his subcommittee's deliberations. It has since come to be called the "Roche schedule," and is an entirely needless schedule. It has the same requirements and controls of schedule three of the bill, or the equivalent of the 1965 DACA controls. Rogers later explained that the additional schedule was put in because of the "scientific and medical judgments" and said Roche had no influence on his subcommittee's decision. When asked which scientific and medical judgments he meant, Rogers said it involved the international drug treaty, which had five schedules, and this was an attempt to keep the U.S. law "in line with the international treaty." Actually, the international treaty has only four schedules of drugs. Califano had little trouble keeping Librium and Valium out of the bill in the House. It was never really an issue there.

Califano was assisted by another Arnold and Porter lawyer as he worked through the spring and summer of

1970 to maintain Roche's interests. "The issue of Librium and Valium," reflected a government lawyer later, "became very intense. The amount of pressure focused on it and the money spent was way out of proportion to other sections of the bill." A Senate aide says: "Roche mounted a hell of a campaign up here. It was one of the most expensive I've ever seen. They were sending up large packets of material on their products to every Senate office and every House office. They weren't all just handouts. Very often they were expensively bound works on Librium and Valium."

Roche had also developed an extraordinarily good communications network in Congress. A House Committee counsel recalls one incident that happened during the summer of 1970: "We were in a general Committee meeting," he says, "and I brought up, rather casually, the Librium and Valium question. I mentioned that I'd heard about it from the Senate side and I wondered if there was any interest in our Committee taking it on. There wasn't much interest. Now, I said that at a private, closed meeting. Only staff people and some members were there. The next day Travis Stewart, Roche's regular lobbyist, visited the Committee office asking to see me. He never mentioned what I had said at the meeting. He just kept saying that he would do anything he could to help. It was rather strange because he had never come to see me before, to my recollection. He said Roche would be glad to give me a presentation of their security set up. I was rather shocked about the whole thing. I never really found out [how Stewart had learned what he had said in the Committee meeting] because everything was so indirect. I suspect that one member of our staff whom Stewart had taken to lunch and buttered up all the time might have told him. One way they operate is, if they cannot get to the members or the key staff people, they'll get to some lower staff member just to find out what's going on."

When the drug bill reached the Senate floor in October, Dodd offered his Librium and Valium amendment, only two hours before Eagleton offered his amphetamine amendment. Dodd spoke before only a half dozen Senators. His speech differed only slightly from the one he had given the previous January when his own drug bill passed. He accused Roche of a wild lobbying campaign to keep Librium and Valium out of the bill and said Roche had outspent his Subcommittee by about three to one. He calculated Roche's annual profits from Librium and Valium to be about $40 million and said the House's exclusion of these drugs was a "triumph of money over conscience." "It is a triumph, however, which I hope will be short-lived," Dodd said. His talk was almost anticlimactic. There was no opposition and the Senate approved his amendment by a voice vote. Roche saved its guns for the House side where Califano rightly figured the battle would still be decided and probably won.

Although the passage of the Eagleton and Dodd amendments were significant victories, they were only partial ones. The full Administration drug bill would now go to a House-Senate conference because the two bodies passed differing versions of the bill. The House-Senate conference is often the quiet burial ground for elements of legislation that are strongly opposed by special interests or are too controversial. No minutes are kept of these sessions, and at their conclusions bland reports are issued describing the final changes made in the bills discussed. After the conference, the House and Senate vote on the report, and approval means the bill—as worked out by the House and Senate—has been passed by Congress. It is then ready for the President's signature.

There was some initial fear that the conference would not be held before the November elections but both House and Senate were anxious for a drug enforcement bill to bring home to the voters. For Dodd the drug bill was especially important. He was a floor manager and its passage would in his eyes be a vindication. His election was three weeks off and he was running as a third party candidate. The conference was set for October 12.

The Senate appointed eleven conferees. Of the eleven, six were in favor of the Eagleton amendment, with Dodd and Hughes taking the lead. Hruska and Strom Thurmond (R.-S.C.) would oppose it. Eagleton, because he was not on the committee that considered the bill, was not appointed. Dodd would try to keep his Librium and Valium amendment, and he expected the Administration support and liberal support on the Senate side.

On October 8 the House prepared to appoint its conferees. Pepper spoke before the House that day and said he favored a motion to instruct the House conferees to accept the Senate amendment. This is a rarely used tactic, calling for a record vote, and there is a serious question as to whether it would have passed. But Pepper and members of the Crime Committee were willing to try it. They were still rankled over the treatment they received on the House floor during the defeat of their amphetamine amendment. Paul Rogers said in response to Pepper that the House conferees, of which he was the key, would give "sympathetic understanding" to the amphetamine amendment. Irrespective of whether the vote to instruct would have passed or not, Rogers wanted to avoid any embarrassment to his Subcommittee. The motion would have, in the words of another congressman, made its opponents "look soft on speed." And this was a record vote. Rogers told Pepper privately that he did not want the motion offered. If it passed, Rogers said, it would tie down the hands of the House conferees and limit their bargaining power. He assured Pepper he would offer only token opposition to the Eagleton amendment to make it appear he was defending the House's position. They would not press it. "It's very hard to get a motion to instruct adopted," Pepper said later. "Rogers kept saying 'you'll get it, you'll get it' so I accepted it." In this way, Pepper reasoned, he would win his amphetamine amendment and Rogers and his people would save face.

The House appointed its conferees. Besides Rogers a full complement of Pepper amendment opponents were named;

Congressmen Jarman, Tim Lee Carter, William Springer, and Ancher Nelson were named; Harley Staggers, the chairman of the House Commerce Committee, would be chairman of the House delegation, but Rogers would be the power. "Staggers has a fear of Rogers as chairman of the Health Subcommittee," a fellow congressman says. "I think in most cases Staggers feels he has to go along with Rogers."

Between the passage of the Senate bill and the conference was a delay of one week. In that time the amphetamine lobby actively tried to kill the amphetamine amendment in the final version of the bill. A letter-writing and telegram campaign was staged for Ritalin, which indicated again that it was organized. "You know, when a congressman gets a hundred letters from people in his district saying that, if you put those controls on Ritalin it will be very hard for us to keep up the treatment for our hyperkinetic child, he listens, even if he knows it's not spontaneous," Perito later explained. "The congressman [receiving the telegram and letters] would then call Pepper. The company knew Pepper would be more sensitive to a call from a colleague than a visit from a lobbyist. It made Claude pause a bit, but he kept going."

Califano was busy sizing up the conference for Roche Labs. He knew most of the House conferees very well. The House Commerce Committee, of which all the conferees were members, handles consumer legislation and Califano, as a presidential assistant, had been involved with the committee members for some years. Califano is a very intelligent and warm man. He leaves a good impression with people, which is an important part of his effectiveness. He put it all to use for his client. "I did a calculation before the conference," Califano remembers, "and I figured pretty well how Librium and Valium would do. We felt quite confident that the House members would be with us."

The conference was held on October 12 and 13. It was obvious that the agreement Rogers had made with Pepper about "token opposition" would be soon broken. The House side, led by Rogers, adamantly refused to accept the Eagleton amphetamine amendment. There was some argument from Dodd and Hughes, but the House side was unyielding. No amphetamine amendment. As one witness inside the conference said: "The House side just didn't seem to think passing that amendment was very important." The conferees did search for something to restore their image of being tough on drugs. The net result was to move liquid injectable methamphetamine, which comprised less than 1 percent of the total amphetamine market and which was sold directly to hospitals and clinics, into schedule two. The conferees could now announce to the world they had stopped speed.

The Librium and Valium amendment went down as well. Dodd was assured of full Senate support but the House side, again led by Rogers, was adamantly against it. Califano's strategy and calculations were absolutely correct. The conference grew heated. House and Senate jealousies, never far from the surface, erupted. Fists pounded tables and there was shouting. Rogers, the most ardent defender of Librium and Valium, sharply cautioned another member of the conference not to use the words "criminal" in connection with them. Harley Staggers followed Rogers' lead. At one point he threatened to take his "boys" (the House members) for a walk and end any hope of a drug bill if the Senate members did not drop their demands on Librium and Valium. It did not resolve itself. A deadlock approached until Senator Hruska—the swing vote—lined up with the House members and on the side of Librium and Valium. Hence, Librium and Valium were not to be controlled in that bill. The conference report said only: "Administrative proceedings for the control of these drugs were initiated in 1966, and final administrative action is scheduled to be taken within . . . weeks . . . The bill provides that if, upon completion of these proceedings—including judicial review—these drugs are listed for control, they shall automatically be included within the coverage of the bill and placed in the appropriate schedule." The drug industry won both battles.

Why had Rogers so strongly opposed the listing of Librium and Valium in the drug bill? Rogers contends that the administrative proceedings needed a chance to be completed. It was unfair, he said, "to include these drugs in the bill before the hearings were finalized." Rogers says he was not influenced by Califano or other Roche Lobbyists, and Roche and Califano claim no undue pressure was applied. Rogers says he opposed the amphetamine amendment because of the imminent action by BNDD and the advice of the "medical people."

The conference report came back to the House and Senate for final passage. The bill, called the Comprehensive Drug Abuse Control and Prevention Act of 1970, was about to become law. The "no knock" provision remained in the bill but the Hughes rehabilitation amendment was stricken out in conference. This was an enforcement bill. It was now the last day of the congressional session before elections. The bill, regardless of its contents, would pass. "If the conference had let my amphetamine amendment remain, the bill would have passed both houses by an overwhelming vote," Eagleton reported later. "Bear in mind it was an anti-narcotic act, and congressmen and senators cannot have a better title on a bill to bring back home. . . . I don't know of many senators or congressmen who would have wanted to go against an anti-narcotic act."

A long-time congressional aide reflects on the legislative process in general and the timing of the drug bill in particular: "String it out, let it sit, and then at the end of the session push it through. By then people finally get so desperate they'll accept almost anything or compromise almost anything to get the bill passed. That's why all the major deals are made in the last few days or hours. Then you are most likely to compromise and everything will get lost in the publicity crush."

On October 14, the House conferees defended their actions

on the House floor. Congressman Springer, who had fought the Pepper amendment on jurisdictional grounds, said the decision on amphetamines was good because it singles out the "worst of these substances, which are the liquid injectable methamphetamines, and puts them into schedule two." Congressman Wiggins spoke for the Crime Committee. He wanted to know why if injectable meth were so bad, weren't the pills—which are easily dissolved in water and shot up— also included in schedule two. Springer admitted there had been "some argument" on that point but said it was best to leave the rest of the amphetamines to administrative action by BNDD. Paul Rogers offered his thoughts; he said the effort to end drug abuse must be sought while also seeking "the best possible way to find and prosecute those who deal in other people's misery for profit." Pepper was blunt: "I am sorry to say that this bill contributes almost nothing in stopping the flow of 'speed' into the veins of the young people of this country."

In the Senate Eagleton denounced the dropping of his amendment. He said that for months members of Congress had been receiving letters from parents who were worried about drugs, and for months Congress had said it would respond effectively. "Yesterday in the conference committee, the drug manufacturers got their way. All amphetamines will remain in schedule three, except for the liquid injectable methamphetamines," Eagleton said. He termed liquid meth a "miniscule" part of the problem of legal amphetamines. It represented something less than 1 percent of the amphetamine legally produced. Even the PMA admitted production of liquid meth was "extremely limited" at that time. Eagleton accused the conferees of dropping his amendment at the "behest of the Administration." "Surely," Eagleton said, "the drug producers are the only winners."

Dodd was back home in Connecticut; he had left the House-Senate conference early to return to the campaign trail. On hearing of the Librium and Valium outcome, he inserted a statement into the *Congressional Record*. "As chairman of the House-Senate conference, I brought up my amendment to include these drugs as controlled dangerous substances. After I brought up my amendment, after extensive debate, and after having been assured by the Senate conferees that we had the votes to include these drugs, I was shocked and distressed to find that the House conferees bludgeoned the Senate conferees into eliminating these 'killer' drugs by threatening to hold up the reporting of this bill from conference. I was stunned to hear that the inclusion of these drugs with a proven history of criminal diversion, illegal use, and multiple fatalities could stop cold the movement of a bill that represents the most far-reaching and comprehensive drug legislation to come before us in fifty-six years."

On October 27, with appropriate pre-election fanfare, President Nixon went to the BNDD offices for the bill-signing ceremony. The bill was much the same as the President had sent to Congress fifteen months earlier. The Justice Department now had new authority, although not as much as originally hoped, and the bill remained enforcement—rather than treatment—oriented. It revised the outdated penalties and made them fairer, and also authorized the addition of 300 new agents to BNDD. With Attorney General Mitchell and BNDD Director Ingersoll at his sides, the President spoke of the bill which declared an all-out war on hard narcotics but only a minor skirmish against drugs which were profitable to the drug companies. He said "in every house in America, in every school in America, in every church in America, the nation faces a major crisis in the increasing use of drugs by our young people." He asked for support to save the "thousands of young people who would otherwise be hooked on drugs." He continued: "The jurisdiction of the attorney general will go far beyond, for example, heroin. It will cover the new types of drugs, the barbiturates and amphetamines that have become so common and are even more dangerous because of their [widespread] use."

After more remarks about the damage from drug abuse, the President signed the bill into law.

The congressional elections were held on November 3. Dodd ran a poor third in his race. The winner was former Congressman Lowell Weicker, Jr., a Republican. Weicker's father had been the president of E. R. Squibb & Sons drug company during the 1940s. Hruska won reelection, as did all of the House conferees. Senator Birch Bayh replaced Dodd as chairman of the Senate Juvenile Delinquency Subcommittee, and he soon fired most of Dodd's old staff, including Carl Perian, the staff director.

Final administrative action against Librium and Valium, which the House conferees announced was only "weeks away," proved to be more elusive than that. Roche Labs won it all. It had succeeded in adding the new drug schedule, which assured Librium and Valium would not be "stigmatized" by being controlled in the same category as barbiturates and amphetamines. Since this had been Roche's stated reason for opposing the DACA controls in the first place, one waited for Roche to end its appeals and voluntarily allow its drugs to be listed in schedule four of the drug law. After all, it was its own schedule. But apparently it was a bit more than the stigma that troubled Roche. There was also that $10 million a year in sales losses to think about. On February 6, 1971, BNDD published its final order directing Librium and Valium to be included in the law now that the hearing examiners in both the FDA and BNDD hearings had concluded for the government and against Roche Laboratories. Roche appealed. In April Roche was granted a stay by the federal court, which meant Librium and Valium would not be controlled until the appeal process was finished. It was now five and a half years since the FDA originally tried to regulate Librium and Valium and no end was in sight.

In 1971, Roche sold 74 *million* Librium and Valium prescriptions in the United States. Valium led with 50 *million* and Librium had 24 million. This represented a total sales volume of slightly less than 3.6 *billion* pills.

POSTSCRIPT I

As the Crime Committee was trying to shut off some of the amphetamine flow, one company was finding a new way to turn it back on again. It came to Larry Reida's attention in mid-October that Lederle Laboratories, a division of American Cyanamid Corporation, had devised a new amphetamine sales gimmick. Called Dexa-Sequels, it was a dextro-amphetamine pill marketed in packets containing a fifteen- to-thirty-day supply. The pills were sealed in plastic blisters and accompanying each packet was a brochure called "The Compact Guide to Weight Loss." The packets were shipped directly from the company to retail drugstores via United Parcel. The reason the company gave the Crime Committee for coming out with them was the ease of packaging.

"I wrote a letter to them asking them in the light of evidence against amphetamines why they chose to come out with a new amphetamine sales idea," Reida says. "I really could not understand it. In the face of so much contrary evidence on amphetamines, Lederle chose to come out with a new way to sell them." The company was unmoved and it continued to market the new packets.

POSTSCRIPT II

In the case of meprobamate, on June 1, 1970, the Supreme Court refused to hear the appeal in the meprobamate case brought by Carter-Wallace. With that denial, all legal avenues for delaying federal controls over meprobamate ended. Carter-Wallace tried an extra-legal one. Thomas "Tommy the Cork" Corcoran re-entered the Capitol Hill scene as Carter-Wallace's "Mr. Fix-It." Five years earlier Corcoran had been on the opposite side lobbying for a barbiturate company to include meprobamate and Librium and Valium in the 1965 act; now he was trying to keep meprobamate free of federal controls. Corcoran, his white hair flowing and his manner bubbling, visited the BNDD offices to make a straightforward deal. In return for delaying the final order to control meprobamate, Carter-Wallace and Tommy the Cork would lobby to put Librium and Valium into the bill. "That's the way the offer was put to us," says a BNDD lawyer at the meeting. "We didn't discuss it much before we turned it down. In my opinion it was unethical for us to accept it." Tommy the Cork was not easily discouraged. He went over BNDD's head. "I'm not sure whether he saw Mitchell or not but he went very high up," another BNDD lawyer said; "maybe it was just Kleindienst he saw." Corcoran maintained good relations with the Nixon Administration and could have seen either. After his high-level meeting, Mitchell called back to BNDD to find out what was going on. It was explained and he told BNDD Director Ingersoll to do what he thought he should do. Mitchell stayed out of it at that point. Meprobamate was finally controlled in schedule four, which required record-keeping but not quotas.

Roche Labs was also pulling some strings to save itself. Michael Sonnenreich of BNDD spoke of a high-paying job offered him by Roche. "It was just before the BNDD hearing on Librium and Valium," a fellow BNDD lawyer said of the offer. "I remember Mike telling us about it." That would have put it in the spring of 1970. Sonnenreich had been pushing to control Librium and Valium at the time. He will not talk of that offer now that he has left BNDD.

19: Plugging Some Loopholes

Watch what we do. Not what we say.
FORMER ATTORNEY GENERAL MITCHELL

PUBLIC pressure is what finally forces politicians to act, or at least appear to act, in the public interest. From the smallest town council to the U.S. Congress, if the public outcry is loud enough something will be done. What is finally done will not always be the best thing or the right thing, but it will be something. Unsafe cars were killing people for years before Ralph Nader made it a matter of wide public knowledge. Then the Congress and the auto manufacturers showed a remarkable reappraisal of their lax policies. The history of amphetamines followed the familiar pattern; not until it became a widely known problem did Congress do much about it, and then it did as little as it could get away with in the face of the power and friendly persuasion of the drug industry.

The Crime Committee had lost twice in the private arena of Congress and, although the last defeat in the House-Senate conference was deeply discouraging, it was not paralyzing.

But it was clear that the only hope of winning finally lay with aroused public concern. BNDD and the Justice Department had promised quick action on amphetamines. If they meant it, all to the good. If they didn't mean it, public pressure might help them change their minds.

Minority Counsel Reida spent much of his remaining time on the Crime Committee to write a powerfully stated case for tough amphetamine controls. It was finished in December but not released until January 2, 1971, just two and a half months after the House-Senate conference. Contained in it was testimony extracted from the committee hearings. It called eight billion amphetamines a year "an incredible over-production of speed by legitimate manufacturers," and it implicated many major drug companies in the diversion of their drugs. Smith Kline & French, Geigy, Strasenburgh, Abbott, Eli Lilly were all named, and evidence was listed of sizable seizures of their drugs. Old medical evidence was cited and also some new material. The Committee found an article published November 5, 1970, in the *New England Journal of Medicine* on *necrotizing angiitis,* a progressive inflammatory disorder of arteries. Ninety percent of its victims die within five years if not treated. The article concerned fourteen drug users who were inflicted with the disease. "Since submitting their article," the Committee report reads, "the doctors have found additional cases at the rate of about one a week at the Los Angeles County Hospital. The fourteen cases had used the typical smorgasbord of drugs—narcotics, stimulants, depressants, and hallucinogens; however, the *only* commonly used drug was methamphetamine. The history of drug abuse ran from three months to five years.

"The findings were:

1. Four out of the first fourteen patients died;
2. Organs affected were the kidney, liver, pancreas, and the small intestine, and damage to their supplying arteries; and

3. Amount of drugs or length of time taken did not appear to be causation."

"Reading that article," Reida said of it later, "was to me just one more instance of what amphetamines could do, and it was one more thing that kept me going." The report issued by the Crime Committee was strong but not hysterical. Information was not distorted to make a point. "You didn't have to distort it, with all the evidence against amphetamines," Reida says. Care was taken to put the report into the hands of knowledgeable and influential people around the country—doctors, scientists, newspaper editors. Reida and Perito together attended the International Drug Symposium in Ann Arbor, Michigan, in December 1970, where Reida spoke. He told those people they had an obligation to look at the facts about amphetamines and push for adoption of a congressional amendment or administrative action to control them.

Several people returning home from the symposium did just that. They wrote letters, and criticism of amphetamines increased and spread. That same month the Utah State Medical Society passed a resolution asking its members to refrain from prescribing amphetamines for weight control. The New York State Commission to Evaluate Drugs held hearings in April on amphetamine abuse. The American Public Health Association and the Washington, D.C., Public Health Association petitioned BNDD and the Justice Department to transfer amphetamines into schedule two. Doctors in Suffolk County, Long Island, voted to voluntarily restrict the prescribing of amphetamines. By mid-1971, when the water had been fully tested, the AMA finally ventured forth with a strong statement against amphetamines. Dr. Henry Brill, then the immediate past chairman of the AMA's Committee on Alcoholism and Drug Dependence, said: "When this stuff gets loose the history of stimulant abuse is that it spreads like wildfire. It becomes a very intense problem with very tragic consequences." The lack of that same sense of history in August 1964 when the AMA opposed the Dodd bill to regulate amphetamines, was one of the reasons its use spread like wildfire. Pepper continued to issue public statements and private letters to BNDD and the Justice Department urging the rescheduling.

On the Senate side, Eagleton had completely taken hold of the issue. He, along with Senators McIntyre, Hughes and Bayh, wrote to BNDD Director Ingersoll also urging the transfer of amphetamines to schedule two. In February Eagleton, with thirty-three Senate co-sponsors, reintroduced his amphetamine amendment in the form of a new bill. BNDD continued to circulate reports that it was about to transfer amphetamines, but no definite decision was announced. On May 18, Pepper reintroduced his amphetamine amendment with nine co-sponsors. It was referred to the House Commerce Committee, thereby seeming to assure it a quiet funeral. But on May 26, BNDD announced it was moving amphetamines and methamphetamines into schedule two, and the companies were given time to respond. The transfer order inexplicably did not include Ritalin and Preludin.

BNDD officials to this day do not concede that public pressure from Congress and others had anything to do with its decision to transfer amphetamines. "It had been in the planning stages for a long time," one BNDD counsel said later. "We were compiling the evidence to make the case." Since nothing in Washington acts in a vacuum, and since the BNDD order followed two bills in Congress, one suspects outside influences as well as considerable public pressure must have had something to do with the decision. Ritalin and Preludin were not included in the order because of lack of evidence, BNDD said, and because of the difficulty of transferring all the drugs at once. The publicity, besides being a prod to BNDD, had another good side effect. It would probably inhibit any of the drug companies from demanding full hearings. The heat of a public hearing would do more damage to the company's image and profits than would the tight regulation of amphetamines.

Eagleton's bill would also transfer Ritalin and Preludin into schedule two. Hearings were set for the bill in mid-July before the Juvenile Delinquency Subcommittee, chaired by Senator Bayh, who was now suddenly interested in drug abuse. On July 7, a week before those hearings and with few objections from drug companies, BNDD made the final order to transfer amphetamines and methamphetamines into schedule two. It was an artful display of timing. Dissension arose among drug companies. Smith Kline & French objected to the transfer of Eskatrol, its amphetamine-tranquilizer combination and biggest seller in its amphetamine line. R. J. Strasenburgh resisted the transfer of Biphetamine and Biphetamine T. But putting most of the amphetamines into schedule two was a major breakthrough. Now they would come under quotas and their production would be limited. The record-keeping would be the same as for morphine and other narcotics. For the first time in their nearly forty-year history, the country would be able to keep track of and limit legal amphetamine traffic. The speculation persists, although the companies deny it, that they had been extended this grace period by the Administration to dispense with their overstocked amphetamine inventories. However, many important details still had to be worked out. How big or small should the quotas be? What medical indications should be allowed? And there were very important details like getting Ritalin, Preludin, Eskatrol and Biphetamine under the same controls. Meanwhile, the omission of Ritalin and Preludin, particularly in light of the drug's history in Sweden, was causing growing concern.

In the early 1940s—two years after they were introduced—Sweden experienced a serious amphetamine epidemic. Within a short time it was estimated that some 200,000 Swedes were amphetamine users and about 3,000 of them were addicts. In 1944, like Japan, Sweden reacted swiftly and put the same restrictions on amphetamines as on hard narcotics. This was twenty-seven years before the United States got around to it. Amphetamines remained medically permissible in Sweden and continued to be prescribed. The tight controls steadily decreased the number of addicts and users, but over a period of years the prescribing became more permissive and the number of users and abusers began to swell. In 1955 Preludin was marketed in Sweden by Geigy Pharmaceuticals of Switzerland for the purpose of weight control. It was not subject to the same tight regulations as amphetamines; hence it was quickly discovered and soon became the "drug of choice" for stimulant addicts. It merely replaced other amphetamines. Preludin abuse brought with it crimes of violence and the familiar pattern of the speed scene. A number of psychological and physical breakdowns were reported and Preludin psychosis was described in Swedish medical journals. In 1959 Sweden put Preludin under the narcotic-like controls, and it was finally withdrawn from the Swedish market in 1965. Three years later, Ritalin, which was creating problems of its own, was withdrawn from Sweden by the CIBA Corporation of Switzerland.

In 1968, the Swedish Committee on International Health Relations convened a symposium in Stockholm on the Abuse of Central Stimulants. At the symposium, Gunnar Inghe, professor at the Social Medicine Institute in Stockholm, told of his country's drug crisis: "From the preventive point of view," he said, "it is especially important to observe that central stimulants are synthesized, manufactured, and distributed by pharmaceutical firms. Without their part in the traffic, the problem would never have arisen. . . .

"Developments in Sweden can well serve as a warning to those countries which still disregard trends already evident within their own borders. Unless they act quickly and with determination, they will soon find themselves in the same situation as Sweden."

There was more evidence showing that Ritalin and Pre-ludin were comparable to amphetamines and demanded the same controls. Dr. Maurice Seevers, then chairman of the pharmacology department at the University of Michigan Medical School, had conducted a series of drug experiments on monkeys for ten years. Seevers, though retired now, is still extremely energetic and active in drug research. He chose monkeys, he says, because they react in a way very similar to man when given psychotropic drugs. His ingenious experiments allowed the monkeys to self-administer the drugs by means of an automatically refilled, motor-driven syringe in the rear of their cage; the monkeys got their drug when they hit a bar. In this way, Seevers and his associates could discover which drugs the monkeys wanted the most by seeing which ones they hit the bar for. One monkey was seen to hit his bar 10,000 times for a cocaine refill. This and other evidence led Seevers to conclude that cocaine was the most "reinforcing" drug he used. By reinforcing, Seevers meant the drug the monkey wanted the most. Seevers also discovered that the monkeys would readily substitute equipotent doses of amphetamine, methamphetamine, and Ritalin and Pre-ludin. "All the stimulants gave a similar pattern," Seevers said of the experiments. "We couldn't tell the difference between cocaine, Ritalin, Preludin, and the amphetamines. Cocaine stands out as clearly the most reinforcing of the stimulants with methamphetamines next and amphetamines after that. But all of the stimulants were much more rein-forcing than the opiates." In other words, the monkeys wanted amphetamine more than they wanted heroin, and they wanted Ritalin and Preludin as much as they wanted other amphetamines.

With this background in mind, the Bayh-Eagleton hear-ings began. They were the only two senators present. Eagle-ton felt the hearings were important because of the gaps in the BNDD rescheduling; he was still angered at the Nixon Administration and BNDD for helping to kill his amendment, and he took it out on John Finlator, the deputy director of BNDD who was to defend the BNDD action. Director Ingersoll was out of the country at the time. Finlator had come to BNDD from the FDA in the reorganization. He was now stuck with the job of explaining why BNDD did not include Ritalin and Preludin in its rescheduling order.

He acknowledged the fact that Ritalin and Preludin had an abuse potential, but that there was not enough evidence to support placing them in schedule two. Eagleton asked a few preliminary questions and brought up his new amphetamine amendment which, if adopted, would foreclose the drug industry's option to stall the controls with hearings and appeals. Finlator said Congress had already "hashed out" that issue and decided against it. It passed in the Senate, Eagleton said, "and Smith Kline & French and other lobbyists had it rejected in the conference committee." "Do you mean to tell me that you, as a dedicated law enforcement agency, would rather go through the long process of administrative and judicial review, that you would rather do it that way than have us do it and get it over and done with?" Eagleton asked. Finlator said yes.

"I am amazed and appalled," Eagleton said, leaning back in his chair and giving Finlator a long, hard stare.

Was there any real street abuse of Ritalin or Preludin? BNDD said there was not, at least not enough to prove anything. The Subcommittee heard differently from a newly organized group called the Task Force on Drug Abuse. Staffed by eager, young law school students investigating the abuse of legal drugs and the drug industry, they had come upon Larry Reida earlier as they sought advice on where to concentrate their investigation. Reida suggested they look into Ritalin and Preludin since it was clear BNDD would not cover them in its transfer. Any evidence they found might change BNDD's mind. The Task Force began a national police survey, and in the Seattle area they found widespread Ritalin abuse.

The two co-directors of the young group, Steve Wax and

Bob Brandon, testified before Eagleton and Bayh. They reported that the Seattle police estimated there to be more than 2,500 Ritalin abusers in the Seattle area alone, and the street price had risen from fifty cents to as much as $2.00 a pill. Ritalin is easily dissolved in water for shooting up, a practice the police said was widespread in the area. In fact, Seattle was called the "Ritalin capital" of the country. Intravenous shooting had one unexpected and very serious side effect. Ritalin contains significant amounts of a filler called talc. When Ritalin was shot up, the task force testified, it caused severe medical complications. One Seattle area clinic reported forty to sixty cases a month of talc-caused abscesses. In one case, a lung had to be removed because of talc clotting. Brandon said the University of Washington Medical School estimated that in mid-1968 there had been thirty-seven cases of Ritalin medical complications, including six deaths that appeared to be traceable to the drug. The police in Portland, Oregon, another area where Ritalin abuse was excessive, reported: "Injection of liquified Ritalin results in abscesses in the area of the body receiving the injections, and death to some persons due to respiratory problems and heart failure. In 1970 four such deaths were attributed directly to the drug." The clear implication was that Ritalin was abused. If amphetamine supplies diminished, users, misusers and abusers would merely switch brands.

Finlator dismissed the findings of the Task Force. He said if the Seattle police reported 2,500 Ritalin abusers, the member of the police department giving that figure was "not getting his facts straight."

Eagleton persisted. "Would you have any objection if Congress went ahead and made Ritalin and Preludin schedule two domestically, or is it more of a problem in Afghanistan?" Eagleton asked.

"I think I said during my speech if you pass this legislation we would certainly enforce it," Finlator said. "However—" at that point Eagleton interrupted.

"As Senator Bayh said, it is lovely for you to say you would enforce the law. I don't think you are conceding much."

The exchange was unusually harsh, as Eagleton came at Finlator like a prosecutor at a defendant.

"If you had your way, would you have it controlled now? . . . As you sit here today, are you convinced that Ritalin is a significant problem, that it has a potential for abuse and that you are firmly convinced that Ritalin ought to be in schedule two?"

Finlator said he was convinced.

"And you are convinced of it today?" Eagleton said.

"Yes sir."

"And if you are convinced of it, you would like to see it there in schedule two?" Eagleton asked.

"Yes sir," Finlator answered, finding no escape.

Eagleton admits he was rough that day. "I couldn't comprehend why BNDD wanted to be so stand-offish about a drug that was subject to great, great abuse. I still can't understand it," he said later.

BNDD explains its resistance to any congressional amendment as being due to its desire to test the transfer mechanisms in the law; some BNDD officials were openly contemptuous of Congress. "Let them put in their amendment and let us put in our transfer order and we'll see who gets the transfer first," one BNDD counsel says. The hearings, however, showed a significant gap in the BNDD information and reasoning. If BNDD people believed there was no significant Ritalin or Preludin abuse, the fastest way to create it was to put the clamps on amphetamines.

The makers of Ritalin and Preludin also appeared before the subcommittee. CIBA and Geigy, two Swiss drug firms, had merged in 1970 to become CIBA-Geigy, Inc.; its U.S. plants are located in Ardsley, New York, and Summit, New Jersey. Ritalin and Preludin were both very salable items in the CIBA-Geigy operation, and the company was opposed to putting them into schedule two. United States sales totaled

$18 million in 1970, with Ritalin at $11 million and Preludin at $7 million; Preludin accounted for 10 percent of the company's sales and Ritalin 15 percent.

Thomas Boucher, CIBA president, told Eagleton and Bayh that putting Ritalin into schedule two would attach a "stigma" to the drug. The argument had a familiar ring. He said 50 percent of the prescriptions written for Ritalin were for hyperkinesis and schedule two controls were unfair because of the "very low level of abuse which has been brought to our attention."

William Howell, president of the Geigy division, said 99 percent of the doctors who prescribe Preludin prescribe it for obesity. Only three cases of abuse or addiction to Preludin have come to the company's attention since May 1966, he testified. Then Howell offered one of the most convoluted reasons yet conceived for exempting Preludin: "I think there are two psychological factors to be considered with Preludin if it is kept in schedule three," he said. "People will not be as tempted to use it because it would indicate that the authorities feel it is not stimulating enough to be abused to any extent. I think if it is put in schedule two, it rather calls it to their attention and points it out as something that has not been abused to this point but might lead them to think that maybe they have been missing a good bet."

That wily reasoning had not fooled the Swedes. If it were to be followed, one might imagine a world where all the most addictive and dangerous drugs would be unrestricted because restriction would only alert the would-be addicts that these drugs should not be passed up. Then, to fool the addicts further, stringent regulations could be placed on candy bars and chewing gum to lure the unknown addict into thinking that's where the kicks are.

Preludin was still the "drug of choice" in Sweden. "I look upon the Swedish situation," Boucher said, "as being a unique situation which we cannot explain."

The CIBA-Geigy spokesmen admitted awareness of some

instances of abuse in the Pacific Northwest, but denied it was of the proportions described by the Task Force. Had they spoken with any of the doctors who developed much of the Ritalin abuse information? They admitted they hadn't, but Dr. Howard Cohn, the CIBA medical director, promised that "one of the first things I will do when I get back to my office is see that someone in my office contacts each of these men."

"They actually did go out there and see some of the people who had given us the Ritalin information," a member of the Task Force said later. "They apparently took some of them out to dinner. A while later the same people who had been telling us about Ritalin's abuse began saying things like 'gee, we're really not all that sure it was Ritalin so much.' They backed off noticeably after the company made its visit."

There were other loose ends to the BNDD amphetamine order. Smith Kline & French was still fighting to keep Eskatrol out. Donald Fletcher, the Smith Kline & French security manager, put on his public relations hat and went before Eagleton and Bayh to explain. According to him, Eskatrol had less abuse potential than plain amphetamines, and it was not diverted. The drug abuse pamphlets he had brought with him were displayed everywhere before the Subcommittee. Eagleton pushed them aside. Smith Kline & French, he knew, had been a major lobbyist against his amphetamine amendment, and Fletcher would have to pay the price. When Fletcher persisted in the Smith Kline & French line of fighting to keep Eskatrol out, Eagleton snapped:

"All you would like to do is stay in the business of selling Eskatrol, and then you would have the market cornered. Eskatrol would be the number one product on the market, and as you pursue this long, protracted appeal process, your product will be the number one product. You will be the Ford, Chevrolet, and Plymouth rolled into one. That is pretty good business and pretty dirty business." Fletcher was silent.

The hearing was over in two days. It attracted wide publicity as the press began belatedly to catch up with the amphetamine story. A week after the Eagleton-Bayh hearings, BNDD announced an administrative hearing on Eskatrol to take place August 16 as its position against amphetamines hardened. The same day BNDD subpoenaed "all studies, reports, tests, and data" on Eskatrol in Smith Kline & French's possession. The fact that combination drugs like Eskatrol were allowed on the market at all was strongly criticized. Dr. John Griffith, whose pioneering amphetamine research helped the country see amphetamine for the dangerous drug it is, said the hazards of the amphetamine combination drugs outweigh the benefits by a thousand to one. Smith Kline & French asked for a delay before turning over the Eskatrol data. A week before the hearing was scheduled, Smith Kline & French representatives came to BNDD headquarters still contending their drug was not subject to abuse, that since amphetamines were to go into schedule two, Eskatrol should be exempted because it is not just an amphetamine. "They also told us that the amphetamine could not be separated out. One of our chemists took some Eskatrol capsules to his laboratory. Within a very short time he devised a way to separate the amphetamine from the tranquilizer," said a BNDD lawyer at that meeting, "and we told the company about it." Smith Kline & French quickly dropped its opposition and BNDD withdrew the subpoena. On August 18, Eskatrol was placed in schedule two. "We didn't want to make a *cause célèbre* out of a good drug," Donald Fletcher of Smith Kline & French tactfully explained.

On September 17, after considerable heat and light had been beamed on Ritalin and Preludin, BNDD announced it was transferring them into schedule two. CIBA-Geigy did not oppose the transfer. BNDD Director Ingersoll wrote Eagleton and Pepper saying "the continuing concern expressed by members of Congress over the proper scheduling of various drugs, has, in no small measure, aided this bureau in its endeavors."

Then the ceiling fell. The FDA announced it was now reconsidering amphetamines for weight control. In December 1971, BNDD announced it would allow a production equivalent to 1.5 billion ten-milligram amphetamine pills for 1972, a figure considered far too high by many authorities; but it was a step in the direction of sanity. BNDD was essentially over a barrel if the FDA still allowed amphetamines for weight control; this was the loophole which prevented a more substantial reduction. Pepper, Eagleton, and others persisted like bill collectors after an overdue account. They continued to write the Justice Department and BNDD to remind them to set the quota lower. The industry was pushing the other way, although not with its old vigor, with more and more people aware of the hazards of amphetamines.

After thirty-nine years it looked like the public might finally be winning. Quotas are the only way to control a diverted and abused drug, because the number that can legitimately be produced is set and not to be exceeded. Excess production—no matter how carefully the records are kept and monitored—creates the source of abuse; the long history of amphetamine abuse was incontrovertible proof. New clandestine labs churning out speed were certain to crop up, but there were laws to deal with them. Perhaps if the United States had enacted the same kind of restrictions over amphetamines in 1944 as did the Swedes, the problem might never have blossomed and clandestine labs would not have been so abundant. But American society had reached its limit of tolerance.

However, as the federal government was making this reasonable policy in Washington, one major drug company would add one final and sorry chapter to amphetamine abuse in the United States.

20: The Corporate Conscience— A Final View

"We are as much concerned as anyone could be. We have children too."

ELWOOD GARNER, PRESIDENT OF THE
R. J. STRASENBURGH CO., IN COMMENTING
ON SPEED ABUSE TO FORTUNE MAGAZINE

WITH amphetamines securely lodged in schedule two and its extremely tight regulations, there came an episode that represents another dark example of the drug industry's corporate conscience. Anomalies in the amphetamine distribution chain could now be readily detected and traced. In the summer and early fall of 1971—only weeks after amphetamines were rescheduled—one glaring anomaly began to appear. Large seizures were made by BNDD field agents of an amphetamine called Bifetamina (a Spanish name). Finally Bifetamina seizures were made regularly enough to suggest they were more than random discoveries. Bifetamina is produced by the Mexico City Branch of the R. J. Strasenburgh Prescription Products Division of the Pennwalt Corporation. Biphetamine was produced for Mexican consumption and was not exportable to the United States, so any Bifetamina pills found in the United States got here illegally. The home office of Strasenburgh is located in Rochester, New

York. It was a family-owned business for more than 100 years until 1960, when it was purchased by Wallace & Tiernan, Inc. In 1969, Wallace & Tiernan was, in turn, purchased by the Pennwalt Corporation, a Philadelphia-based company with fifty subsidiaries in ten states and eleven foreign countries. The Strasenburgh company remained the pharmaceutical division of Pennwalt, with annual sales in its drug line of about $40 million. Its amphetamine sales in the United States in 1971 reached $6.7 million, making it one of the top three amphetamine producers in the country.

The Mexico City branch that began producing Bifetamina in 1967 is a wholly owned and U.S.-managed subsidiary of Pennwalt called Laboratorios Strasenburgh de Mexico. The home office in Rochester shipped only the bulk amphetamine resin to Mexico City where it was inserted into black gelatin capsules and marketed for Mexico. The capsules contained twenty milligrams of amphetamine—double the normal dose—and because of their distinctive all-black capsules they went by the street names of "black mollies," "black beauties," "black widows" and "RJS," the initials of the company printed on the capsules.

Because amphetamine export invoices were now required to be forwarded to BNDD, it was known in August of 1971 that Strasenburgh had shipped 900 kilos of its amphetamine bulk from Rochester to its Mexico City plant, enough for 45 *million* twenty-milligram capsules. The 900 kilos of bulk had been shipped over a period of several months. The last shipment was in June of 1971 and occurred as Strasenburgh was actively fighting the rescheduling of its U.S. amphetamine. The fight was ended by the company on July 13—two days before the Bayh-Eagleton hearing—when it decided to comply with rescheduling.

It was evident that because of their very ample supplies of amphetamines in Mexico City, Pennwalt had relaxed its opposition to the rescheduling. "While we were rescheduling them here, they apparently made an end run around us to Mexico," commented a BNDD lawyer later.

A preliminary intelligence survey was ordered by BNDD. Its results confirmed that sizable quantities of Bifetamina were smuggled across the border and in several areas it appeared to be the "drug of choice" for users. A network of truck routes and truck stops throughout the South and Southwest were the conduits for bringing the illegal capsules into the interior. It was the same network that had operated for decades. The BNDD survey also found several points along the Mexican-American border that served as the major smuggling centers for the capsules. As the evidence arrived, BNDD prepared to move. Between April 1 and October 1, 1971, BNDD agents had purchased or seized 173,000 Bifetamina capsules.

While BNDD was faced with Bifetamina traffic in the West, it was faced with a serious political problem in Washington, a problem that convinced BNDD to take decisive action and to let everyone know about it. A long running feud had simmered for years between the country's two major federal drug enforcement agencies. It began between the old Federal Bureau of Narcotics (FBN) and the Customs Bureau, both of which were under Treasury Department jurisdiction. The basic source of the conflict was overlapping jurisdiction. The Bureau of Customs is charged with protecting the country's borders from, among other things, drug smuggling. The FBN, and later the BNDD, is charged with the task of prosecuting drug dealers within the country's borders. On paper that is a reasonable division of powers, but in reality it has led to a snarling bureaucratic tug-of-war. Customs agents are stationed in foreign countries to investigate and to alert U.S. Customs when a drug smuggler is coming through. BNDD agents also investigate in foreign countries to alert their U.S. agents of incoming shipments so BNDD can arrest the major dealers when the drugs reach their destination. The agencies quarreled over which agents had jurisdiction in which foreign countries, and for a while they appeared to grant one another their own spheres of control. But clashes continued over whether Customs should let the drug shipment go through so BNDD could arrest the dealer or whether it (Customs) should make the arrest at the border and receive the credit. An FBN agent in 1959 told the Juvenile Delinquency Subcommittee that the Customs Bureau's international policy was a "dog-in-the-manger policy." Once Customs was on a case, FBN could not come near it. FBN also froze out Customs. Former Senator John Carroll of Colorado was at those hearings and promised at the time to "knock some heads together" to end the "bureaucratic bungling."

Heads were knocked together time and time again but it only raised welts. In 1968, when BNDD was created and the two rivals were no longer under one roof at Treasury, it was hoped the conflict would ease, but it did not, as one case shows. A charter boat captain out of Miami was approached by a drug dealer and asked to bring in a large shipment of cocaine. He then reported it to BNDD, who told the captain to proceed with the shipment. They would watch it and when it reached the inland dealer they would make the arrest. Customs was requested to allow the charter boat to pass through, but when the boat came into Miami, Customs seized and impounded it. The BNDD investigation was stopped cold and the captain was left to wonder what it all meant.

How often these kinds of incidents have happened over the years is difficult to estimate, but they have happened often enough to seriously cripple federal drug enforcement. Some officials guess they may have interfered with 20 percent of the federal drug cases. The war continues to this day and one reason for BNDD's decision to take decisive action in the Bifetamina case was to move one step ahead in slowing this everlasting bureaucratic battle.

Another reason was the fact that BNDD, although publicly

proclaimed as the new super drug enforcement agency, was then and is now in danger of a premature death. Talk persisted of folding BNDD into the FBI—which has since happened—and many BNDD officials regarded themselves as being involved in a fight to survive as an agency. There was also the plain fact that the loose controls over the Bifetamina capsules were a threat to the public health and an apparent violation of the law. So, in the fall of 1971, BNDD acted not only to stop the Pennwalt-Strasenburgh operation but to protect itself and, as one BNDD lawyer put it, "to stop any other company from trying the same stunt."

On November 8 at the BNDD regional office in Dallas, Texas, "Operation Blackjack" was inaugurated. It consisted of a task force of eleven BNDD agents from different parts of the country called together to buy and seize enough capsules to make a strong case against the company. Considerable internal debate arose at BNDD headquarters regarding the course of action once the case was made. Some of the younger lawyers talked of suspending or revoking the Rochester plant's license to produce controlled drugs. There was talk of possible criminal conspiracy charges against members of the corporation. The lesser option was to attempt to revoke Pennwalt's amphetamine-export license. This would stop Bifetamina production in Mexico because the plant there had no capacity to produce bulk amphetamine. It was this option that was selected; it would be the easiest to accomplish and would also effectively stop the Bifetamina traffic. Under the 1970 act, Pennwalt was required to apply annually for its export license renewal. When the application was submitted in January, the company would be hit with an order that would demand that the company "show cause" why its export license should not be revoked.

Operation Blackjack moved quickly. January 15 was the cut-off date. Robert Rosthal, BNDD deputy chief counsel and a veteran of eighteen years in the Justice Department, was in overall charge of the investigation into Pennwalt. A gruff, acerbic man, Rosthal would lay out the case once the evidence was gathered. "We had a lot to begin with, having the Bifetamina picked up in the incidental seizures of the previous few months. But we wanted enough to really ice the case," he said later. There would be no question of the origin of the capsules once they were seized. Sophisticated "pillistic" tests, like ballistics tests for bullets, can determine the origin of the capsules by examining microscopically the brush and groove marks on the Bifetamina capsules; when compared to a known quantity, these marks would prove they came from the Mexico City Pennwalt plant and were not counterfeit.

BNDD agents contacted informants, made connections, and set up buys. It was already known from the intelligence report that the pills were shipped from the Mexico City plant to a handful of Mexican pharmacies along the borders, some of which are no more than adobe shacks with "farmacia" signs in front. Many were located in rural poverty areas of little population. Yet they were receiving thousands of these capsules. Once in the stores, the capsules, all properly labeled and sealed by Pennwalt, could be purchased in huge quantities and smuggled across the border into the United States. Smuggling could be done a variety of ways. In Reynosa, Mexico, a taxi fleet that made frequent border crossings was known to bring in Bifetamina; air strips were used for smuggling via light planes; private cars and trucks brought them in. The major U.S. points of entry were five Texas cities, El Paso, Del Rio, McAllen, Laredo and Brownsville. One truckstop in El Paso was known to handle shipments in the hundreds of thousands.

At each step along the way the capsules were sold at nearly 100 percent markup. The initial cost to the drugstore or pharmacy was approximately nine cents, the smuggler paid fifteen to twenty cents, and in turn sold them in the United States for about thirty-five cents. They were sold on the street for seventy-five cents and some buys were made at $2.00 a capsule. Bifetamina was showing up in many states and as far north as Boston, Massachusetts.

The case was building for the massive diversion of Bifetamina. Three days before the formal organization of Operation Blackjack 20,000 capsules were seized in Atlanta, Georgia, in their original bottles. The agent who attempted to arrest the peddler was nearly run over as the peddler tried to escape. A week later in Glendale, Kentucky, 40,000 Bifetamina capsules were seized and three men arrested. In two separate cases in El Paso, both concluded on January 11, 122,000 capsules were seized and three men arrested. Smaller seizures were also mounting. Ten thousand at a gas station in Waco, Texas. One peddler told a BNDD undercover agent he could get him 30,000 Bifetamina capsules a week out of McAllen, Texas. Another said his supply was "unlimited." In all, between November 8, 1971, and January 15, 1972, a period of nine weeks, a total of 896,000 Bifetamina capsules were seized or bought by BNDD agents and thirty-nine individuals arrested. It came to about 100,000 capsules a week. Since April 1971, a total of more than 1.2 million Bifetamina capsules had been seized or bought in twelve states. How many had been smuggled in undiscovered is anyone's guess.

Care was taken throughout Operation Blackjack not to alert Pennwalt. At the end of November, however, a "leak" was reported along the Texas-Mexican border and there was some fear the company might find out and do something to blunt BNDD's case. The source of the leak was not found but one BNDD lawyer pointed his finger at BNDD's old rival, Customs, and said: "I wouldn't put it past those bastards to go down and tell Pennwalt just what we're doing."

Fortunately, the leak never reached the company and BNDD retained the element of surprise. BNDD had wanted to seize a million Bifetamina capsules in Operation Blackjack before the "show cause" order. Although they fell a little short, it was enough to suggest that Pennwalt knew what was happening to its capsules. "There's no way they can get around it," Deputy Chief Counsel Rosthal said at the time. "I don't know what kind of an excuse they'll offer, but you can't produce that many pills in a country that small and that poor and still think it is all going for legitimate medical purposes." The traffic pattern always returned to the few Mexican drugstores, and BNDD estimated that these eight border drugstores had been shipped 13 *million* of the 17 *million* Bifetamina capsules manufactured during 1971.

In late December Pennwalt filed its application with BNDD as expected for renewal of its export license. On January 14, BNDD served Pennwalt with a notice "to afford you an opportunity to show cause as to why the Bureau of Narcotics and Dangerous Drugs should not deny your application, dated December 27, 1971, for certificate of registration to export amphetamine . . . ." A hearing was scheduled for February 23 in case the company wanted to appeal.

It was a dramatic move. BNDD's action was a complete surprise to the company. BNDD had taken pains to insure wide press coverage. Television networks and key newspaper reporters were tipped in advance as the word went forth that BNDD was nailing a major U.S. drug company for its role in allowing diversion of its dangerous drugs. Much of the publicity was orchestrated for BNDD's own purposes, and to forewarn other companies that the same could happen to them. It proved that BNDD had a law to work with and had used it.

The first reaction from the company came from William P. Drake, president of Pennwalt. He said the show cause order was "baseless." The industry-funded "Pink Sheet" howled its protest. A headline in its January 24th issue said: "Justice's BNDD 'creams' Strasenburgh at news conference on flow of illicit Bifetamina from Mexico to United States; Unveils show cause & subpoena procedures." It called BNDD's news conference an "attack" and said it was a sharp warning of BNDD's power to obtain a "press conviction" against any drug company. A few days later Pennwalt issued a full press release stating that all Bifetamina sales in Mexico were legal, that none were exported to the United States, and that the company "has no knowledge, nor is it aware that any of its employees have been charged with having knowledge that its products were being sold into illicit channels of distribution in Mexico or the United States." Pennwalt promised to "cooperate fully" with the government. The release also noted one other thing BNDD had expected. As of January 20, the Mexican government was placing very stringent regulations on amphetamines and they were to be phased out of production within six months.

Pennwalt had been caught in a double squeeze from the United States and Mexican authorities, and soon conceded. It would not reapply for its export license, and it would not suffer the embarrassment of a hearing. Elwood Garner, president of the Strasenburgh division, said the company was discontinuing its foreign manufacture of amphetamines because "the local governments don't have controls to prevent their being smuggled back into the United States."

In its initial press release after the show cause order, Pennwalt promised to launch a continuing study to review the Mexican amphetamine sales in order to determine "whether there has been any failure on the company's part." On February 2, the company was given an opportunity to discuss that "failure," when the House Subcommittee on Public Health and Environment asked company representatives to testify. The subcommittee was then and is now chaired by Paul Rogers. A year and a half earlier Rogers had opposed the Pepper and Eagleton amphetamine amendments at least in part because of his stated belief that the industry was doing a good job of policing itself. It would be difficult now to congratulate the industry for its self-regulation.

Dr. William P. Head, vice-president of technical operations for the Strasenburgh division, was sent to defend his company's policy before the subcommittee. The subcommittee members had been primed by Rosthal and other BNDD lawyers and given all the evidence. Head testified. He contended that all Bifetamina sales in Mexico were legal. The arrests of peddlers and the massive seizures of the capsules and the show cause order were all a surprise to the company. He said the Mexico City plant ceased amphetamine production and the fact that the company withdrew its export license renewal served to "demonstrate a full awareness of the seriousness of the matters . . . ." Head then stated: "We feel that we must be candid with you in saying that our investigation, to date, has disclosed to us a growth in the sales of our product in Mexico that seems out of proportion to what the normal expectations for that product should have foreseen."

Dr. Head then supplied sales figures of the Mexico City amphetamine operation for the prior three years. In 1969, Bifetamina sales were $354,000. In 1970 they nearly doubled to $619,000. In 1971 they nearly doubled again to more than $1.2 million. The number of Bifetamina capsules being manufactured jumped proportionately. In 1969 3.3 million were distributed. By 1971 it had jumped to 17.6 million. In three years the sales of Bifetamina had gone up fourfold. Dr. Head was asked what this incredible growth in sales suggested to Pennwalt. He replied that "it seems evident to us that the rate of growth was sufficiently fraught with risk so that it might well have raised questions of qualitative analysis for our personnel to consider."

Peter Kyros, a Maine Democrat, asked Pennwalt why it said in its statement that the illicit traffic in Bifetamina was "alleged." Pennwalt counsel Matthew Broderick said that because Pennwalt did not contest the BNDD charge, "as far as we know today, it is still an allegation and not an established fact."

Kyros asked Broderick if he really meant that Pennwalt had no knowledge of illegal amphetamine traffic until the arrival of the BNDD show cause order.

"That is true, sir," Broderick said. "The first knowledge we had of this investigation which the order to show cause refers to as commencing in April, and Operation Blackjack, commencing in October or November, was through the press, and then we received the order to show cause." Broderick said the earlier seizures "were not brought to our attention."

Kyros recalled the drug industry's promise to the subcommittee two years earlier that it would keep a close watch on its sales to better monitor illicit traffic of its drugs. He pointed to the doubling and then the redoubling of Bifetamina sales in three years and then asked: "I would think that would cause a question in your mind as to the extent of the distribution and what is happening. Why is there such a growing market of amphetamines in Mexico? Wasn't that question once raised in your corporation?"

"No, it was not, Mr. Kyros," answered Dr. Head. He said the 1969 to 1970 sales had not doubled and said only now were the 1971 sales figures available.

"I will agree with you that if you look at all three figures, right now is the point where the alarm bell is ringing, and I think I did cover that in my statement," Dr. Head said.

To only make an annual check on sales of a product is to contravene accepted business practices, especially for a major corporation, but Dr. Head insisted that only within the past few days had Pennwalt realized what was happening.

Paul Rogers began to question Dr. Head. He wanted to know if the large bulk shipments of amphetamine from Rochester to Mexico City in March and June had triggered any concern. Dr. Head answered that the bulk was intended for the 1972 inventory and said the company was also planning to export amphetamine to South American countries from its Mexico City plant. This did not seem to assuage Rogers, although he did not pursue it in any depth. Congressman James Symington, the son of Senator Stuart Symington and a liberal Democrat from Missouri, then went after Dr. Head with a series of questions. He inquired about the cost of the bulk amphetamine and noted that the bulk material in 1969 cost $12,716, which resulted in sales of $354,000 for the capsules. In 1971, Symington pointed out, the bulk cost a little more than $20,000, resulting in sales of $1.2 million and an even greater markup ratio. The capsules were selling for sixty times the cost of the amphetamine material. Dr. Head explained that processing, quality control and packaging must all be added into the cost as well. He admitted these costs were far cheaper in Mexico than in the United States. He could not account for the increase in the profit ratio in the 1971 sales figures over the 1969 sales figures.

Symington inquired about the enormous jump in sales in such a short span of time and what it suggested to the company. This was the crucial issue.

"Do you have conventions where various people are given awards for the number of pills they have sold in the market or given other appropriate recognition?" Symington wanted to know.

"There have been sales meetings, yes sir," Dr. Head answered.

"The person who is responsible for the success of your Mexican subdivision, doesn't he write home about how well he is doing?" Symington pressed.

"No, sir; not to my knowledge," Dr. Head answered.

"He just kind of does it all by himself. That is unusual," Symington mused.

Rogers and Tim Lee Carter, two of the most ardent opponents of the Pepper amendment, asked some questions to demonstrate their toughness with the legitimate drug industry. Carter said it was "rather strange" that the company did not notice the quadrupling of its sales in four years. Rogers, who later said he was "greatly surprised" by the Pennwalt episode, wanted to know how long the company had been selling Bifetamina to the border pharmacies. Dr. Head responded that since BNDD did not advise Pennwalt which pharmacies were involved in the diversion, "it has not been possible to obtain individual sales figures for those pharmacies."

Symington wanted to know what the company learned from the case. "What does it have to teach you? Just tell us, basically."

Dr. Head answered: "Well, despite the size of this market in regard to Pennwalt's total volume, we still are, and will continue to be deeply concerned about this entire problem of drug abuse, both here and abroad. We certainly deplore our product coming back into this country or, for that matter, even being diverted within Mexico." It was not much of a lesson.

The Pennwalt case brought into the open the gravest questions of corporate responsibility in a free enterprise society, particularly a society in which drug abuse had become of such critical concern. The full depth of the company's complicity in the Bifetamina diversion was not fully aired at the hearings nor were they ever documented by BNDD, which kept an open and active investigation for several months. Once the company dropped its request for an export license, BNDD dropped its subpoena and the matter more or less ended. No criminal conspiracy charges were ever made. Pennwalt later informed BNDD that the vice-president of its international operation and the general manager of the Mexican plant had resigned, and the request for early retirement from Elwood Garner, president of Pennwalt's Strasenburgh division, had been accepted. The company exonerated itself by choosing scapegoats. The resignations had a certain public relations charm, but the central issue of corporate responsibility or irresponsibility was not squarely faced. What happened was not the work of a small, quick-buck drug company —the kind to which the major companies had pointed an accusing finger for years—but a major U.S. corporation with a listing on the New York Stock Exchange and a solid rating from Dun & Bradstreet. "The fact of the matter is," a BNDD lawyer said later, "they just didn't give a damn. Here they are, a bunch of bluebloods sitting in their Philadelphia office. They say sure, a few fat housewives abuse the stuff, but that's all they'll admit. After they make it and sell it they don't care where the pills end up."

What did Pennwalt lose? It lost its license to export amphetamines and the publicity did little for the company's image. By no longer being able to export amphetamines, the company lost about $4 million in sales a year. But Pennwalt could continue to export other drug products. The gross sales of Pennwalt in 1970 were nearly $414 million, meaning the amphetamine export loss meant less than 1 percent of the corporation's total annual sales. Pennwalt even assured its stockholders the loss would be of no consequence. Pennwalt continues to produce Biphetamine and Biphetamine T for United States domestic consumption. Although the House Health Subcommittee held up the printing of its hearing on Pennwalt for several months to await additional material specifically requested by its members, much of the material was never sent. Pennwalt did not forward its ten-year amphetamine sales records, the record of the objections by some of its stockholders about the company's amphetamine production, nor did it send an accounting of the promotional costs of its drug division. The hearing book was finally printed without these additions a year after the hearing ended.

Robert Rosthal, the BNDD counsel who led the case against Pennwalt, spoke before the American Bar Association conference on drug abuse and law enforcement two months after the Pennwalt-Strasenburgh case came to an end. The meeting was held in Rosthal's native New York. Rosthal participated in the criminal investigation of Teamster Union president Jimmy Hoffa and the Billy Sol Estes swindle while he was in the Justice Department. While preparing his notes for the ABA conference, he wrote a note of caution to himself when he reached the section on Pennwalt's case. "It reminded me not to get carried away when I talked about

Pennwalt," Rosthal says. He said to the convention: "The drug problem in this country is usually thought of as street traffickers and pushers but there is also a drug problem in terms of legitimate industry. In my eighteen years in the criminal division of the Justice Department, including some aspects of organized crime and the infiltration of legitimate business, I've seen an awful lot. But imagine this situation. Imagine if Sam Giancanna, Joe Profaci and Joe Bonanno had invaded the 120-year-old drug division of the Pennwalt Corporation and devised a scheme to smuggle drugs back into the United States or at the very least allowed it to happen. Imagine the uproar from the people. But I'll tell you something, those old dons could learn something from some manufacturers in the 'legitimate' drug industry."

Epilogue

THIS year, 1973, the Bureau of Narcotics and Dangerous Drugs permitted a total of about 650 million amphetamine, methamphetamine, Ritalin and Preludin pills to be put on the market. While this is a substantial cut from the uncounted billions that were flooding the country just three years ago, it is still millions more than what most responsible medical authorities consider necessary. Amphetamines are still prescribed for weight control although in early 1973 the FDA issued a stiff warning on the hazards of the drug. Ritalin enjoys more than a third of the amphetamine market. It is prescribed in large quantities for hyperkinesis, the childhood malady that still escapes a precise medical definition. The use of stimulants for hyperkinetic children is under stronger and stronger criticism, even from former proponents of such drug therapy.

The FDA moved belatedly to ban amphetamine combination drugs—considered for years by the best medical opinion to have no medical value at all—and on February 12, 1973, the FDA published its intention in the *Federal Register*. Almost unnoticed in that published statement was an accusation that Smith Kline & French Laboratories had "deliberately failed" to make required reports. The language was strong by FDA standards. What the FDA had discovered was that a report on the drug Eskatrol, Smith Kline & French's leading amphetamine combination drug, had revealed serious cases of street abuse. Part of the report, which was commissioned by Smith Kline & French, surveyed housewives who used Eskatrol for dieting. The survey said that they appeared to handle the drug well and experienced few problems. However, the other part of the eleven-state survey found street and school abuse of Eskatrol. As required by law, Smith Kline & French submitted to the FDA the first part of the report on the housewives (which showed Eskatrol in the best possible light), but Smith Kline & French deliberately withheld the second part of the report since it reflected badly on this profitable pill. The FDA later learned of this deception. To compound it all, Smith Kline & French has since requested a hearing to fight the FDA ban on Eskatrol. "Smith Kline & French tried to tell us that they were not required to submit that second part of the survey to us," an FDA spokesman said, "but our lawyers say all of it must be submitted."

It was merely another episode in the long and sad history of amphetamines where the drug company, regardless of whether something were legally required or not, did something contrary to public health for the sake of profit.

After several years of dormancy, the AMA Council on Drugs, which is made up of independent doctors, asserted itself by publishing a provocative book called the *AMA Drug Evaluations 1971* as a guide to doctors. The book took a hard line against a number of drugs. It said the amphetamine combinations, and other combination drugs as well, were "not recommended," and it seriously questioned the use of amphetamines for weight control because of their "untoward effects." The book also questioned drug company claims in regard to a number of other drugs.

The drug industry was not pleased. The Pharmaceutical Manufacturers Association (PMA), which has continued its very close relationship with the AMA, put up a mighty roar. It demanded many changes and offered to pay for them. The Council on Drugs stood firm and the book was published as written. But as the second edition loomed, the PMA intensified its opposition and in a showdown—this time with the AMA— the PMA and the drug industry won and the Council on Drugs lost. The new edition of the *Drug Evaluations* omits any mention of a drug being "not recommended." In fact, the AMA went a step further and placed the final writing and editing of the drug evaluation book in the hands of AMA staff people, thereby removing it from the hands of the independent members of the Council on Drugs. The entire Council on Drugs was disbanded, ostensibly for economic reasons. Dr. John Adriani, past chairman of the Council on Drugs, is a respected and outspoken doctor and was a prime mover in the first drug evaluation book. He said this of the disbanding: "The Council on Drugs was dissolved primarily because of the pressure from the drug industry. The drug evaluations book did not make the drug industry very happy and they were even more unhappy with how the second edition was turning out. We were going to say flatly in that edition that in some instances a drug was not indicated for anything at all. The AMA said publicly that we were dissolved because of economic reasons. Hell, we didn't cost them much. There were ten of us on the Council and we worked for nothing. We met three times a year and the only thing we cost them was traveling expenses. It's sad really because one of our jobs is education and that is what we were trying to do. It just means now that the AMA has relinquished another leadership role in medicine and it means someone else will take it over, most likely the government." The Council on Drugs had been in existence since 1905.

In the area of ethical drug advertising, the FDA has moved against some of the most offensive drug ads. One ad for Serentil recommended it be taken "for the anxiety that comes from not fitting in." The company, Sandoz Pharmaceuticals, was required in 1971 to publish a correction for advertising that the drug be used for everyday anxiety situations. Many drug companies, however, still manage to promote their mood drugs as being solutions for almost everything we encounter in our day-to-day lives, despite FDA efforts to limit this practice.

The link between drug advertising and drug abuse has been explored in little depth and there is still no direct link between the two. The only indirect link seems to be that the wider *use* of drugs among parents, has produced more drug *abuse* by their children. Clearly, one reason the parents are taking more drugs is because of advertising. At a conference of the National Council of Churches Drug Advertising Project in November 1972, no direct link was discovered and both the AMA and PMA indicated no willingness to do a study to see if a direct link existed. That, apparently, is someone else's concern. Television drug advertising also has an unmeasured effect on our national willingness to see pills as panaceas.

As a nation, we are now purchasing, according to some estimates, more than 250 million mood drug prescriptions each year. This has many consequences, many of which are known and many are unknown. One of the subtlest and potentially most insidious effects which is just now emerging is called the "amputation" effect. In essence, this means, if the theory is correct, that if we take barbiturates to lull ourselves to sleep, we may in fact be "amputating" or short-circuiting, the body's normal ability to induce itself to sleep. This same principle would hold for amphetamines, which might impair the body's normal ability to raise its energy levels, and it would also hold with tranquilizers, which, if taken regularly, might impair the body's normal ability to overcome stress. In their highly respected book, *Mystification and Drug Abuse,* the four doctor-authors discuss the use of amphetamines to temporarily boost the energy level. They suggest this pattern might result in "at least temporary impairment of the ability of the organism to regulate its own energy expenditures and to deal with fatigue . . . ." They go on to suggest that the impairment might be permanent. The impairment or amputation of normal functioning is not a result of drug abuse, but is a result of drug use at recommended doses. The clear implication is that a person must continue the use of a mood drug in order to cope with a situation because he is no longer able to cope with that situation without the drug. It is not drug addiction in the classic sense, but if the amputation theory is true it is a form of drug reliance.

One example related to this is the frequent case of the young wife who is sedated immediately after learning of her husband's untimely death. It is a common practice that disregards the question of what the sedation and suppression of grief may eventually do to the woman. Dr. Daniel X. Freedman, chairman of the department of psychiatry at the University of Chicago and a noted drug authority, testified before Senator Gaylord Nelson's Monopoly Subcommittee that "grief is very important to normal experience, and . . . stunted grief, stunted emotional working through of these problems, can lead to a serious psychiatric problem." In other words, the sedation, stunting or tranquilizing of grief, while offering temporary relief, may lead later to serious problems because the grief was not fully expressed at the time it was most painful. So along with the amputation drug effect, we also may have the suppression effect, both of which may cause more problems than would have been encountered if the drug had never been taken at all.

On March 28, 1973, the Third District u.s. Court of Appeals in Philadelphia issued a forty-four-page decision on the Librium and Valium case. In it, the court noted the evidence that Librium and Valium produce euphoria, tolerance, withdrawal and paradoxical rage, that they are diverted illegally and have a substantial potential for significant abuse, was ample. But, the court said, at the very beginning of the FDA hearing in 1966, FDA counsel James Phelps did not submit to Roche Laboratories the report of the FDA Advisory Committee which included mention of Librium and Valium. The report did not contain information which would have materially changed the case, but the appeals court said the denial of the report to Roche Labs was a denial of due process, and it therefore reversed the hearing examiner's ruling against Librium and Valium. So, after hearings, lobbying battles and court proceedings lasting about eight years, Librium and Valium succeeded in escaping regulation. "We won everything but the case," a government lawyer remarked on the appeals court decision. "The failure to turn over the advisory committee report was plain stupid. It would have made no difference in the case." Now that the functions of federal drug enforcement have been reorganized again, there is little likelihood that the government will move quickly to control Librium and Valium amid the difficulties of this newest reorganization. So Roche Laboratories has won. "The total package, in terms of Roche's lobbying in Congress, the way they promoted the drug and the way they defended themselves in the agencies and in court is one of the best I've ever seen put together," said an admiring government attorney; "it was really a masterpiece." The only thing missing was a similar concern for the public health.

Few of the personalities described in this book have remained where they were during the bouts with the drug industry. Congressman Claude Pepper is still chairman of the House Select Committee on Crime as of this writing, but there is very little chance the committee will remain as a committee for the duration of the 93rd Congress. It has trodden on the jurisdiction of too many other committees to stay alive and will probably be dissolved.

On December 4, 1972, Pepper's relationship with Dr. Max Jacobson, which earlier had almost undermined the Committee's efforts on the amphetamine amendment, was made public when the *New York Times* broke the story of Dr. Jacobson and his alleged amphetamine injections. By the time the *Times* published the story the Crime Committee's amphetamine investigations were over and the embarrassment to Pepper was far less than it would have been earlier. Pepper publicly denied he had ever been given amphetamine injections by Jacobson. The *Times* article mentioned that the BNDD investigated Dr. Jacobson several times over a period of five years and the investigations indicated large amounts of amphetamine purchased by Jacobson were unaccounted for. The article did not mention, however, that on at least one occasion Pepper intervened with BNDD on behalf of his old friend. Jacobson said that he had injected only "small quantities" of amphetamine into some patients. Despite this, Pepper has continued to demand a cutback of amphetamine production.

Larry Reida, the Crime Committee minority counsel and mainstay in the protracted fight to tightly control amphetamines, is now legislative counsel with the Interstate Commerce Commission. Paul Perito, the chief counsel who, along with Reida, diligently sought amphetamine controls, was for a while the deputy director of the Special Action Office for Drug Abuse Prevention until he resigned in early 1973. He is now a consultant. Congressman Paul Rogers, who undercut so much of the Crime Committee's attempts to put the clamps on amphetamine production and controls on Librium and Valium, is chairman of the House Health and Environment Subcommittee, and his power grows continually. Dr. Tim Lee Carter, the Republican Congressman from Kentucky whose medical authority was used to support the drug companies' bid to keep the controls off amphetamines, received an AMA plaque in 1972 for his "wise and able counsel in shaping programs to improve the nation's health." Carter accepted the award, saying he was dedicated to serving humanity but added, "I am tilted toward the AMA," whatever that might mean.

Senator Thomas Dodd, who had a history of heart trouble, died at his home in Old Lyme, Connecticut, on May 24, 1971, only a few weeks after telling a friend he thought he did not have much longer to live. His long labors to control many drug industry practices were scarcely mentioned in the obituaries. Carl Perian, who led so much of Dodd's drug investigations, is now an aide to Congressman John Murphy of New York.

Senator Birch Bayh, who assumed the chairmanship of Dodd's Juvenile Delinquency Subcommittee, has asserted himself strongly in the area of drug abuse and has held important and substantive hearings on barbiturate abuse and the abuse of methaqualone, a non-barbiturate sedative now abused by many young people. Bayh's efforts have been instrumental in focusing attention on these drugs and speeding up BNDD's attempts to move fast-acting barbiturates and methaqualone, both generic names for a number of brands, into the tightly controlled schedule two of the 1970 drug act. Some of the drug companies are objecting, arguing that their drugs are not dangerous or addictive or abused. The dialogue makes one recall what the amphetamine companies were saying ten years ago.

This book has examined the drug industry's role in drug use and drug abuse along several lines. The vast overproduction of dangerous drugs, the inexcusably sloppy way in which they were allowed to fall into the black market, the continued push, through promotion, production and advertising, to create a drug-acculturated society, a society so ready to take drugs and often so immune to their hazards that it has become an accepted way of life. The book has also described how effective political muscle has consistently outweighed considerations of public health. For me, the book has raised more questions than it has demonstrated solutions. I will pose what I think should be some of those questions.

How can the interlock between the AMA and the drug industry be untangled? Why should this once independent and honorable medical society remain beholden to and the servant of the drug industry? The doctors themselves, who make up this organization, should offer their own guidelines for economic and political disengagement. But the interlock is a two-way street, because the millions of dollars the drug industry puts into the AMA treasury with any advertising is reciprocated by the AMA, which has invested almost $10 million of its retirement fund in the drug industry.

Should doctors continue to be allowed to hold stock interests in drug companies, particularly when their practices include the prescribing of drugs produced by that company? Should doctors be required to list their holdings in their offices with signs saying "Let the patient beware?"

Should mood drugs be continually promoted for every conceivable problem suffered by man? Why are tight limits not created, requiring that drugs be promoted only for medically treatable indications? And why should the drug industry annually spend three to four times as much money on promotion as it does on research?

Must drug companies be allowed to produce and distribute dangerous drugs until the public health problem becomes so virulent that any remedy is too little and too late, as in the case with amphetamines? Perhaps a special tax to the drug company of a penny a pill should be placed on all drugs that are potentially addictive.

Where are we to find the corporate conscience? If it is not in the corporate board rooms, then where is it located? Demands by conscientious stockholders for some kind of social responsibility from the drug companies have in the past been brushed aside by corporate officers. The government finally becomes not only the easiest answer but, by default, the only answer, as unsatisfactory as that answer might be.

Should drug sampling be allowed to continue under such loose and unenforceable controls? Recently the State of California enacted a law whereby doctors desiring drug samples must request them of the company in writing. It is a good idea for the entire country.

Should drug companies continue to be allowed to select and often seduce the drug researcher who conducts clinical trials of their new drugs? This implicit conflict of interest has created a situation where new drugs are ushered in on waves of high praise, and only later are their problems and side effects made known.

Should the infestation of the medical profession by the drug industry be allowed to continue unabated? Laws can do very little to prevent this, but the doctors themselves must be obliged to face the question and abide by a code of ethics to prevent the kind of mutual back-slapping and favoritism that is so deeply imbedded in this interchange.

Should medical education continue to pass so lightly over the area of drug usage and pharmacology? Why, when most practicing doctors spend much of their time prescribing drugs, should their knowledge of drugs remain so minuscule? Why should a drug company detail man, who may have a degree in education, have more detailed knowledge about a drug than a doctor who prescribes it for his patients?

Why should drug pricing continue to be so out of line with the cost of the drug? When markups are five, ten, twenty times the cost of material and labor, it is clear that the public, and usually that segment of the public least able to afford it, is getting skinned.

In the area of political questions, why should the penalties against drug corporations remain so weak and so seldom enforced? As long as any drug company can bend the truth in its advertising, and successfully claim innocence when its drugs are widely abused, any "war on drugs" is doomed to failure.

Why should administrative hearings and court reviews take so long when questions of the public health are involved? The Librium and Valium case dragged on for eight years and there is still no end in sight. This process must be speeded up. Perhaps congressional hearings could be held. Evidence could be turned in, testimony heard, and a decision rendered in a matter of weeks. Then it could go to court, again within weeks or months. In the case of Librium and Valium, it was well over five years before the case even reached the appeals court.

The process by which large corporations have easy access to our political leadership will continue as long as political campaigning is so expensive and is paid for by special interests. Why cannot public financing be arranged? Or at the very least, why do the laws continue to allow for such obvious loopholes that the sources of contributions can be hidden?

These are questions which lack easy answers, but there are some glimmers of hope. Senator Gaylord Nelson continues, to the chagrin of the drug industry and the hope of the public, his relentless and courageous probing of the drug industry in his position as chairman of the Senate Monopoly Subcommittee. Usually working by himself, with only economist Benjamin Gordon as his full-time aide in the investigations, Senator Nelson has introduced in the Senate an omnibus drug bill which would rectify some of the existing defects. Among the many provisions needed in the bill are stricter regulations of drug sampling, drug testing, drug advertising and a host of other practices now only loosely regulated. The drug industry is digging in to fight Nelson. It has a $6-billion-a-year industry to protect and to draw upon in the battle. As the drug industry continues to both forestall and weaken the effectiveness of the laws, and at the same time fails to adequately regulate itself, it maintains for itself uninterrupted profit. But this attitude could allow another major and sudden drug catastrophe like thalidomide, a catastrophe which some government officials now privately predict is inevitable. This attitude is also leading our country more deeply into a drug-reliant and drug-accustomed society. But as we move closer to a system of socialized medicine and the government assumes a larger role in health care, it may also be forced to assume direct control of the drug industry. After its long succession of victories, this finally may be a demand the drug industry will find difficult to defeat.

Index